I0762728

FRAMING FATHERHOOD

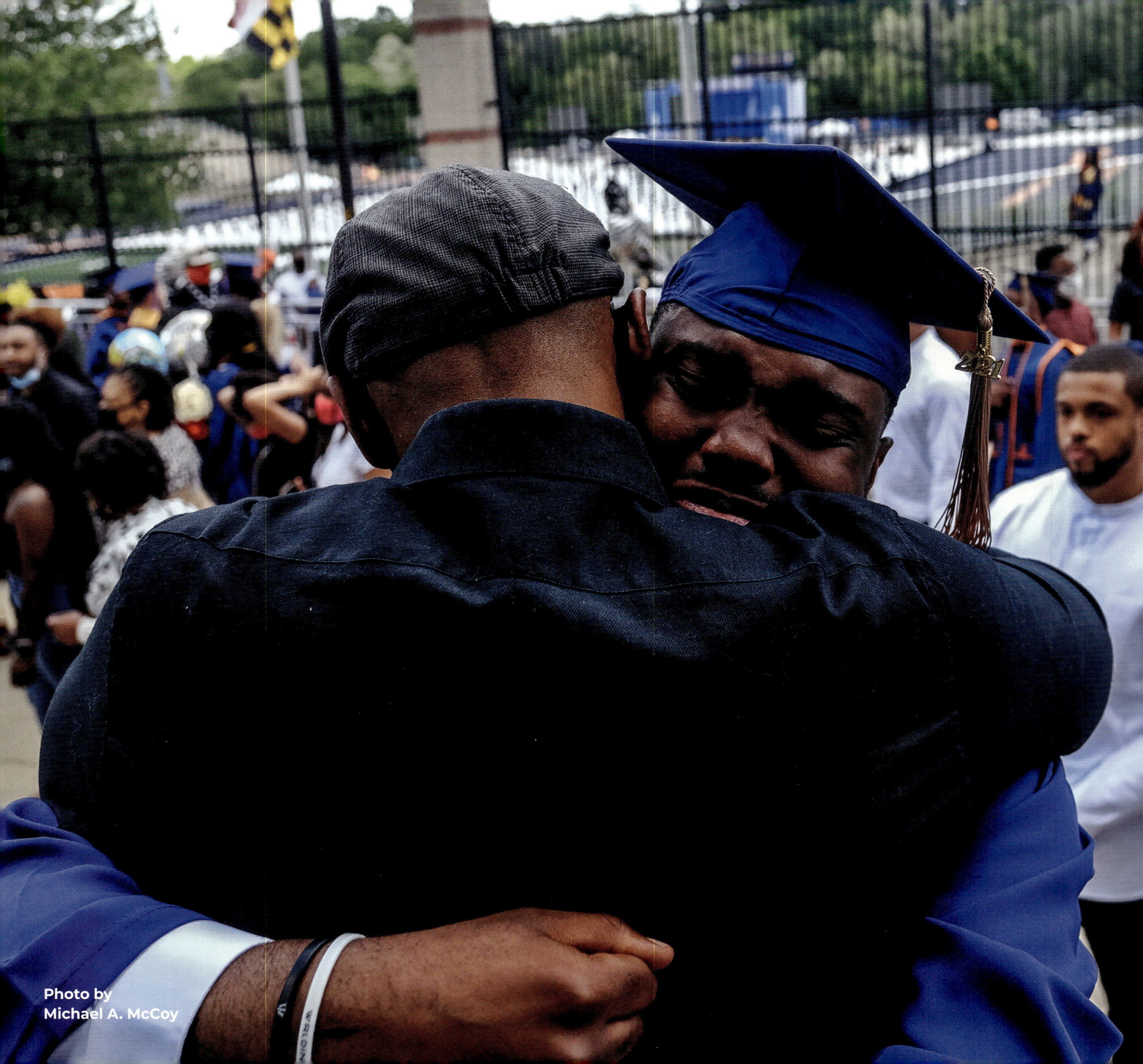

Photo by
Michael A. McCoy

IMANI M. CHEERS, PHD

FRAMING FATHERHOOD

A CELEBRATION OF BLACK FATHERS

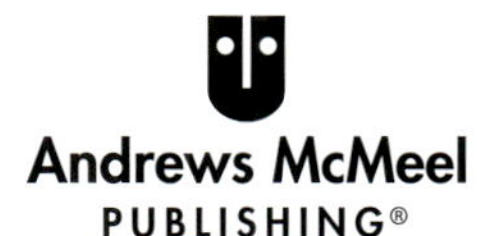
Andrews McMeel
PUBLISHING®

The authorised representative in the EEA is Simon and Schuster Netherlands BV, Herculesplein 96 3584 AA Utrecht, Netherlands. (info@simonandschuster.nl)

Andrews McMeel Publishing
a division of Andrews McMeel Universal
1130 Walnut Street, Kansas City, Missouri 64106

www.andrewsmcmeel.com

25 26 27 28 29 POA 10 9 8 7 6 5 4 3 2 1

ISBN: 979-8-8816-0029-7

Library of Congress Control Number: 2024952686

Editor: Danys Mares
Art Director: Diane Marsh
Designer: Brittany Lee
Production Editor: Kayla Overbey
Production Manager: Julie Skalla

ATTENTION: SCHOOLS AND BUSINESSES
Andrews McMeel books are available at quantity discounts with bulk purchase for educational, business, or sales promotional use. For information, please email the Andrews McMeel Publishing Special Sales Department: sales@andrewsmcmeel.com.

To my son, Isaiah Milton Cheers, I pray this depiction of Black men and their children inspires you to be the type of man your great-grandfathers, Milton Cheers and Ernest Hayes, were. Men of honor, filled with faith, and focused on their families.

INTRODUCTION

Framing Fatherhood is a celebration of Black joy. Focused on Black fathers and their children, this book highlights the intimate moments and introspective messages between father and child. The timeless tenderness. The unapologetic and unrestrained vulnerability that strengthens one's soul. These images by twenty-one prominent Black male photographers capture the love that legacies leave.

Coming from the point of view of a cultural curator and content creator, *Framing Fatherhood: A Celebration of Black Fathers* is a love letter to Black men, their children, and the young people their love impacts. A glimpse into the gentleness that spans generations. A peek into the poignant and purposeful pathways from boyhood to manhood, childhood to adulthood.

Dedicated to my son, Isaiah, and his great-grandfathers, Milton Cheers and Ernest Hayes, this work exemplifies Black excellence.

This coffee-table book is composed of photographs from the original exhibition of *Framing Fatherhood*, which premiered at the Corcoran School of the Arts and Design in Washington, DC, on June 19, 2022. During its six-week run, *Framing Fatherhood* welcomed over thirty thousand visitors, setting a record for the gallery. The exhibition was profiled nationally on *CBS Mornings* and in *The Washington Post*, as well as by local Washington, DC, media, including WTOP Radio, FOX 5, and WUSA9. The exhibition showcased over seventy-five photographs from fourteen prominent Black male photographers from across the country. This book features more than one hundred twenty-five photographs from twenty-one photographers as well as essays and poems from ten Black authors and poets. The goal of this book is to celebrate Black men and fathers through the lens of iconic Black male storytellers who make up our creative village.

In solidarity,
Imani M. Cheers

TAU BATTICE

Lifelong lover of photography and its power to preserve the moment, proclaim nuance, and propel humanity to positive action

above: **Mikey, Michael, and Mitchel, 2021**

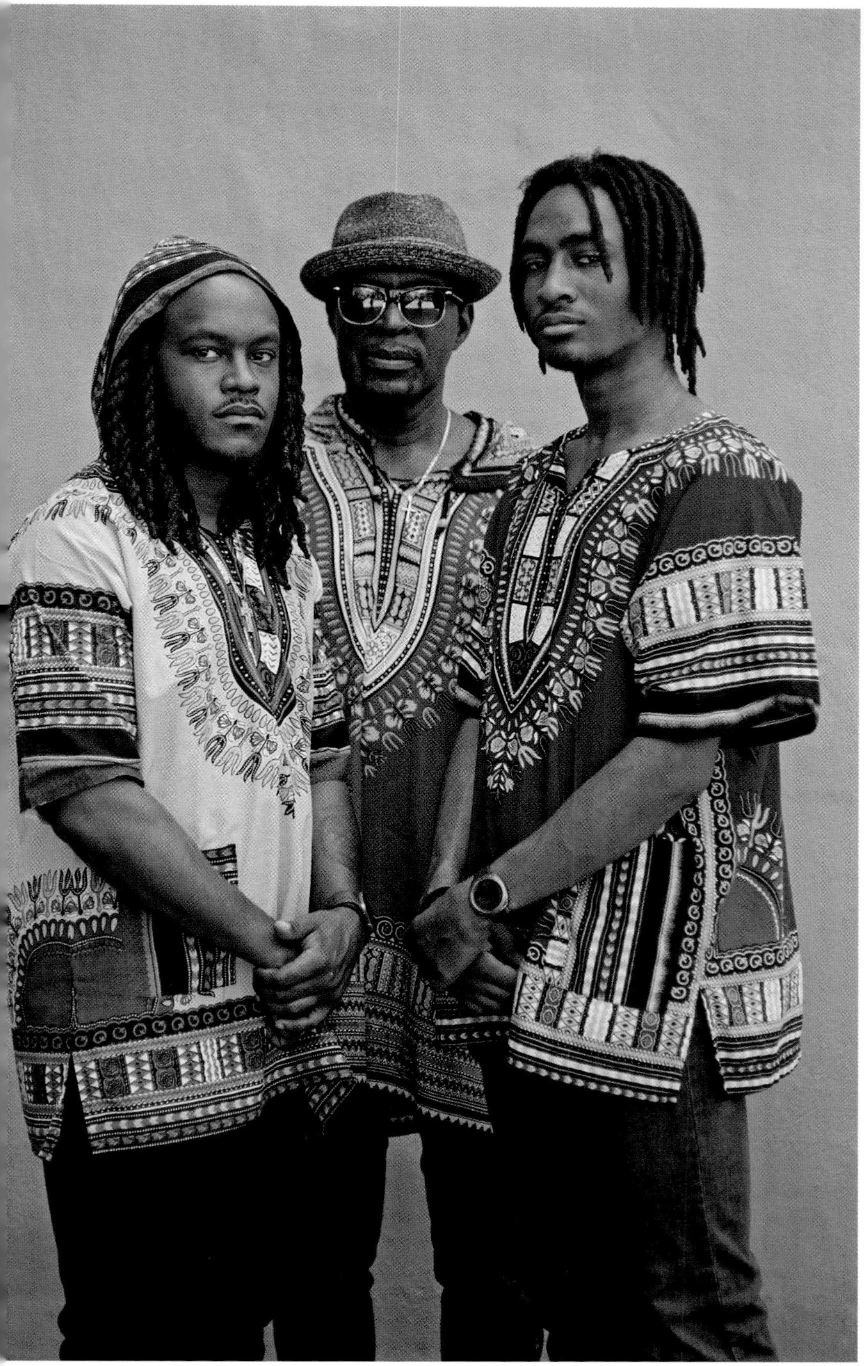

right: **George, Miles, and Max, 2019**

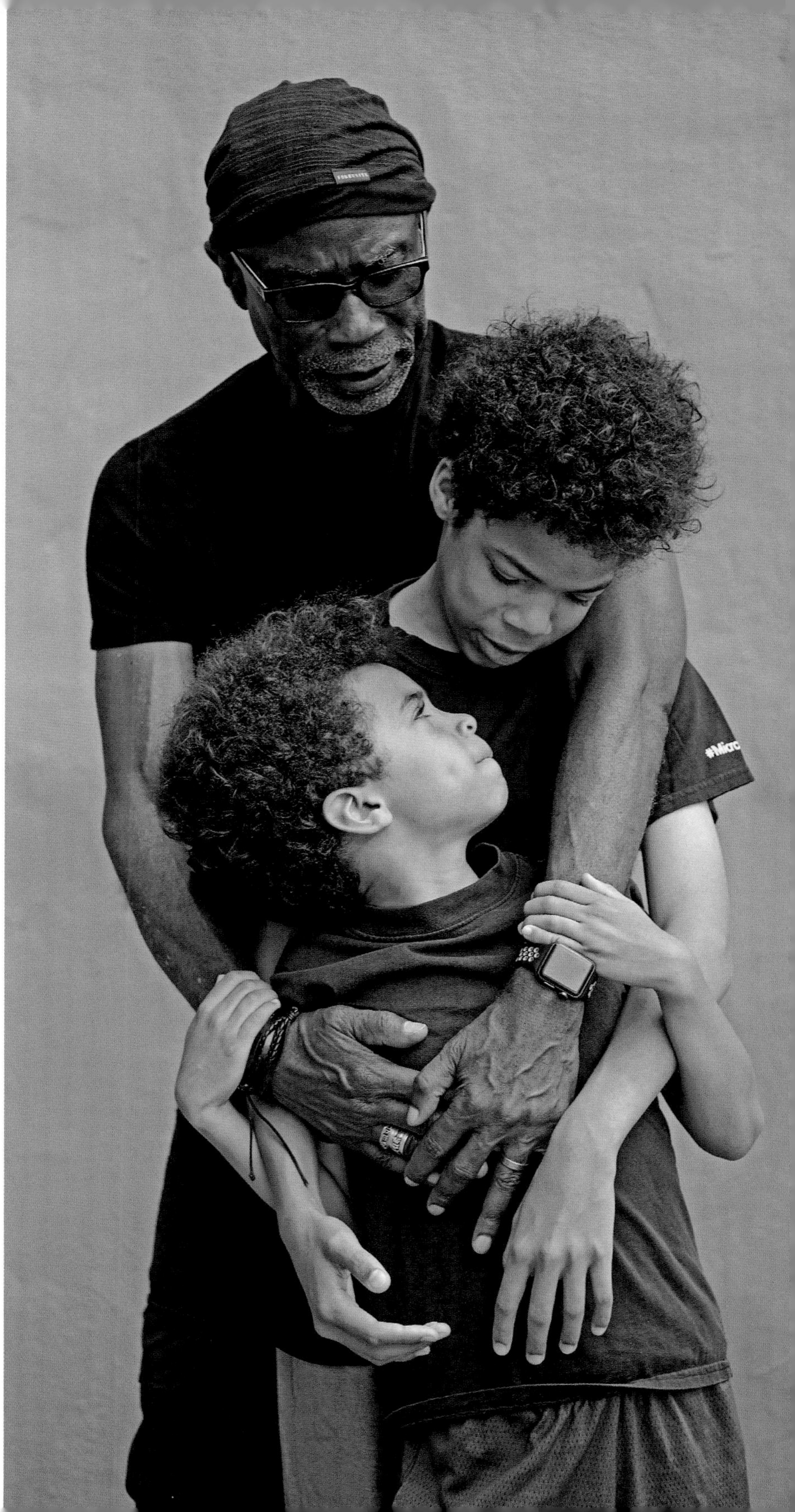

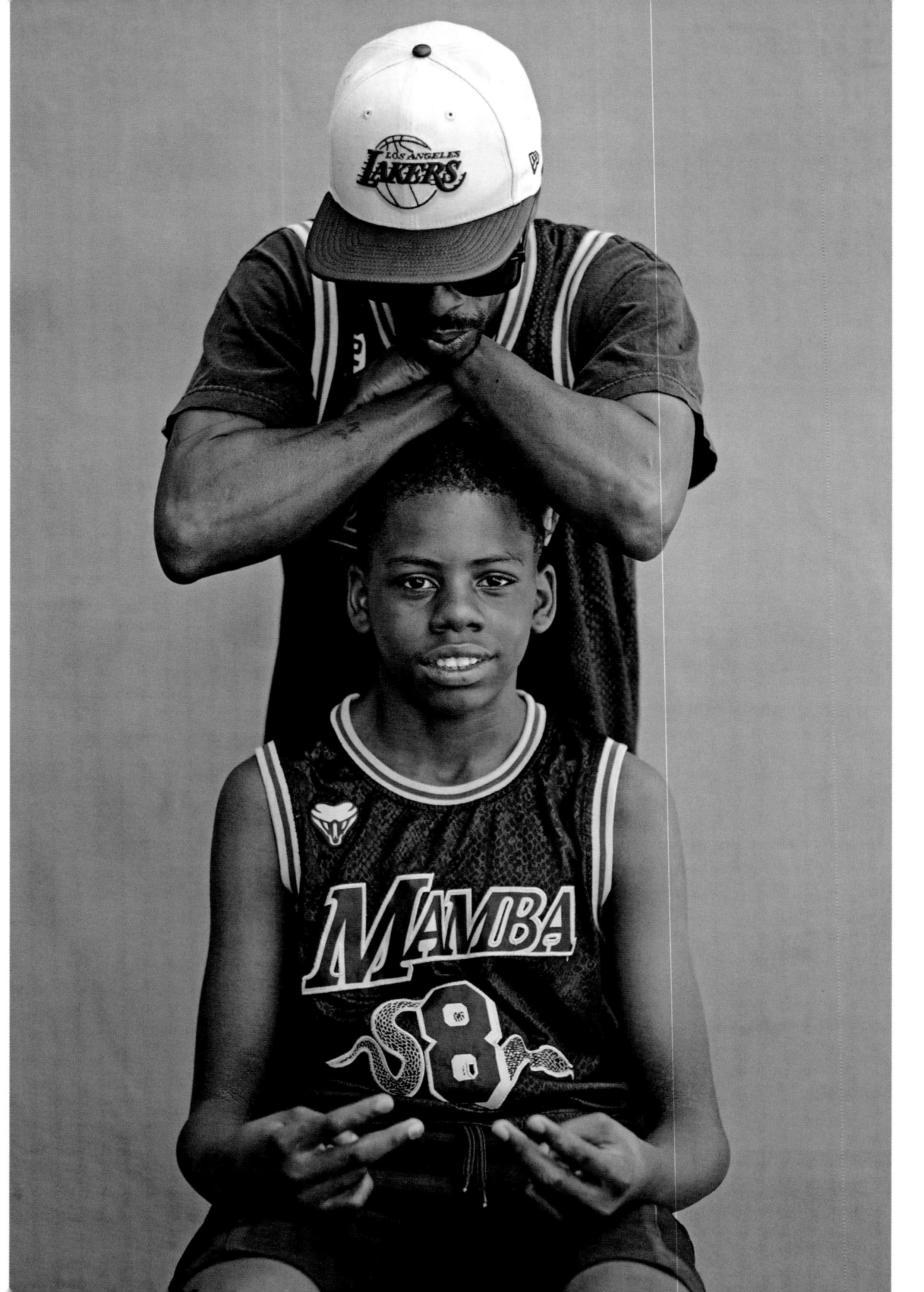

left: **Damion and Damion Jr., 2024**

opposite: **Daniel and Nathaniel, 2023**

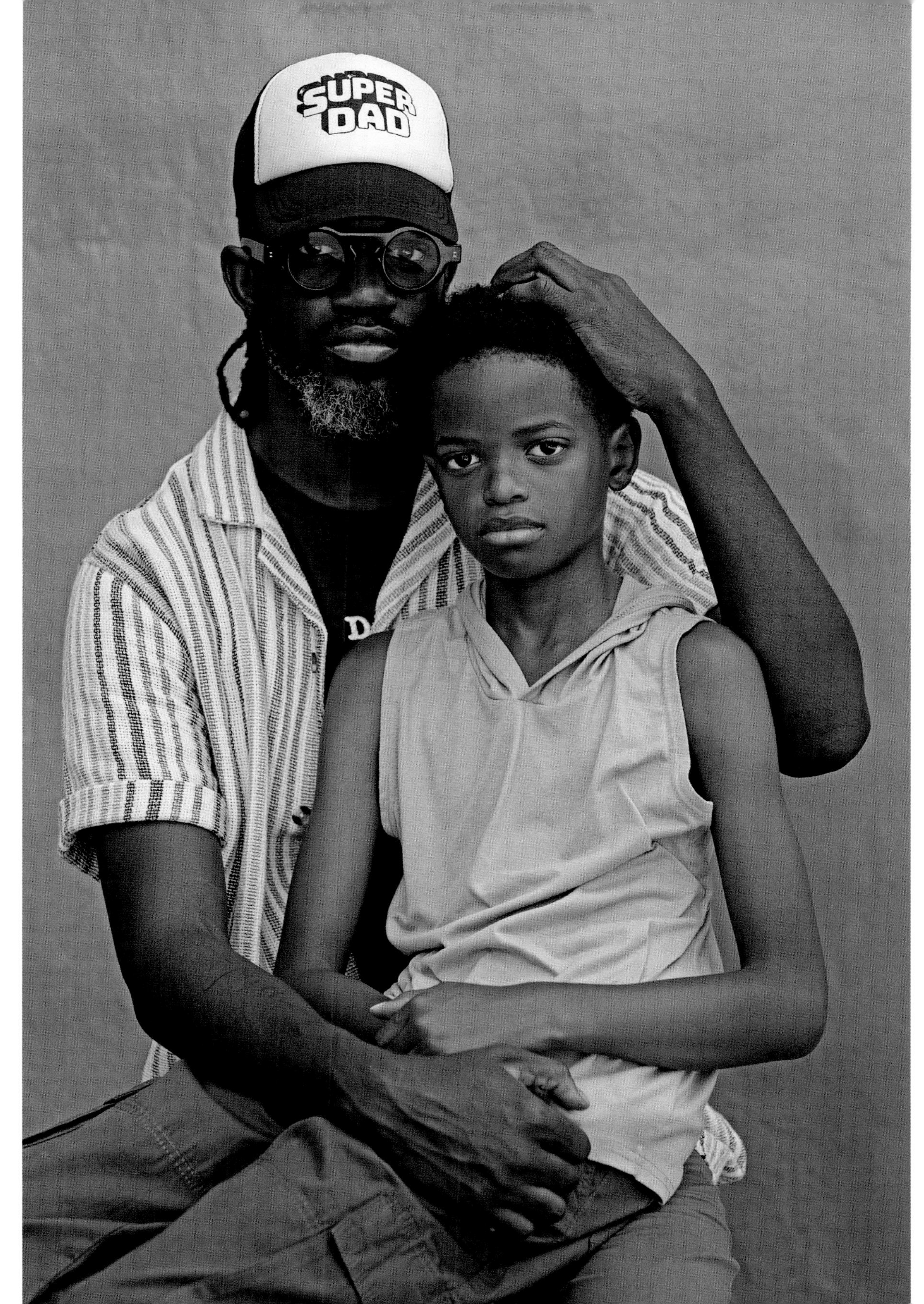
SUPER
DAD

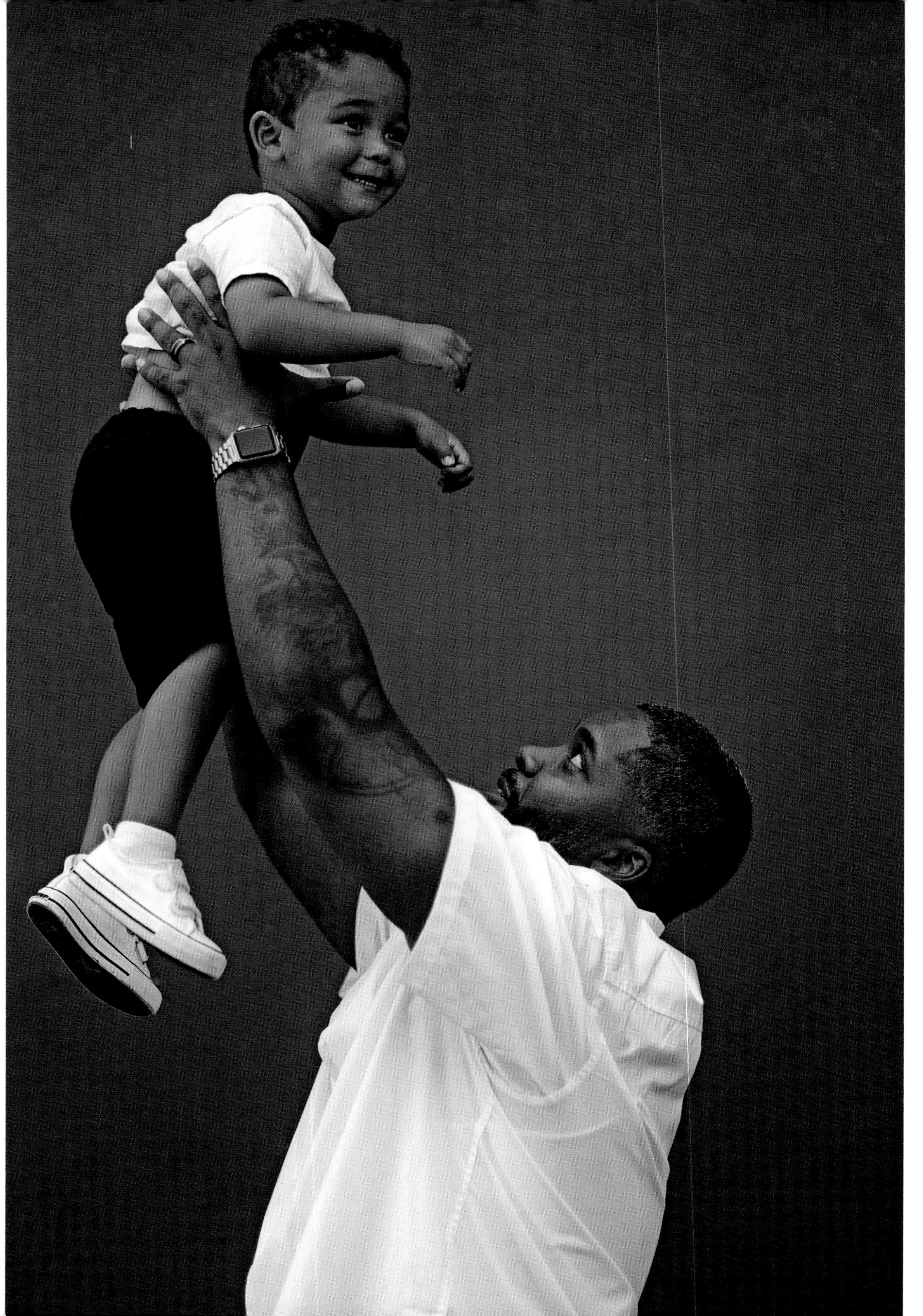

left: **Erix and Erix Jr., 2023**

opposite: **Allan and Allan Jr., 2023**

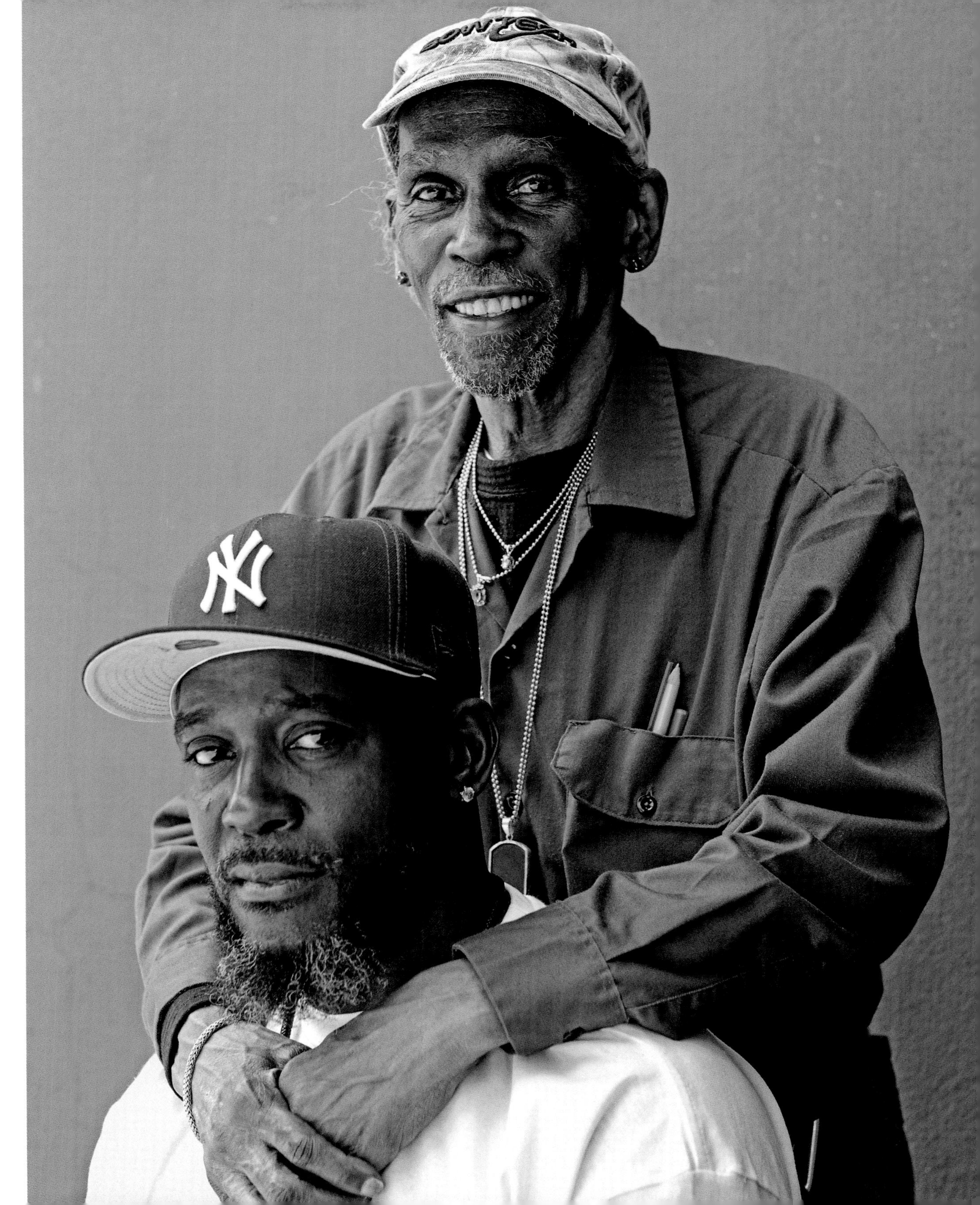
NY

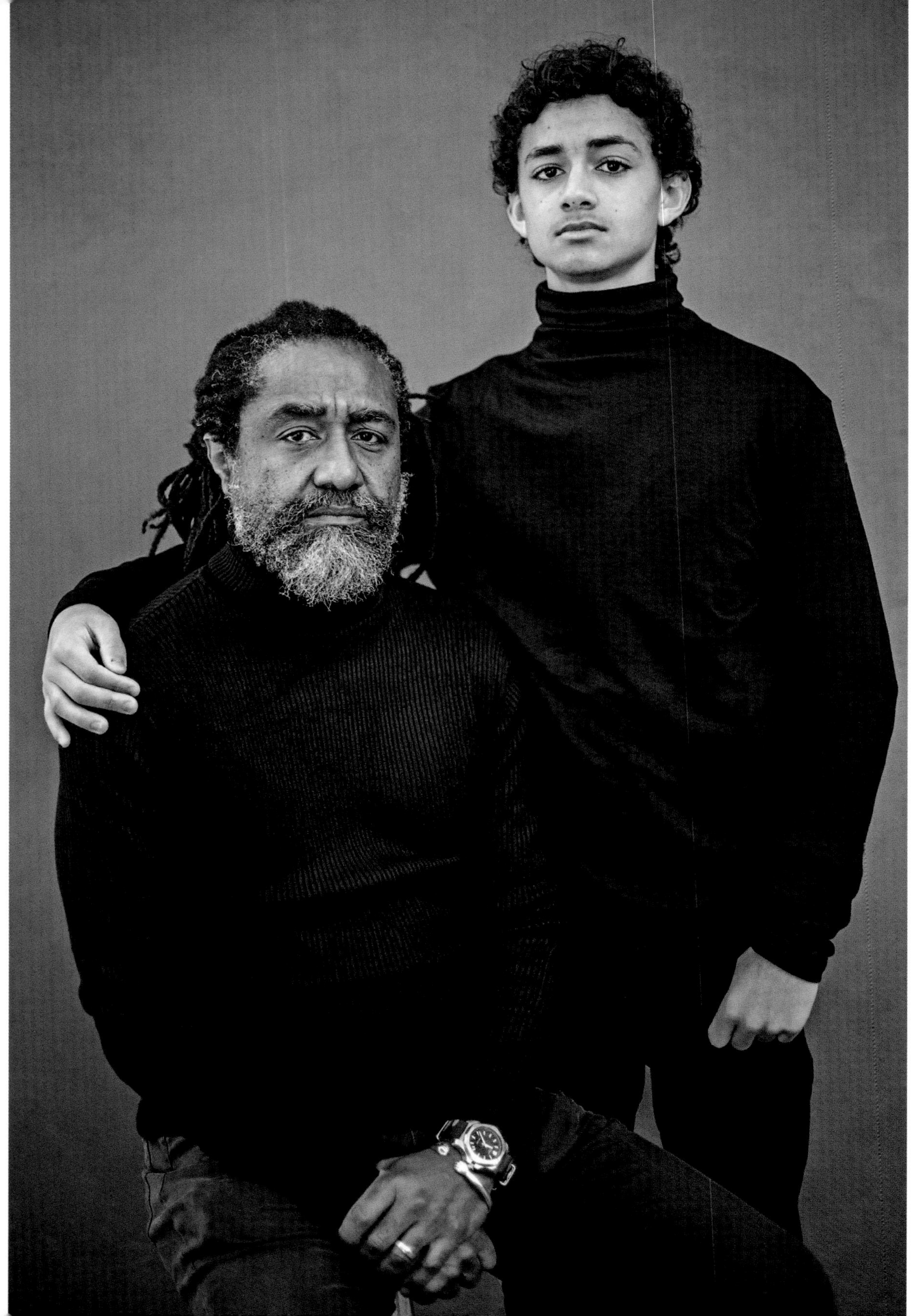

left: **Herbert and Declan, 2021**

opposite, left: **Karlton and Jacari, 2014**

opposite, right: **Tosin and Elijah, 2021**

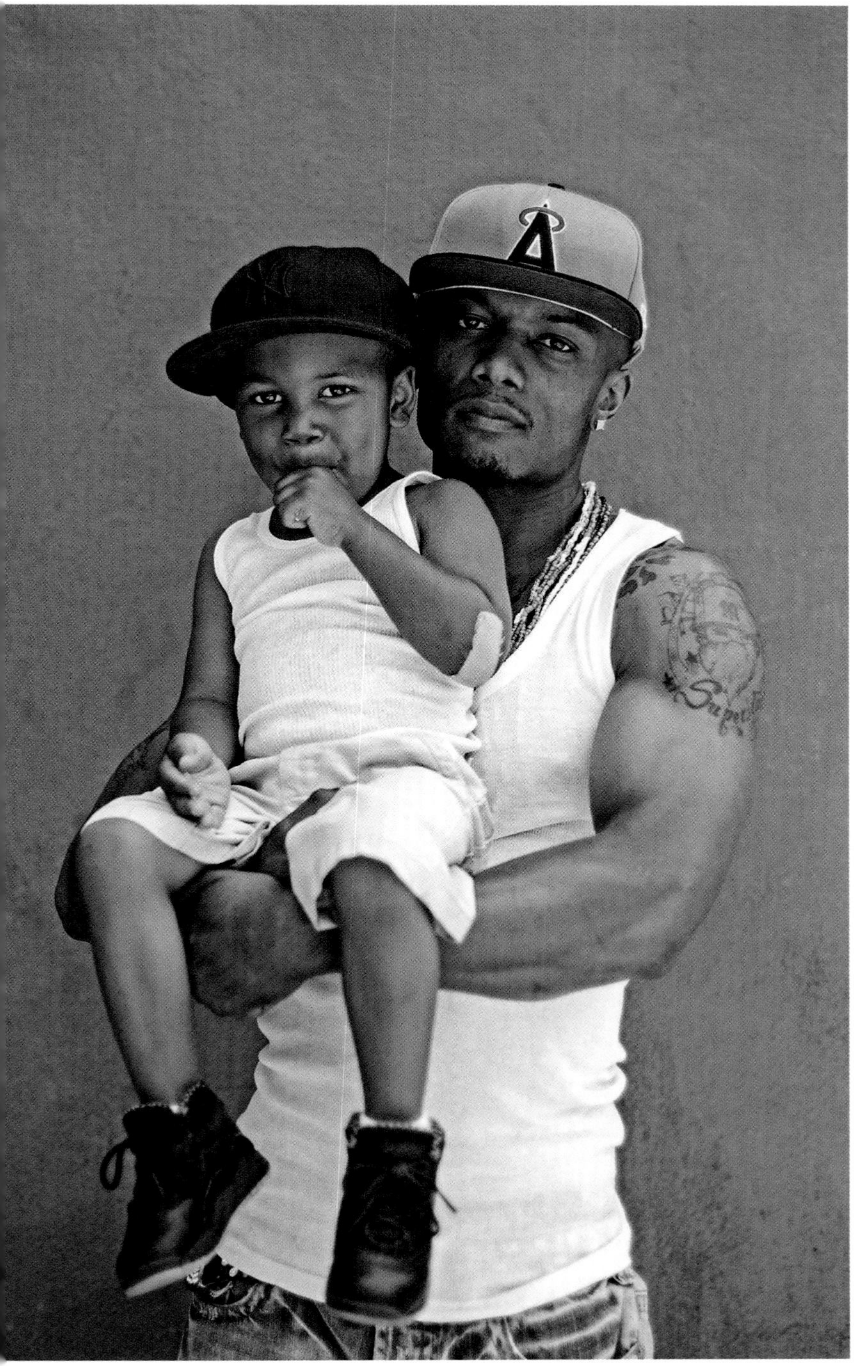

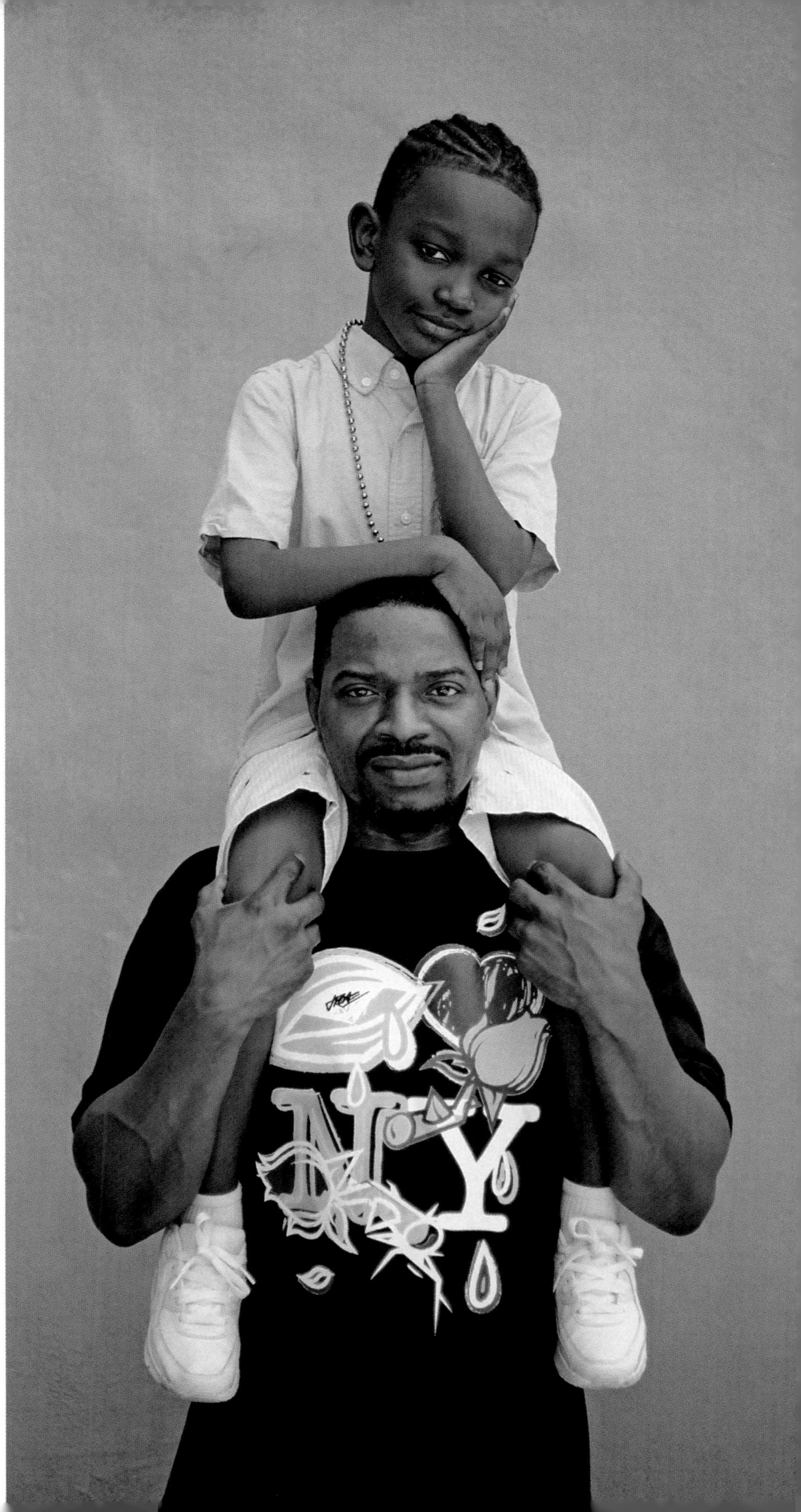

DADDYING

TAU BATTICE

For me, "Daddy" is the most important title. Beyond every educational and material achievement, it is the appellation that moves my deepest being, emotionally and socially. With these portraits, I aim to preserve "daddying" moments in which fathers are fully present and nurturing healthy relationships with their sons. In the collected split seconds composing this body of work, I strive to amplify the transference of manhood from father to son, the warmth, the tenderness, the intimacy, the stewardship, the pride. Joyfully!

West 125th Street, Harlem, just east of the world-famous Apollo Theater, is where I photograph said relationships with an eye for simplicity and approachable majesty. My hope is that the images made in this beacon of Black America relay the regularity and diversity of Black father-son relationships even as they encourage more wholesome relationships for men of African descent and their sons. Such relationships are not as anomalous and rare as some popular media would have us believe; instead, they are the lived realities of many Black families. I started intermittently photographing "daddying" ten years ago on a Harlem street corner. To date, I have photographed thirty fathers with their sons in what is really an homage to the beautiful relationship I have always had and still have with my own father.

New York City is where I have lived most of my life. My mother moved here in 1987 from Saint Kitts and Nevis; I first came in 1992. This city has formally educated me, blessed me with my children, and fostered my thriving career as an educator and visual anthropologist. Harlem is where I photograph Black men and their sons. This tough city is home: a notion that, for me, implies both guidance and sanctuary. Not surprisingly, solid fathers in their daddying provide these same qualities to their sons. Strolling through Harlem, I am always in deep admiration of fathers commuting with their sons. Particularly when these fathers are of African descent, I have wondered how they father in an America that can sometimes be unkind to Black men. Though I am a father myself, I am a "girl dad" to daughters. I do not have a biological son, but I do have a stepson whom I had the good fortune of raising since he was four years old. These images allow me to spread the energies of positive Black father-son relationships. My psychological self-excavations have made me realize that not having a biological son of my own leads me to pour positive energies into healthy father-son visuals.

Indeed, making these images of everyday fathers has been key to my development as a more empathetic man. Hopefully these photographs reflect that love of the common father and the common people.

"MY HOPE IS THAT THE IMAGES MADE IN THIS BEACON OF BLACK AMERICA RELAY THE REGULARITY AND DIVERSITY OF BLACK FATHER-SON RELATIONSHIPS."

JAMEL SHABAZZ

Celebrated New York City photographer whose goal as an artist is to contribute to the preservation of world history and culture

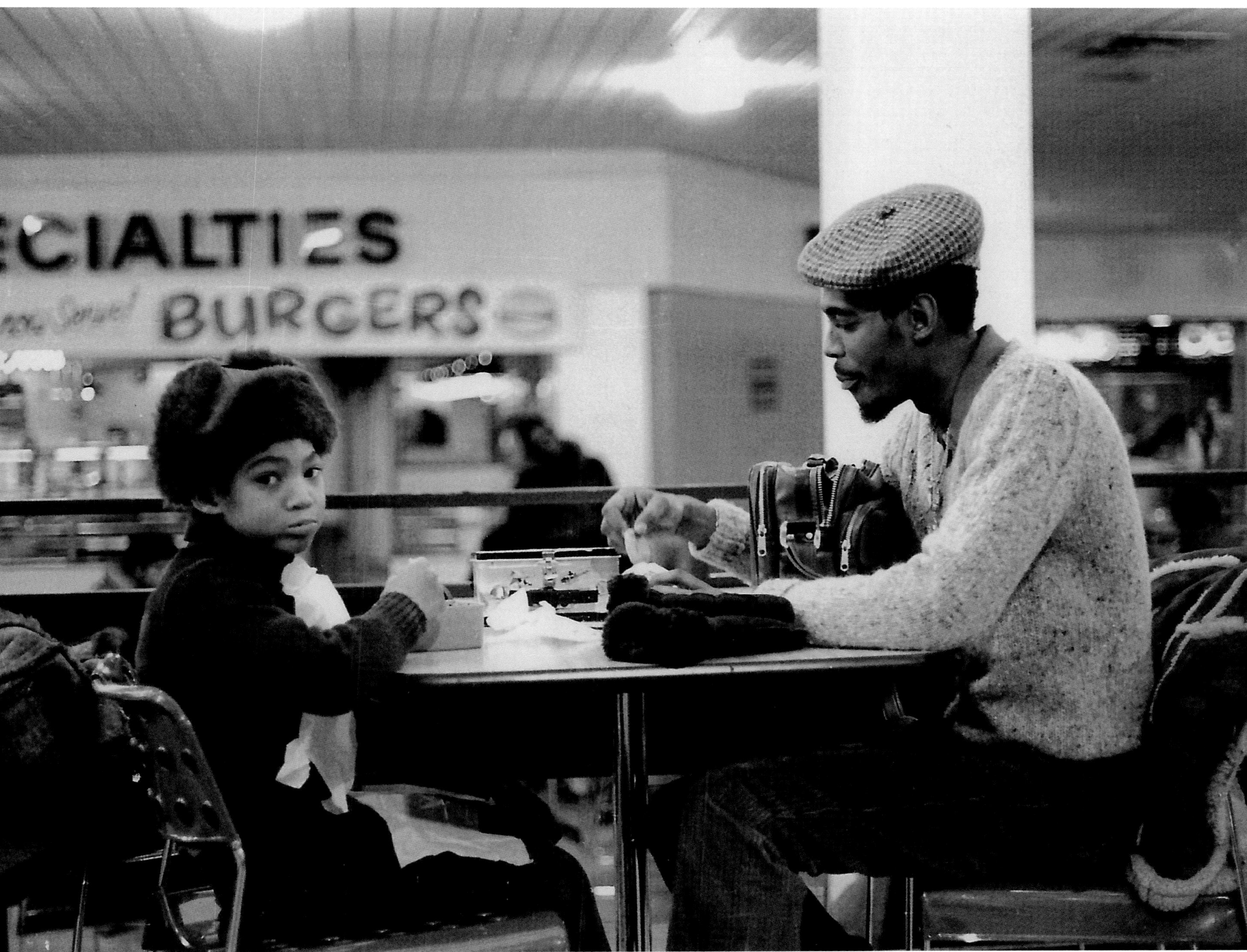

Father-and-son time, Brooklyn, New York, 1982

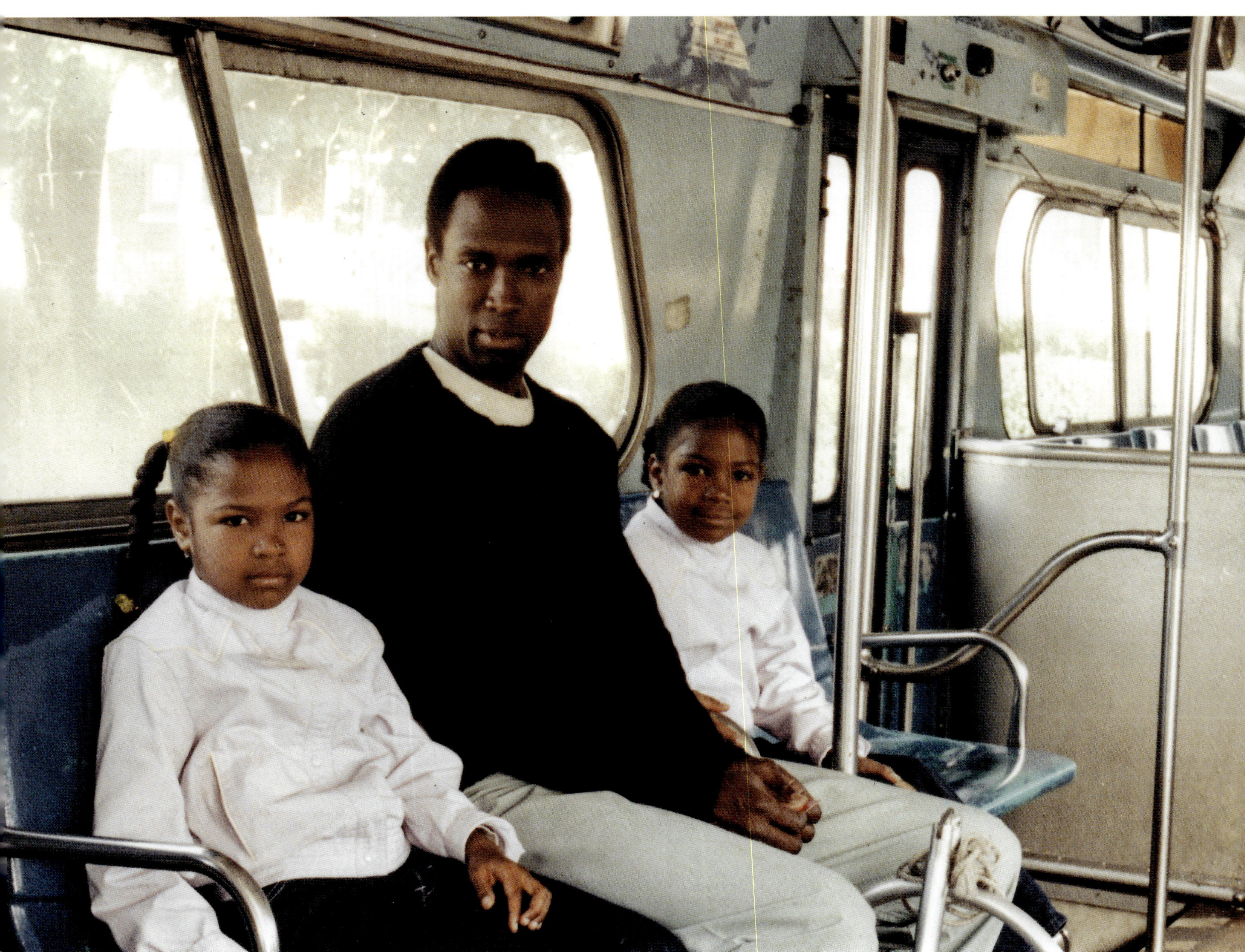

Daddy's little girls, Crown Heights, Brooklyn, New York, 1980

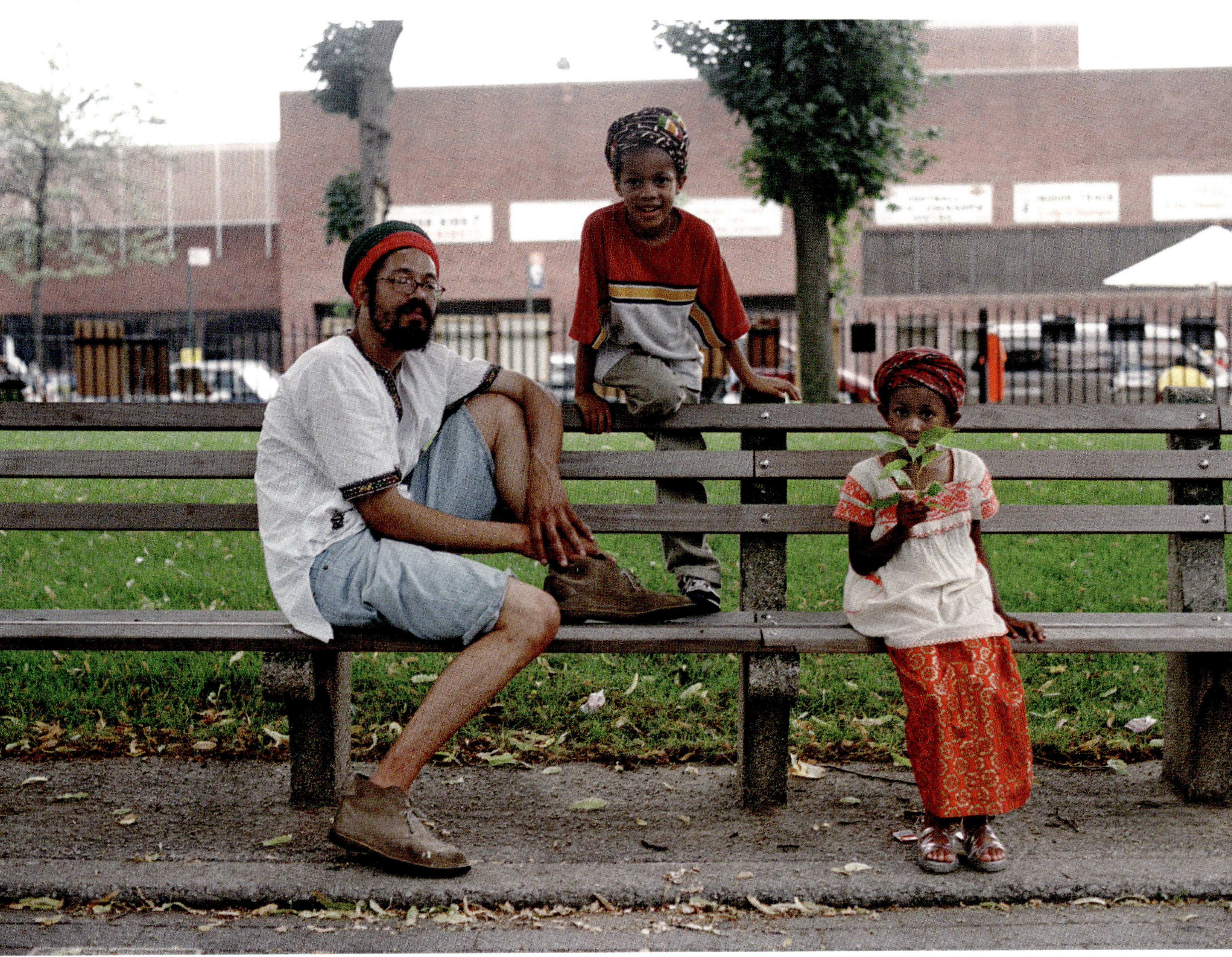

Father and seeds, Brooklyn, New York, circa 1990

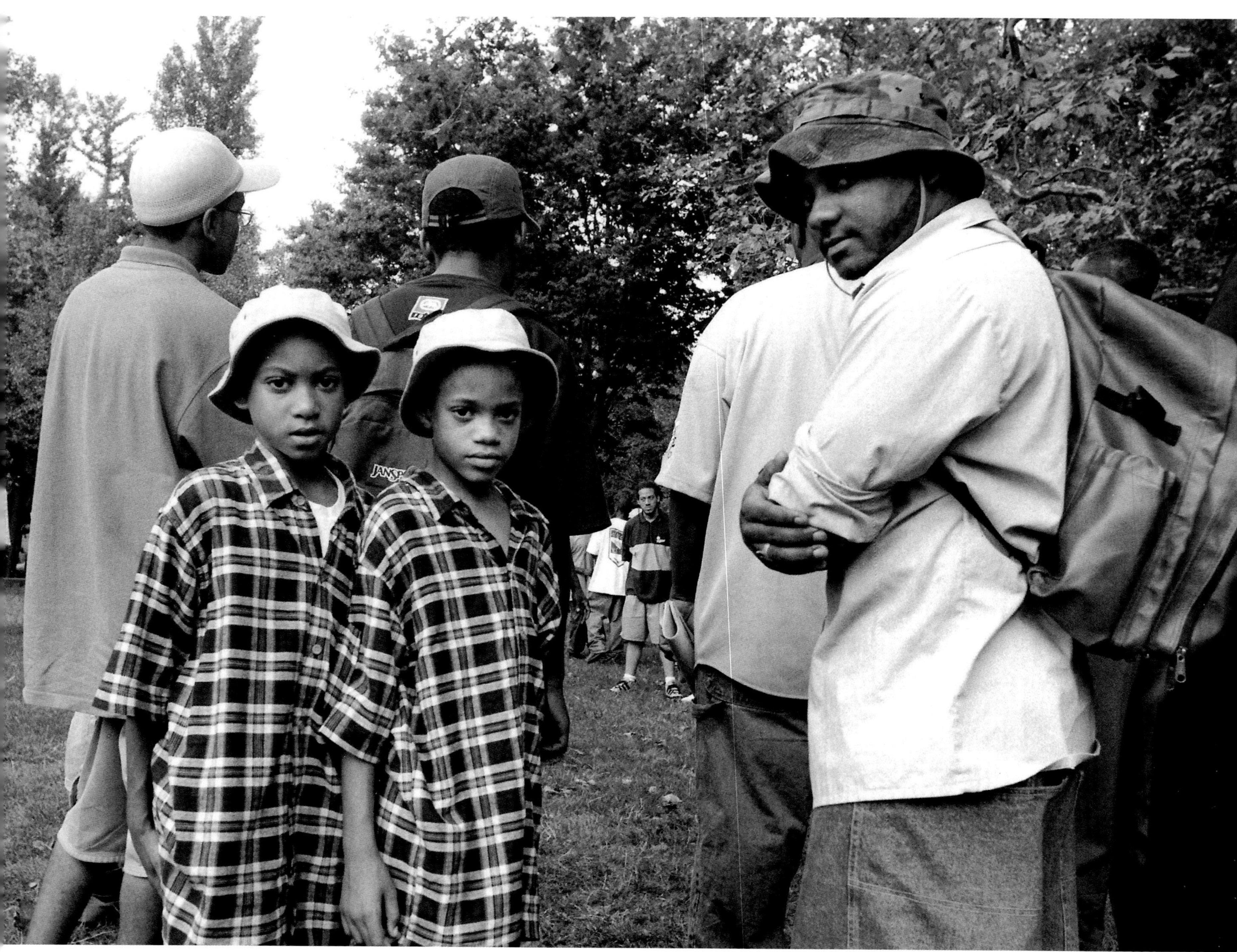

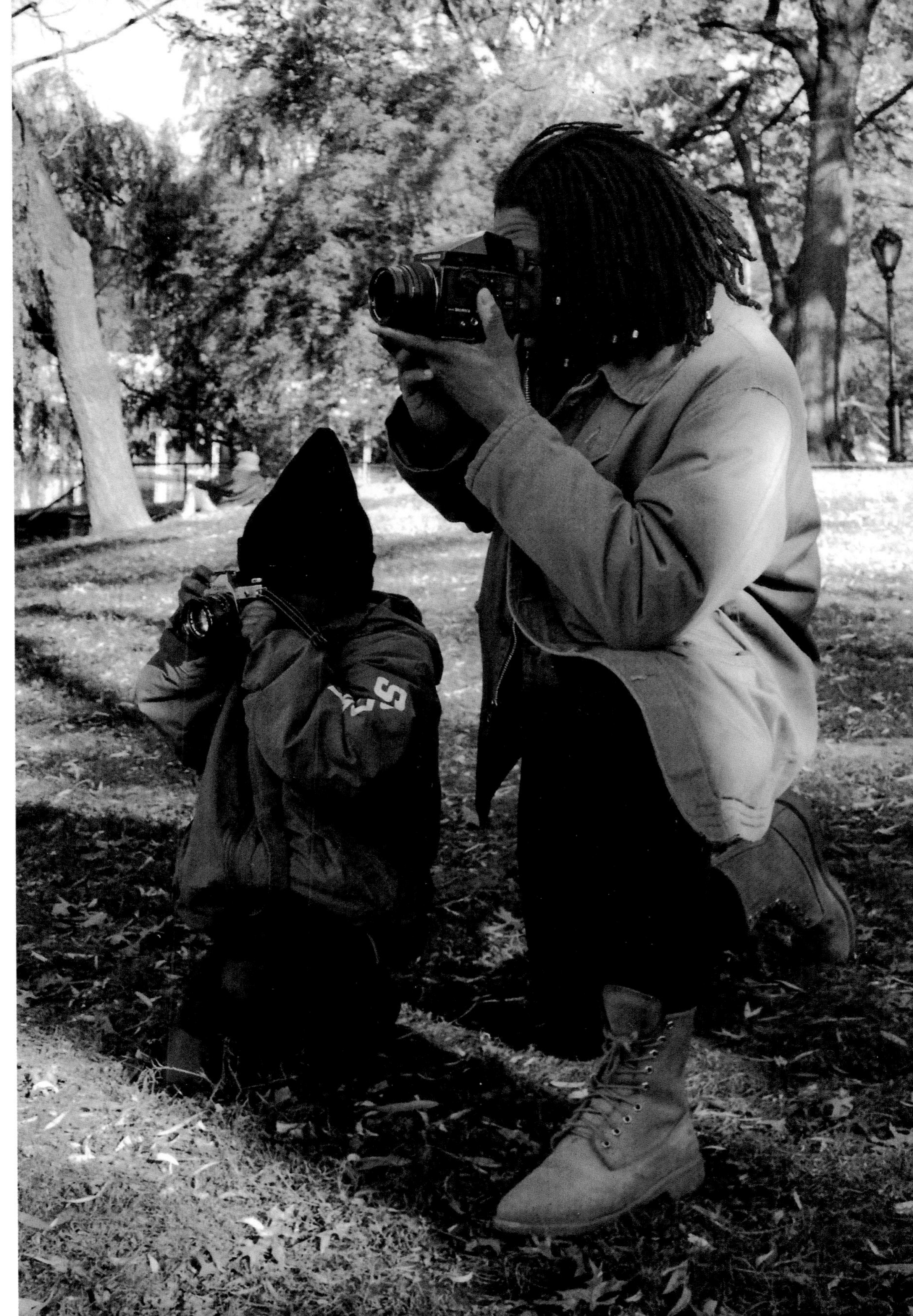

opposite: **Fathers and sons, Brooklyn, New York, 1997**

right: **The teacher and the student, New York City, New York, 1995**

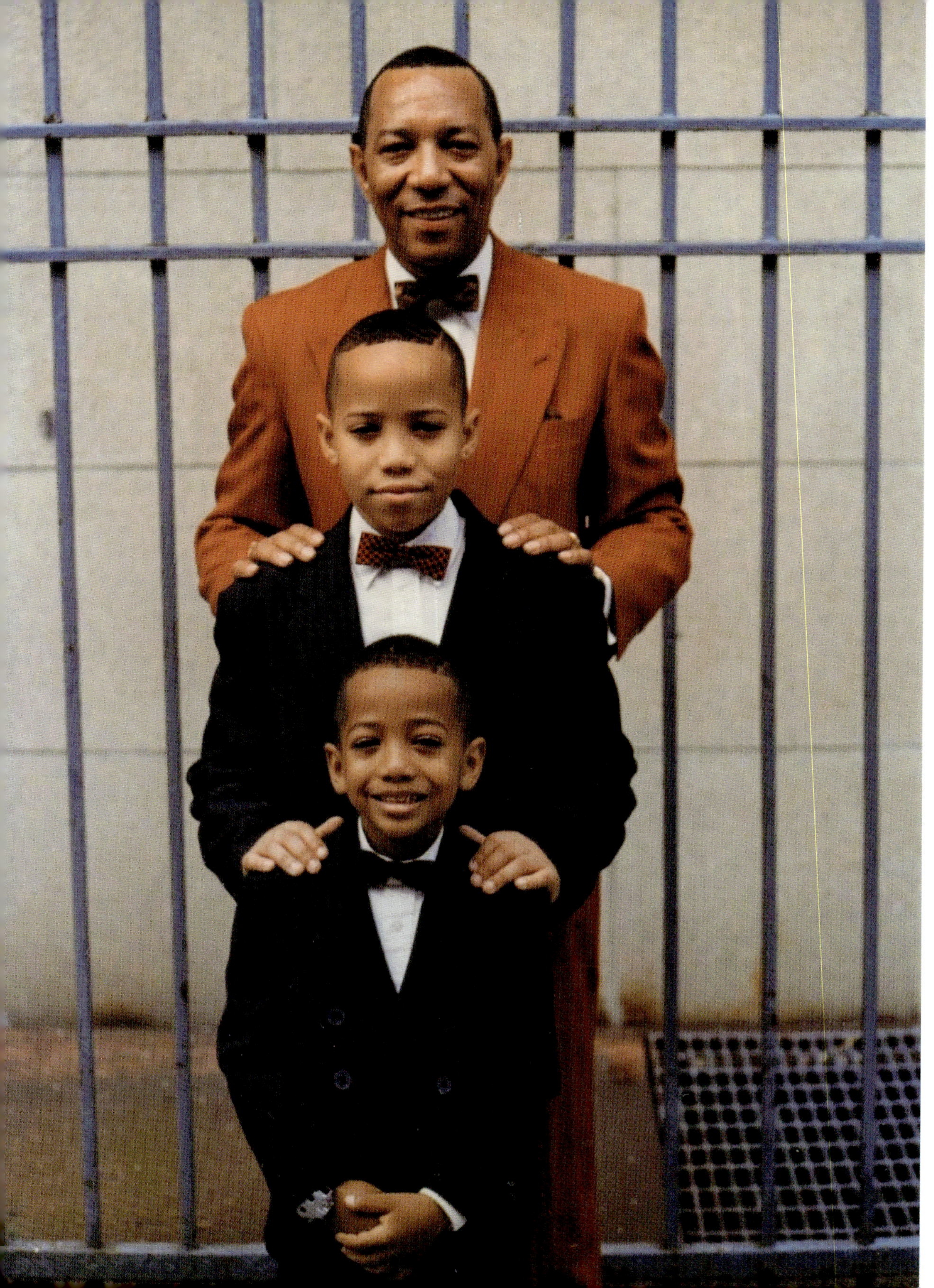

left: **Three stages of life, Harlem, New York City, 1994**

opposite: **It takes a village, Philadelphia, Pennsylvania, 1994**

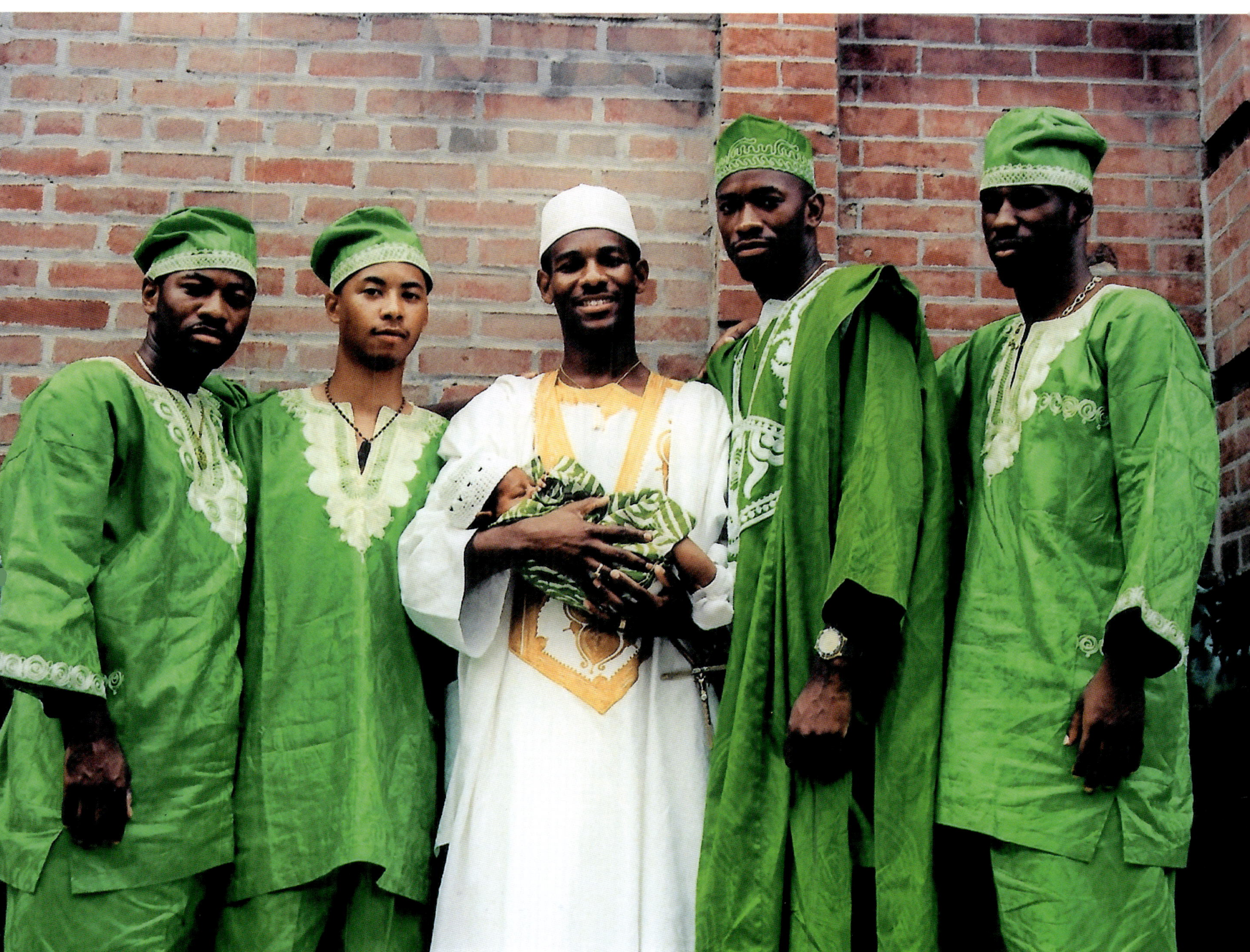

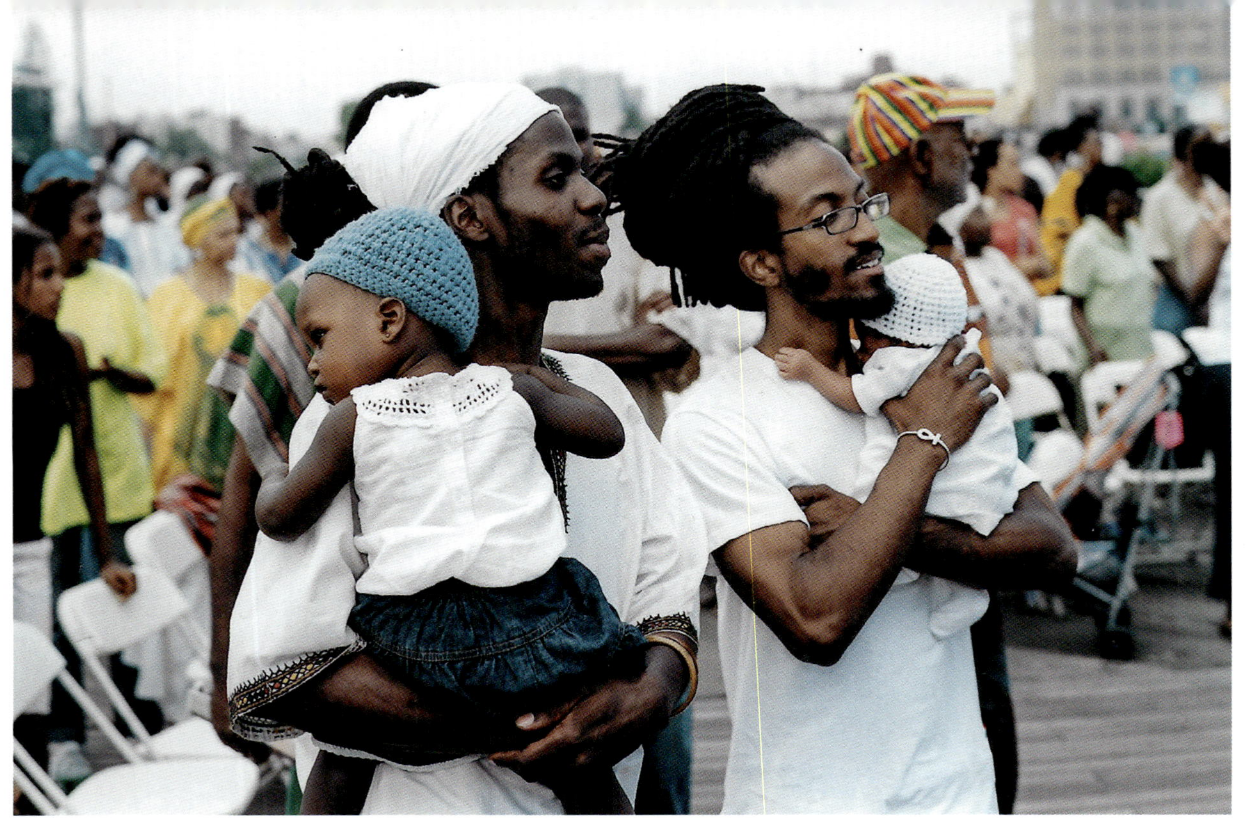

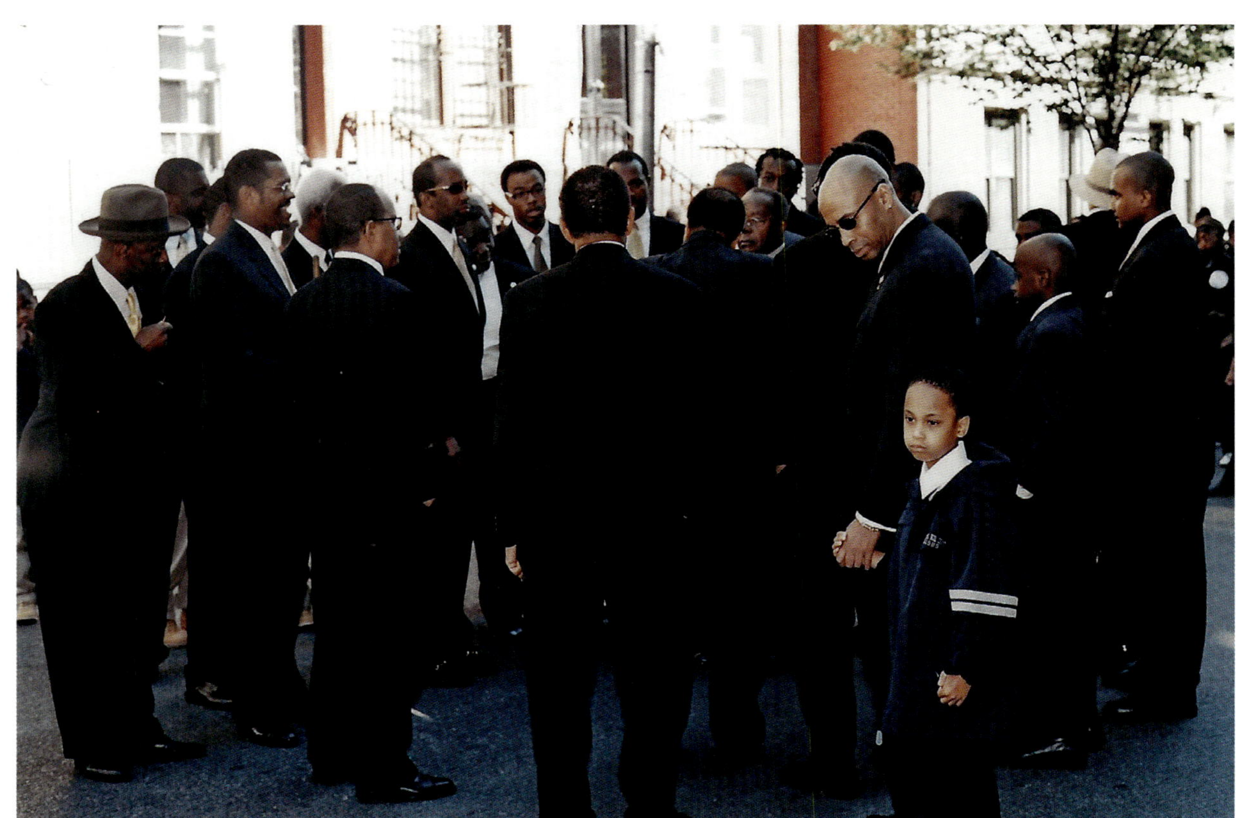

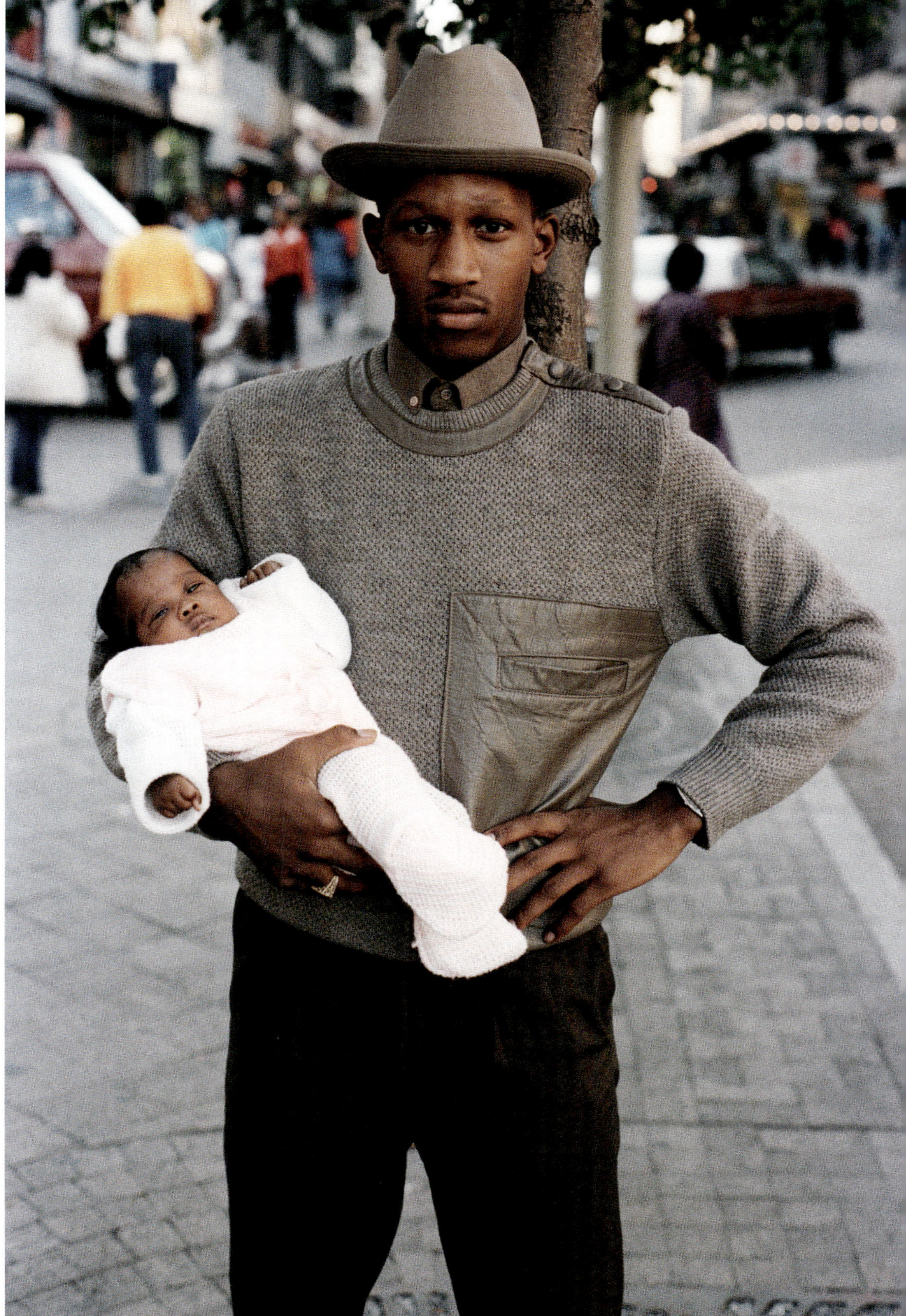

opposite, top: **Men of honor, Brooklyn, New York, 2004**

opposite, bottom: **Reflection of a father, Brooklyn, New York, 1990**

right: **Dupreme and Ebby, Brooklyn, New York, 1985**

FATHERHOOD
DEREK MORGAN

As a Black man, fatherhood means actively refining my strengths and redefining my weaknesses to evolve both myself and my family legacy. I learned from my dad the importance of demonstrating love through unwavering support, which has shaped my approach to parenting. Since becoming a father, I have committed myself to improving my verbal expressions of love. It is my responsibility to build on the legacy my dad created for me.

My dad set the gold standard for being an active and supportive role model, not just for me but also for my teammates and friends. His steadfast support for anyone on my team was remarkable; he took on many roles, from serving as a scoutmaster to participating in the Parent Booster Club. Whenever I run into an old friend from my sports or scouting days, they immediately ask, "How are you? How is your dad/are your parents?" I take pride in that impact and aspire to leave a similar mark on my sons and their community. To honor my father's example, I actively volunteer as a coach or team parent. You can count on me to be present at every game—I'm often the loudest voice in the gym or on the field—championing my boys and their teammates regardless of the outcome. When other parents ask me, "How and why do you do it?" I confidently reply, "My dad taught me to show up and show out from a young age."

While my dad showed love through actions, he struggled to verbalize his feelings. Daily affirmations like "I love you" were rare; my mom often provided those instead. Although my love for my dad remains unwavering, I recognize that our bond could have been even stronger if we had exchanged those words more frequently. Because of this, I have made it my job to redefine that aspect of fatherhood. It is important to tell my sons that I love them every single day. I start and end each day with a good-morning or good-night hug, a forehead kiss, and an "I love you." I refuse to let my sons ever wonder, "What if?" when it comes to my love for them. I want them to constantly seek ways to improve themselves and their relationships as they grow.

My fatherhood journey began in 2016, but the foundation for this role was established well before I ever considered having children. My dad provided me with the solid groundwork that helped me navigate the daily challenges of being a father. Given that his design is constantly being polished and reevaluated to suit my journey, it remains a guide. The invaluable lessons I have learned along the way have helped me grow as both a father and a man. I have chosen to be intentional with supportive actions and emotional investments in my children. My goal is to nurture the next generation so that they ultimately become in touch with their emotions. While this journey is my own, I do this in honor of my dad, as I constantly strive to be a more evolved version of him.

> **“SINCE BECOMING A FATHER, I HAVE COMMITTED MYSELF TO IMPROVING MY VERBAL EXPRESSIONS OF LOVE.”**

D. MICHAEL CHEERS

Award-winning photojournalist, filmmaker, and educator dedicated to the uplifting of Black communities worldwide

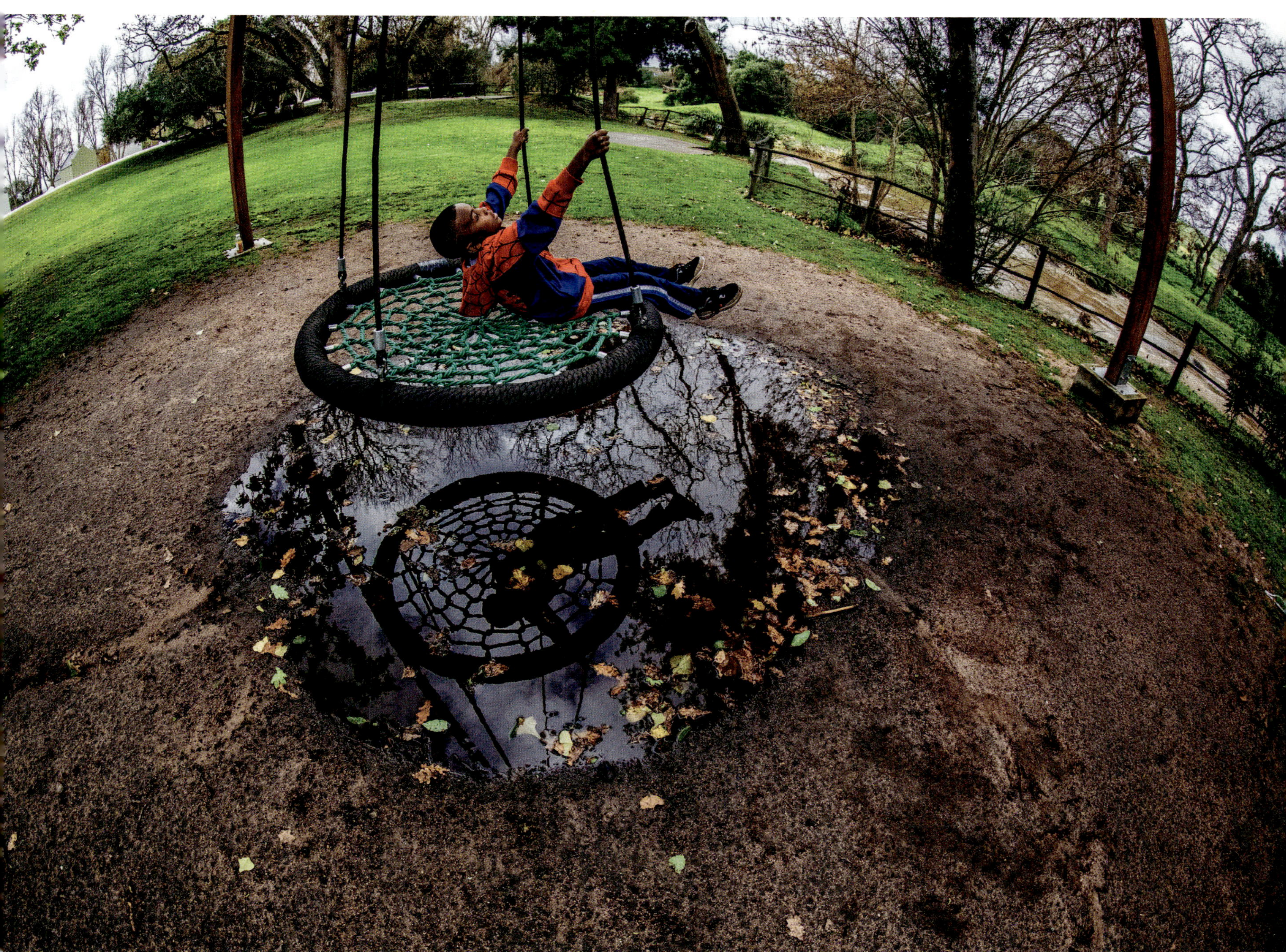

Isaiah enjoys a swing outside the Spier Wine Farm in Cape Town, South Africa, in 2018.

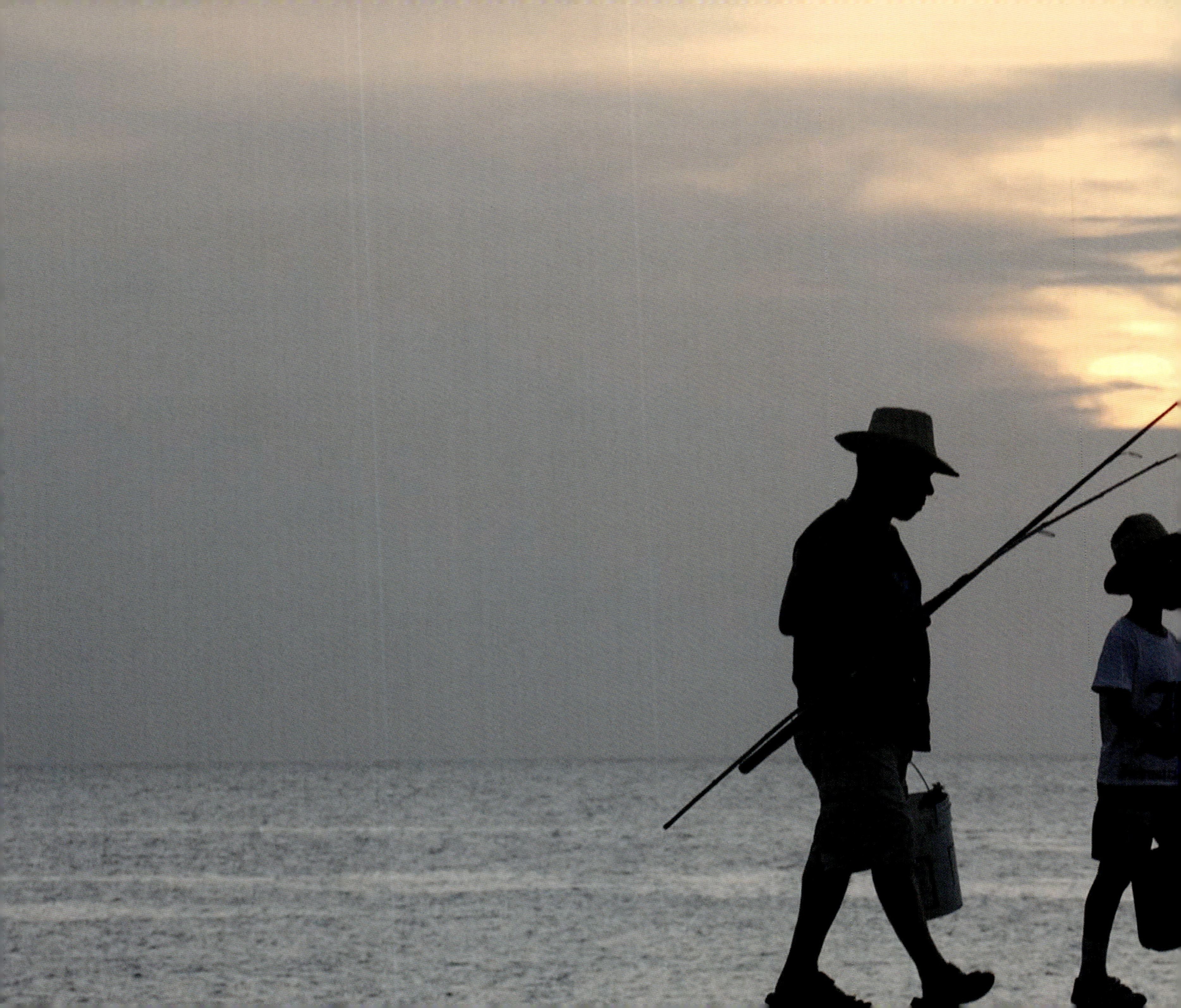

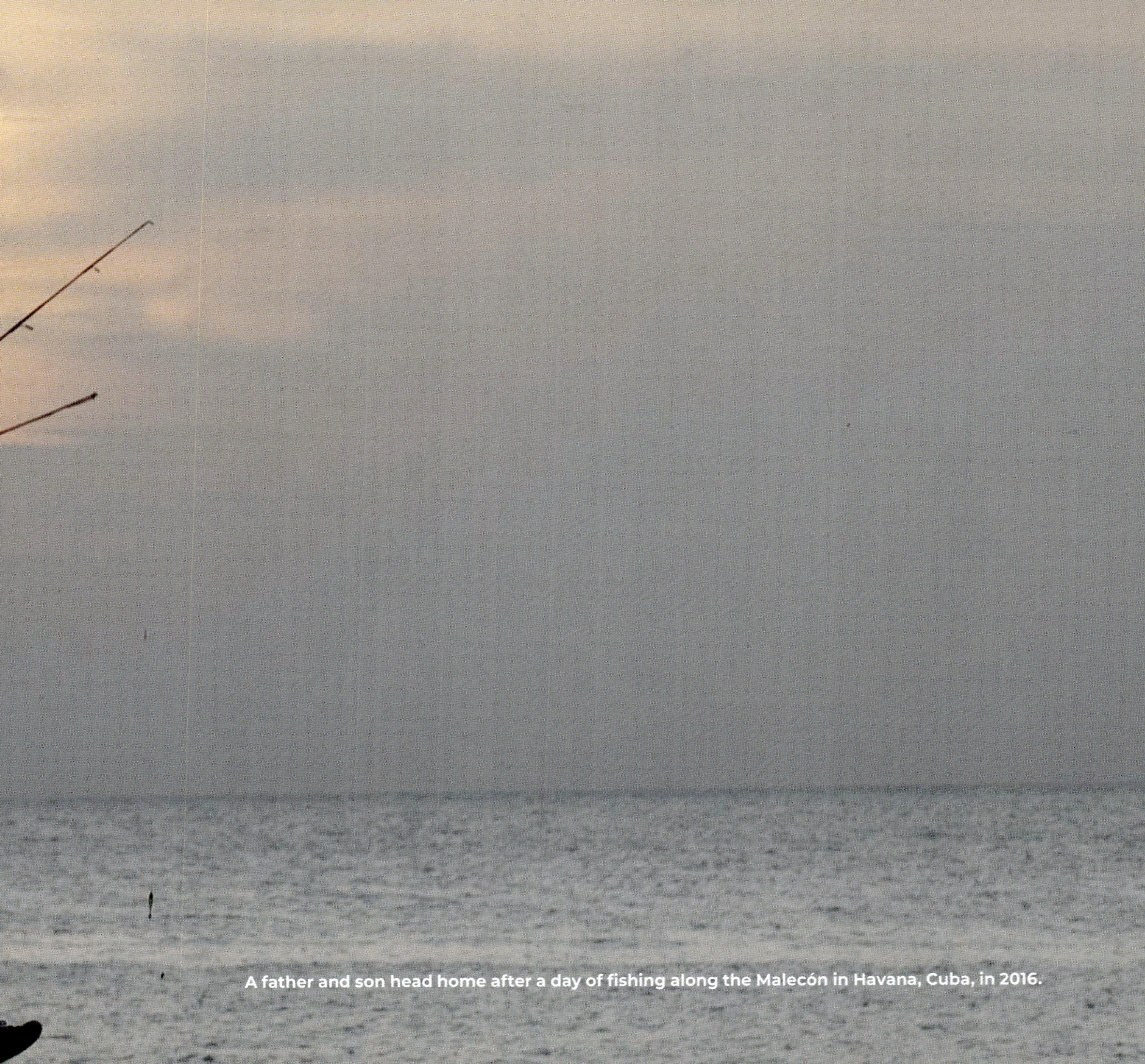

A father and son head home after a day of fishing along the Malecón in Havana, Cuba, in 2016.

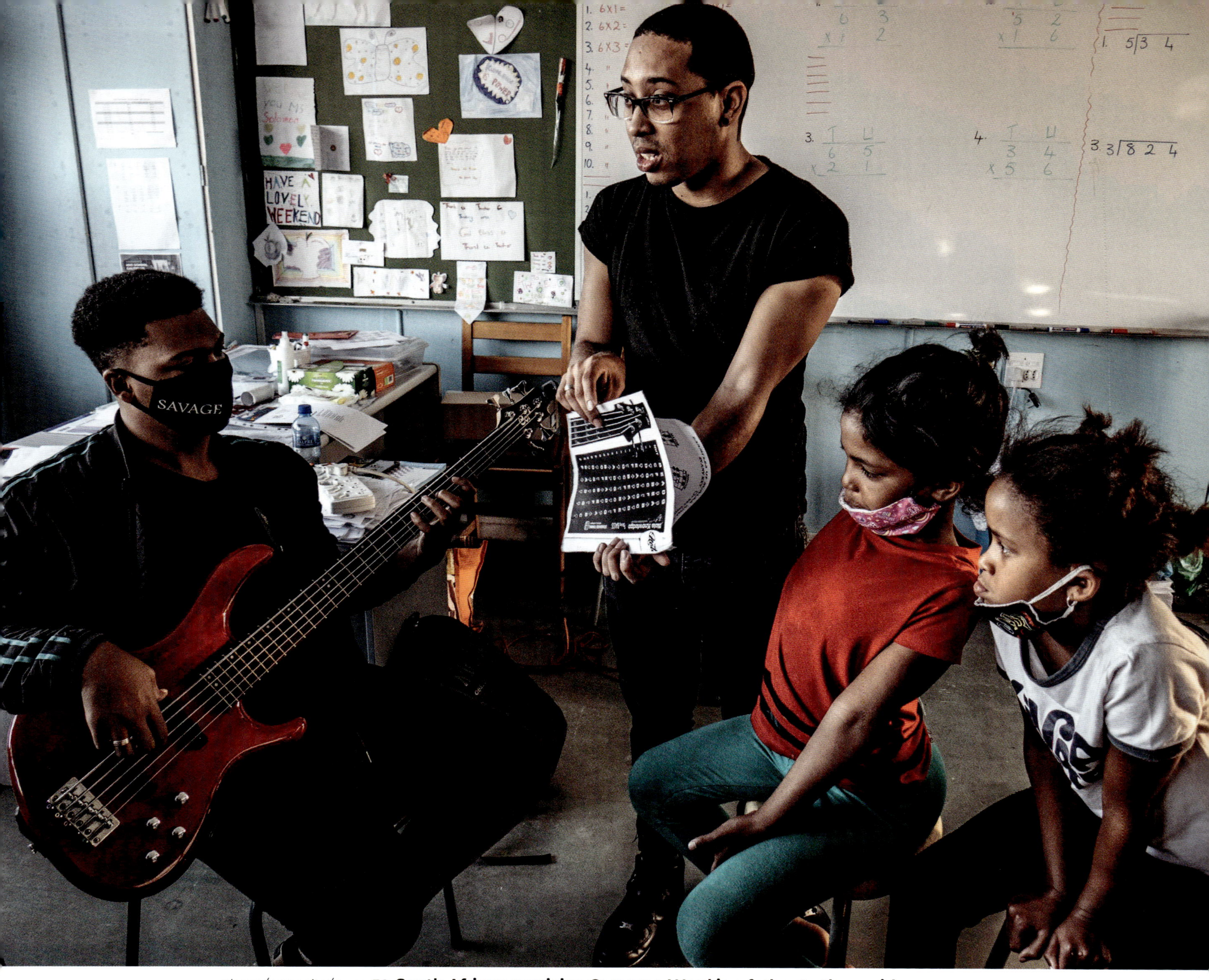

above/opposite/page 30: **South African musician Cameron Ward is a father to three girls, but he is everything to the marginalized youths in his Cape Flats community in Cape Town, South Africa. He started the Cameron Ward Music Foundation in 2018.**

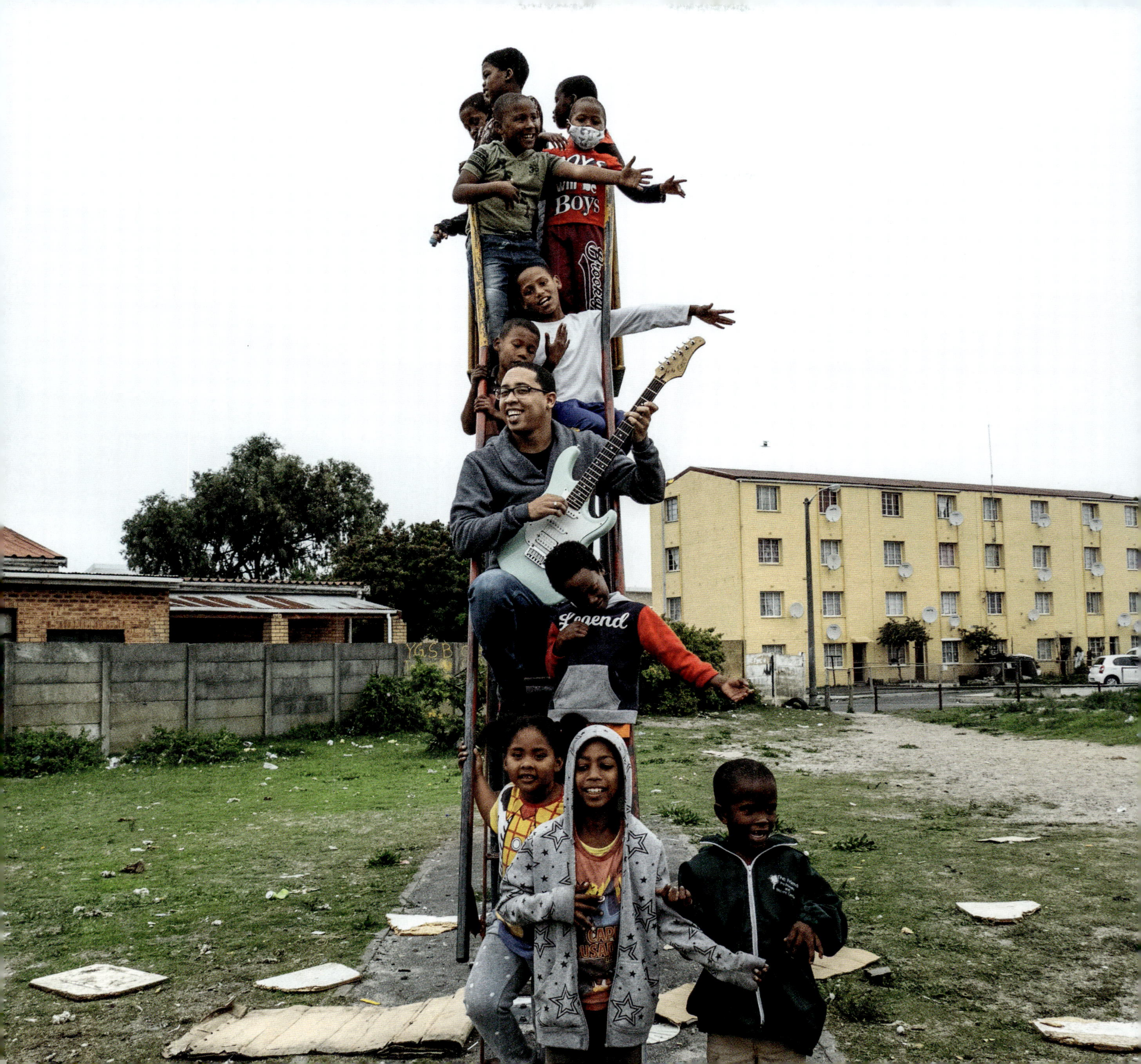
Boys
Legend

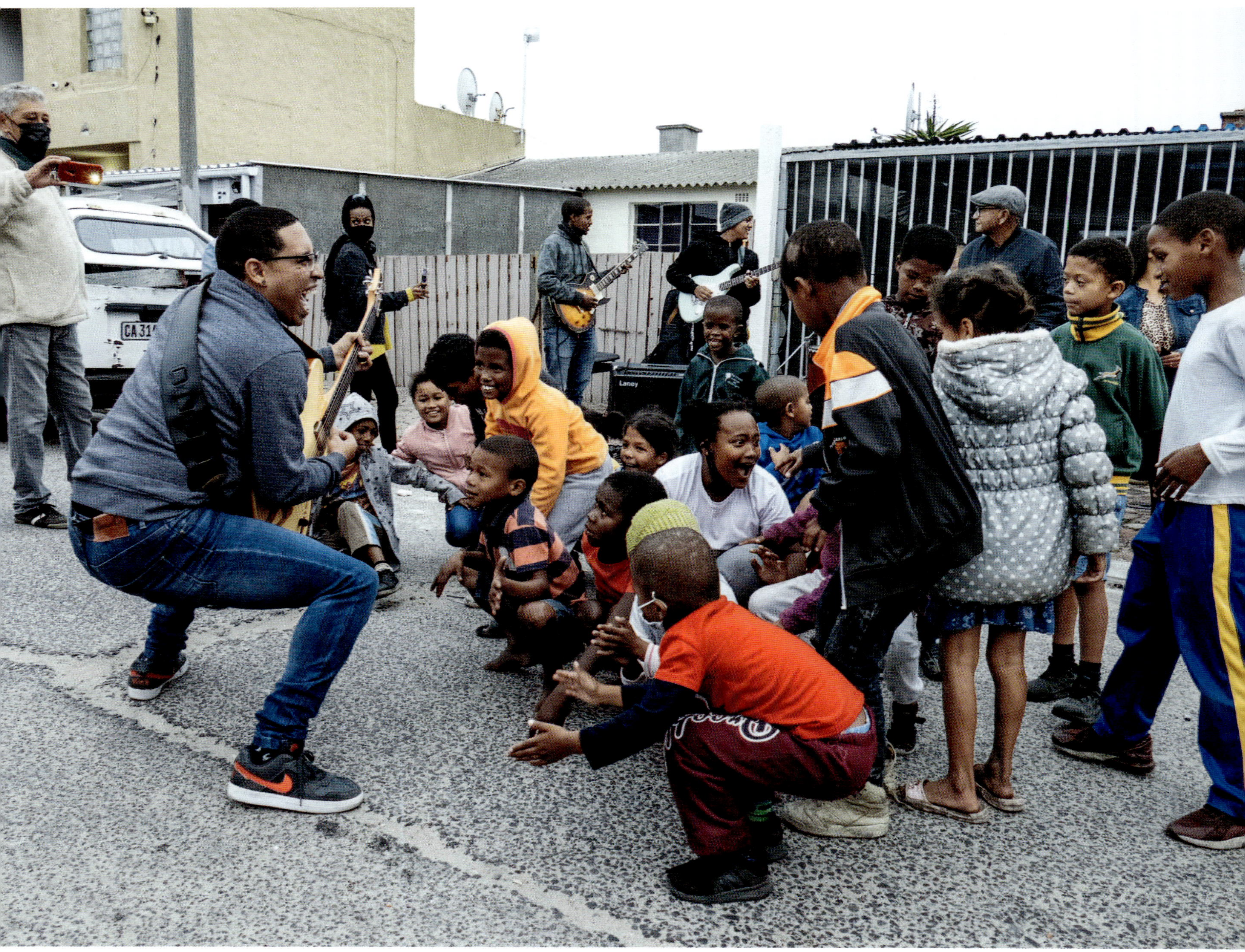

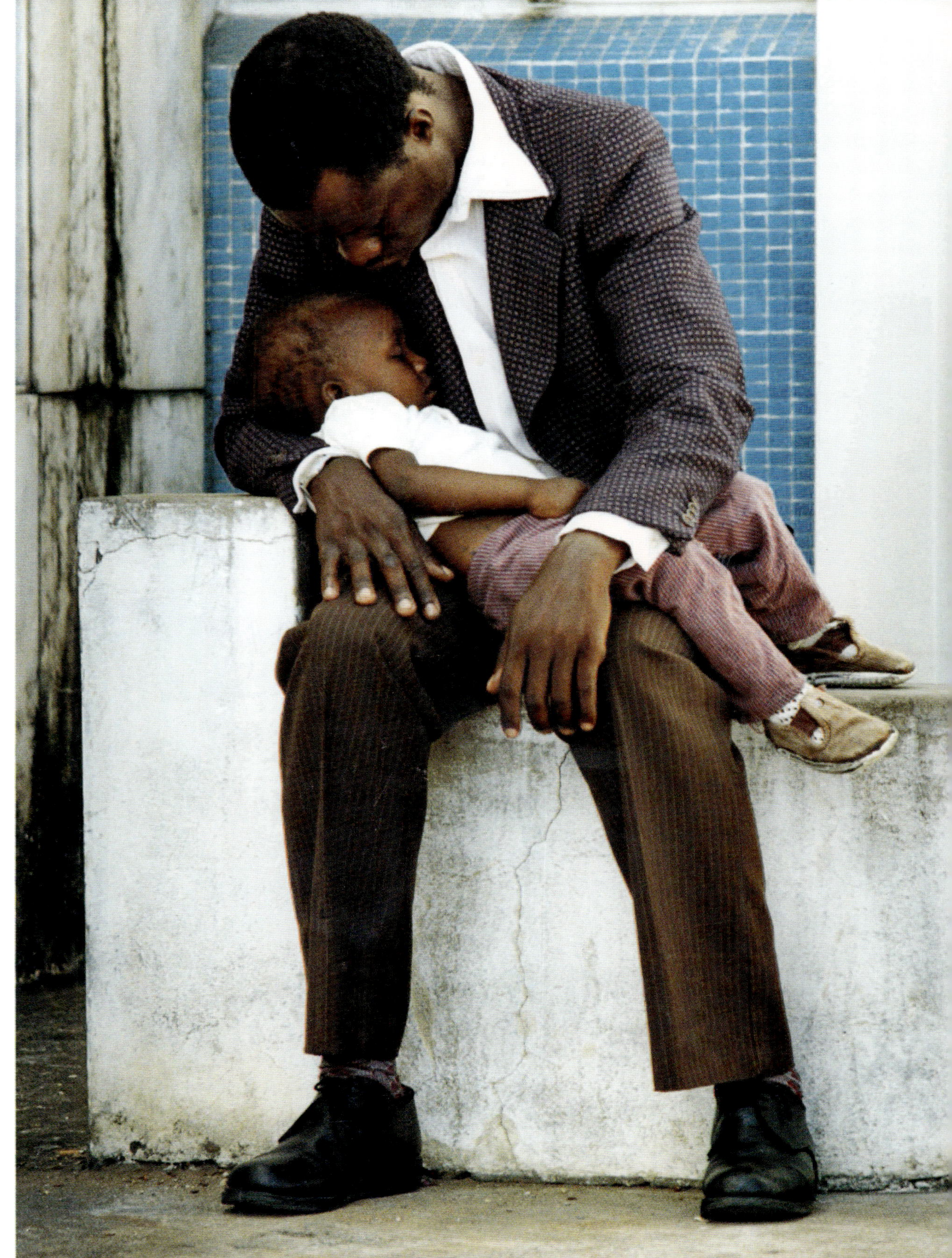

right: **A father and son nap outside a medical clinic in Dodoma, Tanzania.**

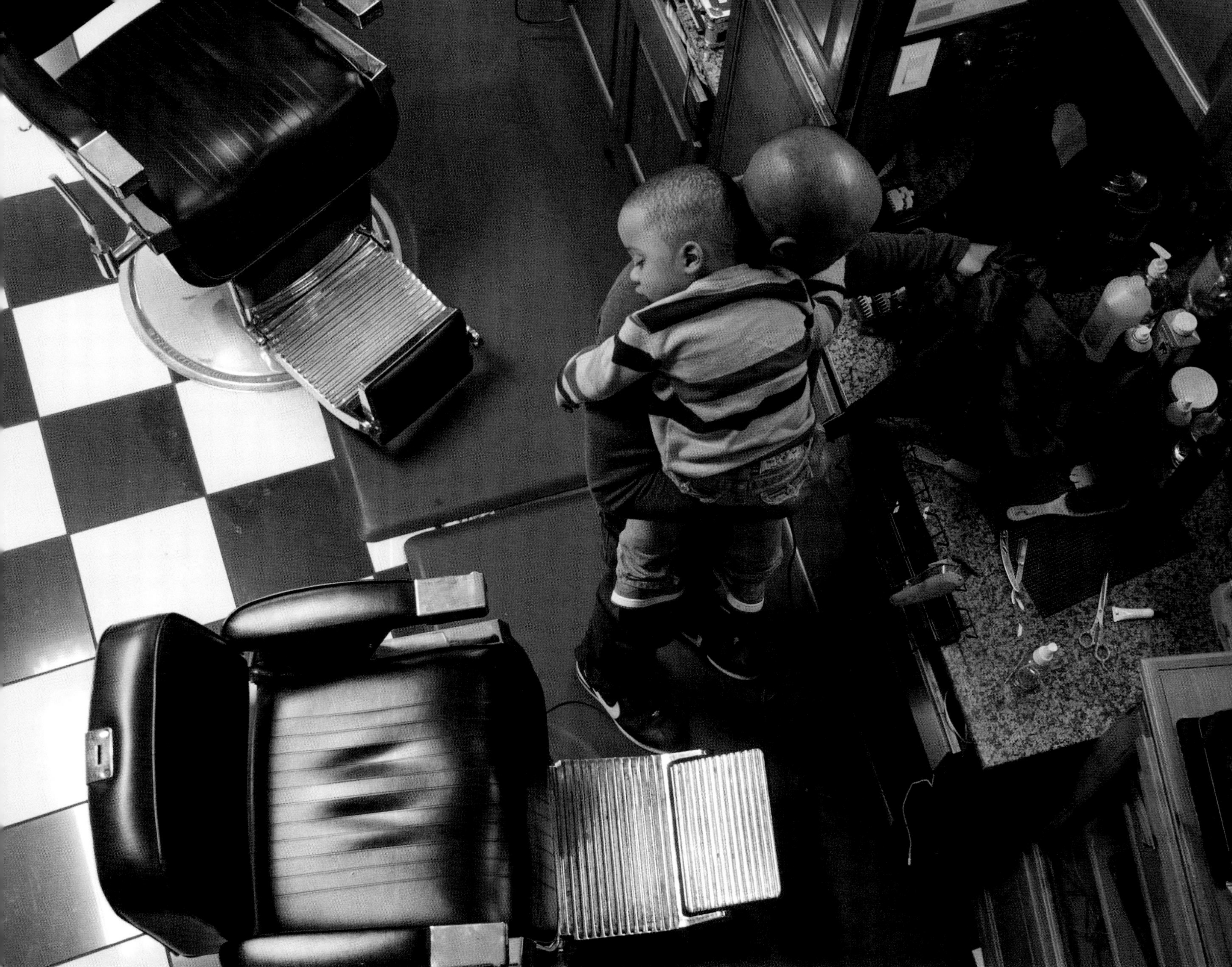

The Barbers Inc hairstylists Nicholas Loftis (*above*), shop owner Dave Diggs (*opposite, top*), and Alfonzo Jordan (*opposite, bottom*) pull double duty as fathers and babysitters.

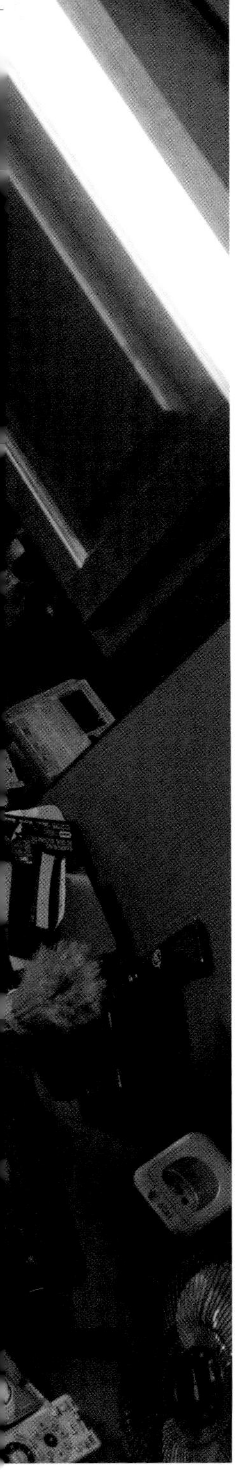

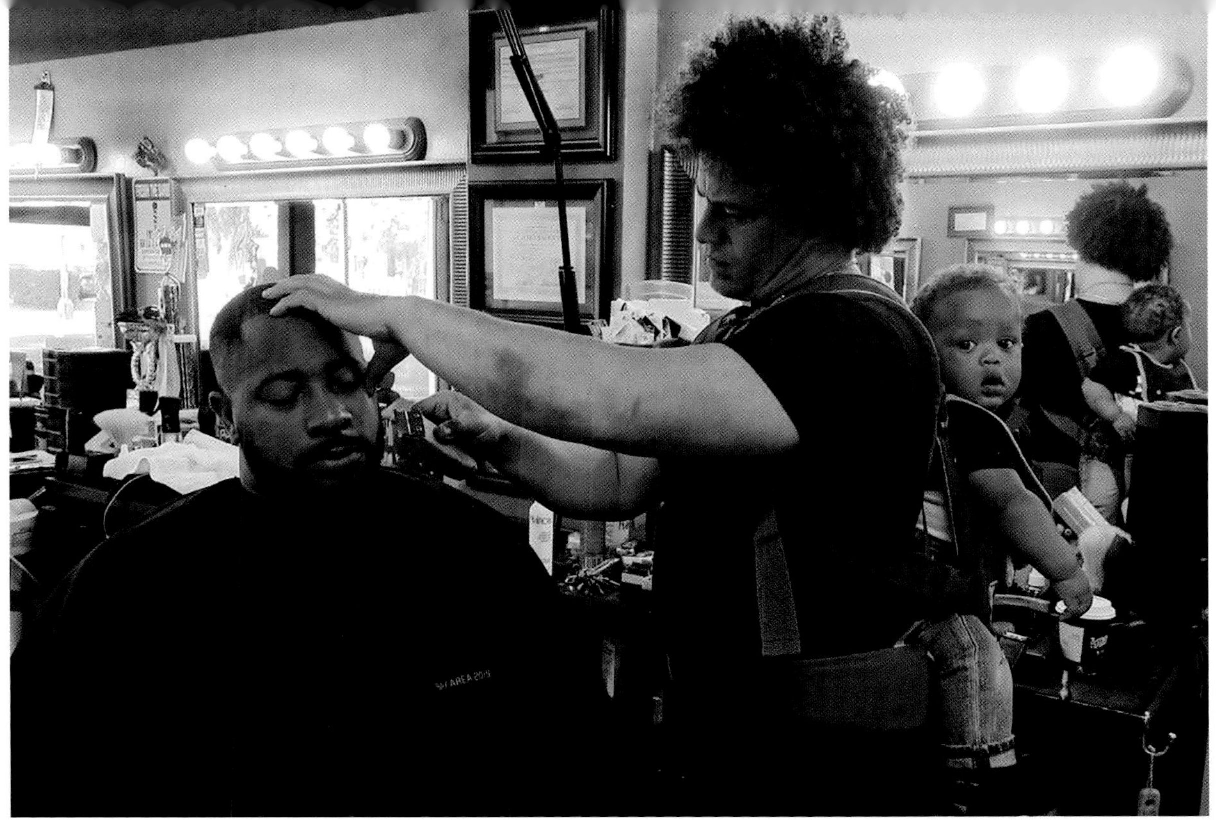

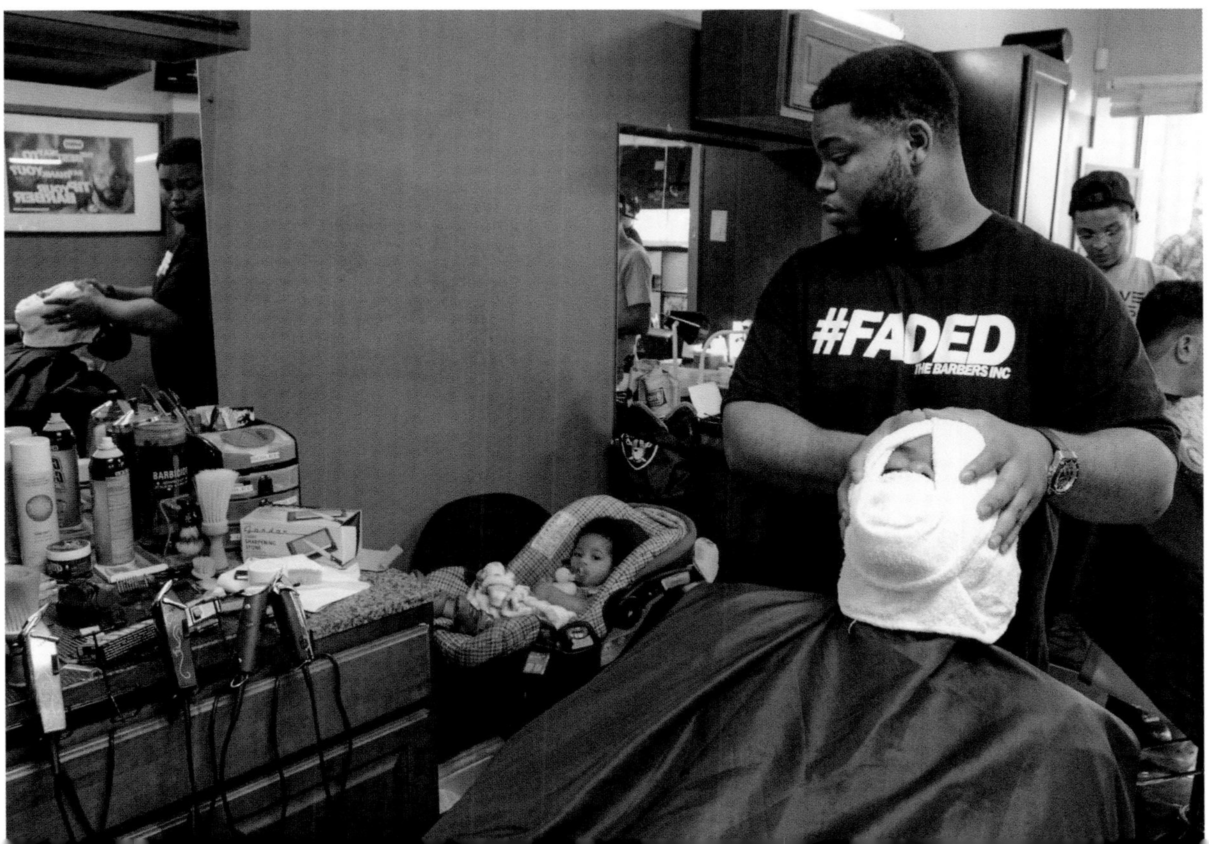
#FADED
THE BARBERS INC

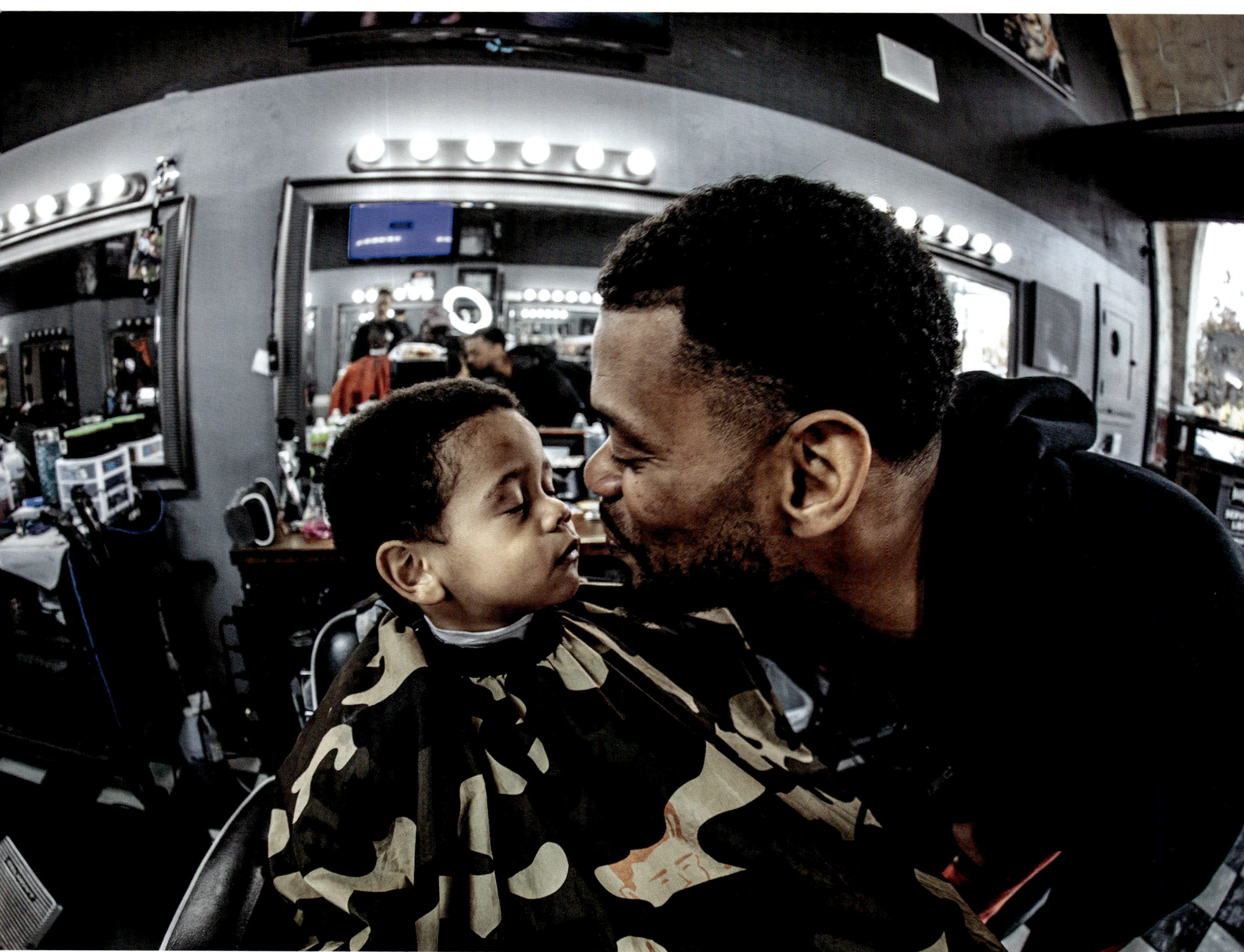

There's nothing a kiss from Dad can't fix.

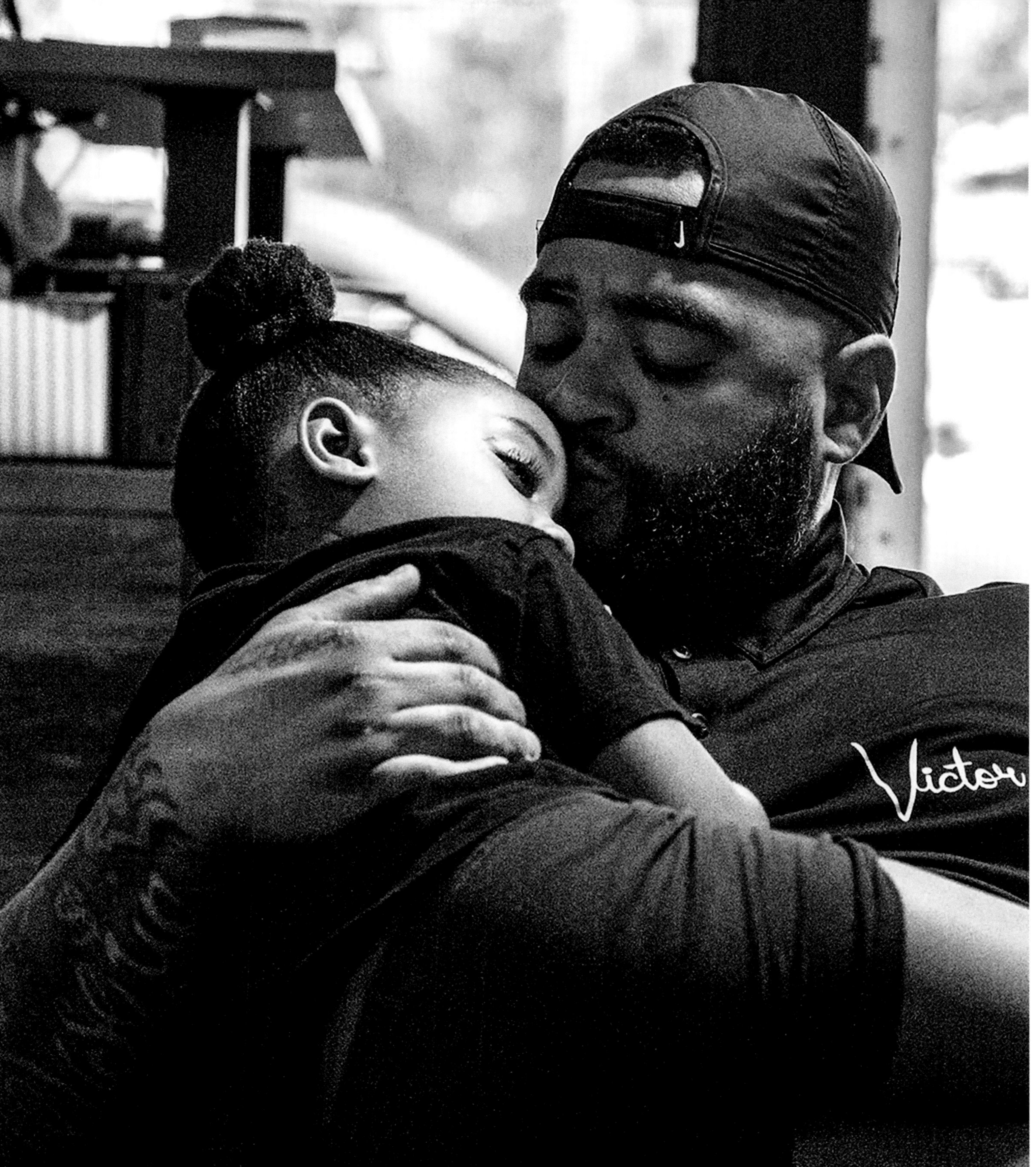
Victor

BREAKING CYCLES:

MY JOURNEY TO FATHERHOOD AND HEALING

DELAN STONE

Becoming a father for the first time changed my world. It was a perspective-shifting, mind-altering, lifelong realization. A realization that tapped into some of my biggest insecurities from childhood that I later realized had nothing to do with me. Insecurities that were given to me unknowingly by my biological father and that he inherited from his father.

Growing up in Portland, Oregon, I didn't have a meaningful, significant relationship with my biological father. My mother got pregnant with me at sixteen and had me at seventeen years old. I am her firstborn. A year later, she had my sister. She and my father split up shortly after my sister was born. After the split, the relationship between my dad and me could be best described as strained, with infrequent visits. Due to his absence, there was always a void inside me that could never be filled. I had plenty of men in my life who did their best to help fill that emptiness by spending time and imparting wisdom where necessary—from my maternal grandfather, my uncles, my stepdad, mentors from my Rites of Passage program, and countless role models along the way. But no matter how excellent the guidance, something was still missing. The person I needed most was missing. My father was absent.

At some point, I decided that when I got the opportunity to be a father, I would be the most committed, loving, and involved father ever. Despite my father's absence and lack of commitment, my goal was to honor the duty of being a father. But whenever I thought about the promise of fatherhood, I felt the fear of becoming my father in the pit of my stomach. I was afraid that I was destined to continue the generational trauma and make the same mistakes my father made and his father made. No matter how great a father I wanted

“I AM RESPONSIBLE FOR TEACHING HIM TO BE STRONG WHEN TIMES GET TOUGH, HOW TO FIGHT FOR HIS BELIEFS, HOW TO STAND ON PRINCIPLE WHEN THE TIME COMES, AND HOW TO RETAIN HIS JOY.”

to be, nothing could remove the feeling I had that it was probable that I would somehow mess up the relationship with my future child. I had encouraging conversations with close family and read books on removing the doubt, but nothing helped.

I got married in 2012. My wife and I had difficulty conceiving, and we didn't have a child until 2022. During the ten years before my son was born, I started the slow process of reconnecting with my father. Through that painful but rewarding journey, much of my doubt slowly disappeared—the healing process in one relationship allowed for a clear path to form and a new relationship to begin. The universe shifted when my son was born, and my vision, duty, and responsibility crystallized.

Being a Black father means that I am responsible for raising a Black boy into a man, and that is something I don't take lightly. I am responsible for teaching him that he comes from a rich, beautiful heritage, regardless of what the world may say about him through media, policies, literature, or other influences. I am responsible for teaching him to be strong when times get tough, how to fight for his beliefs, how to stand on principle when the time comes, and how to retain his joy.

It means I am responsible for giving him all the tools necessary to help him fulfill his life's purpose, whatever that may be. I am also responsible for holding myself accountable when I make mistakes and modeling what that looks like for him so that he may, in time, do the same. I am responsible for showing him how to love and soften up when necessary. I am his blueprint.

Being a Black father means the world to me!

BRANDON RUFFIN

Oakland, California–based visual storyteller whose photography provides a mirror for people to observe who they are now and who they can be

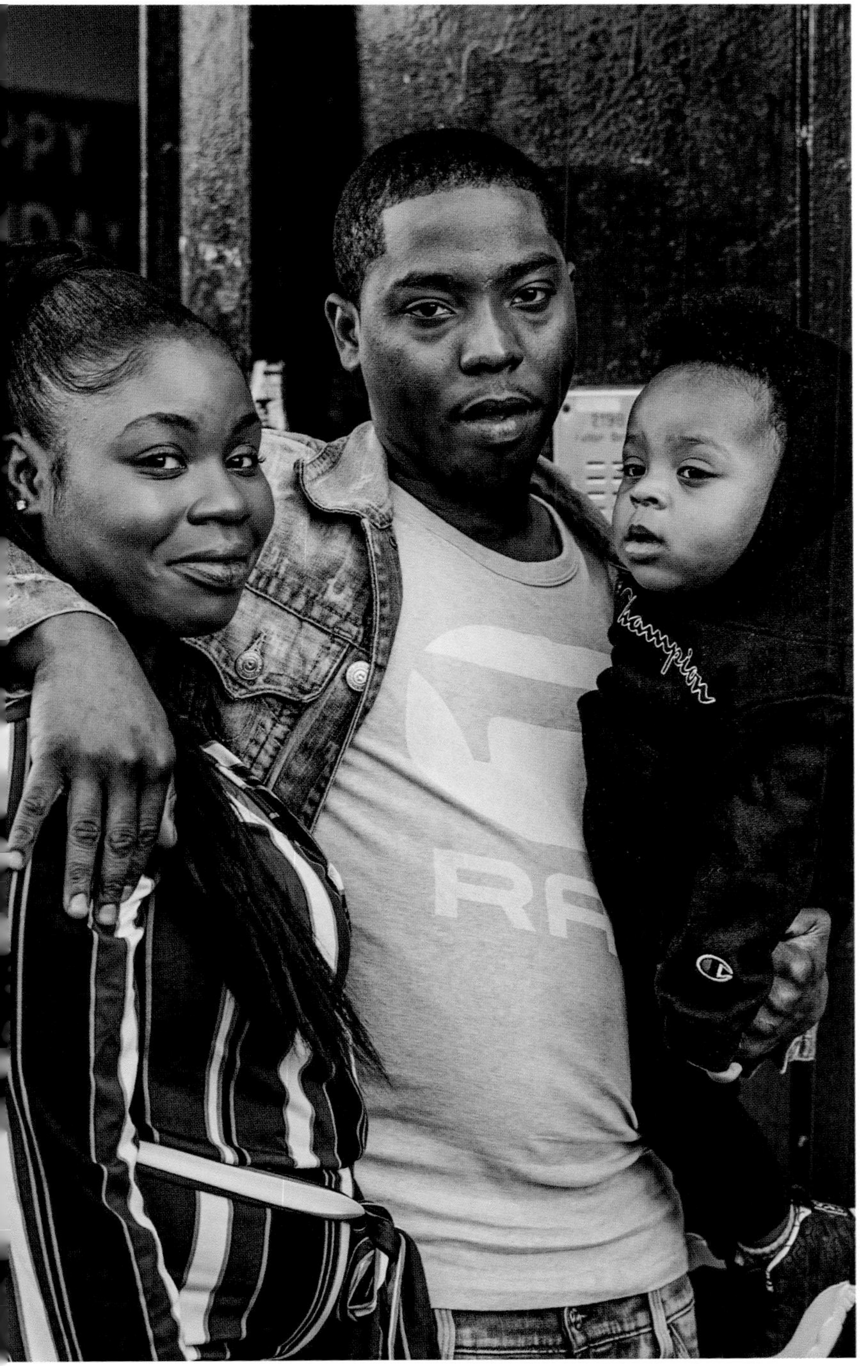

Our family, our world

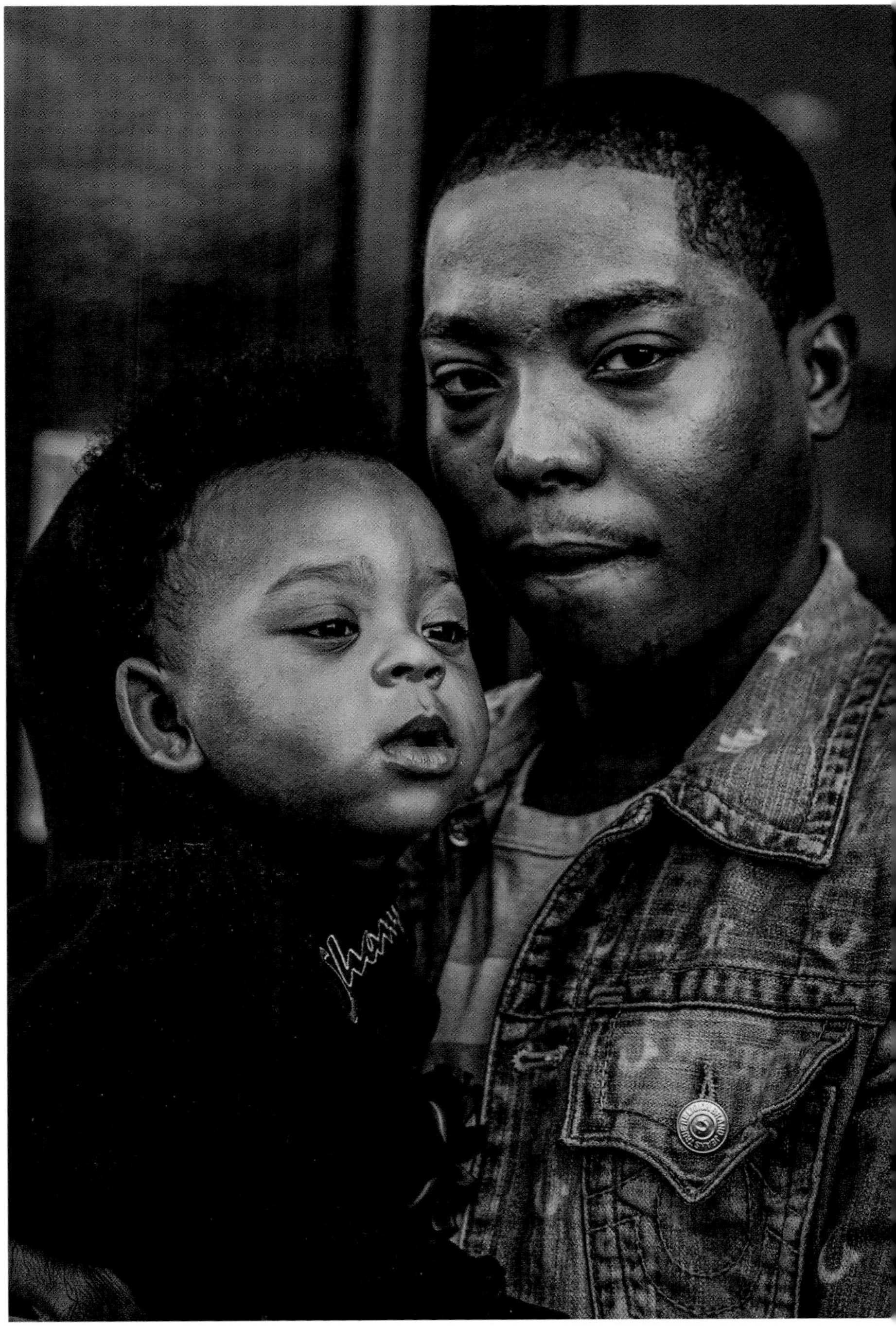

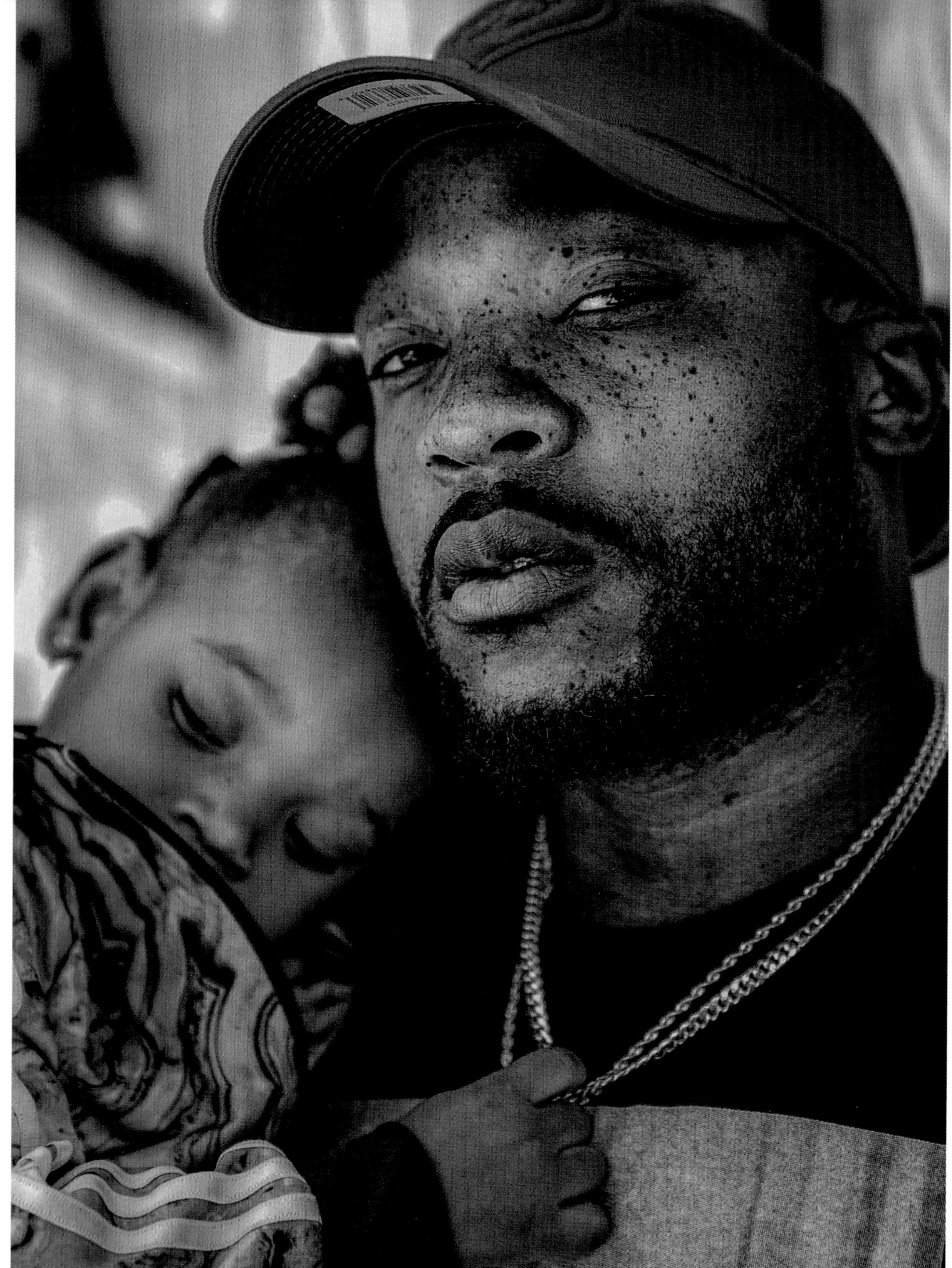

BRANDON RUFFIN

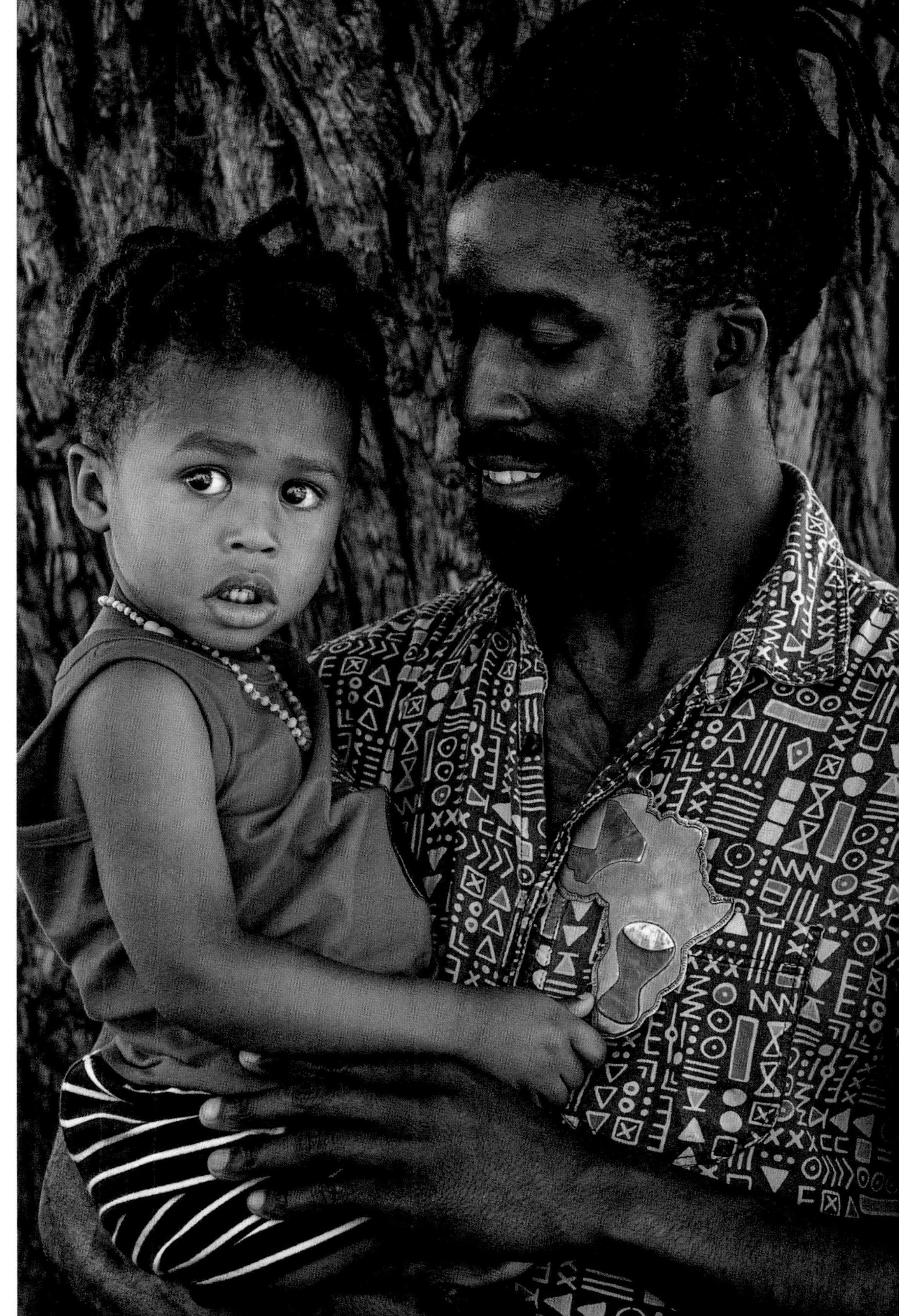

In Dad's arms

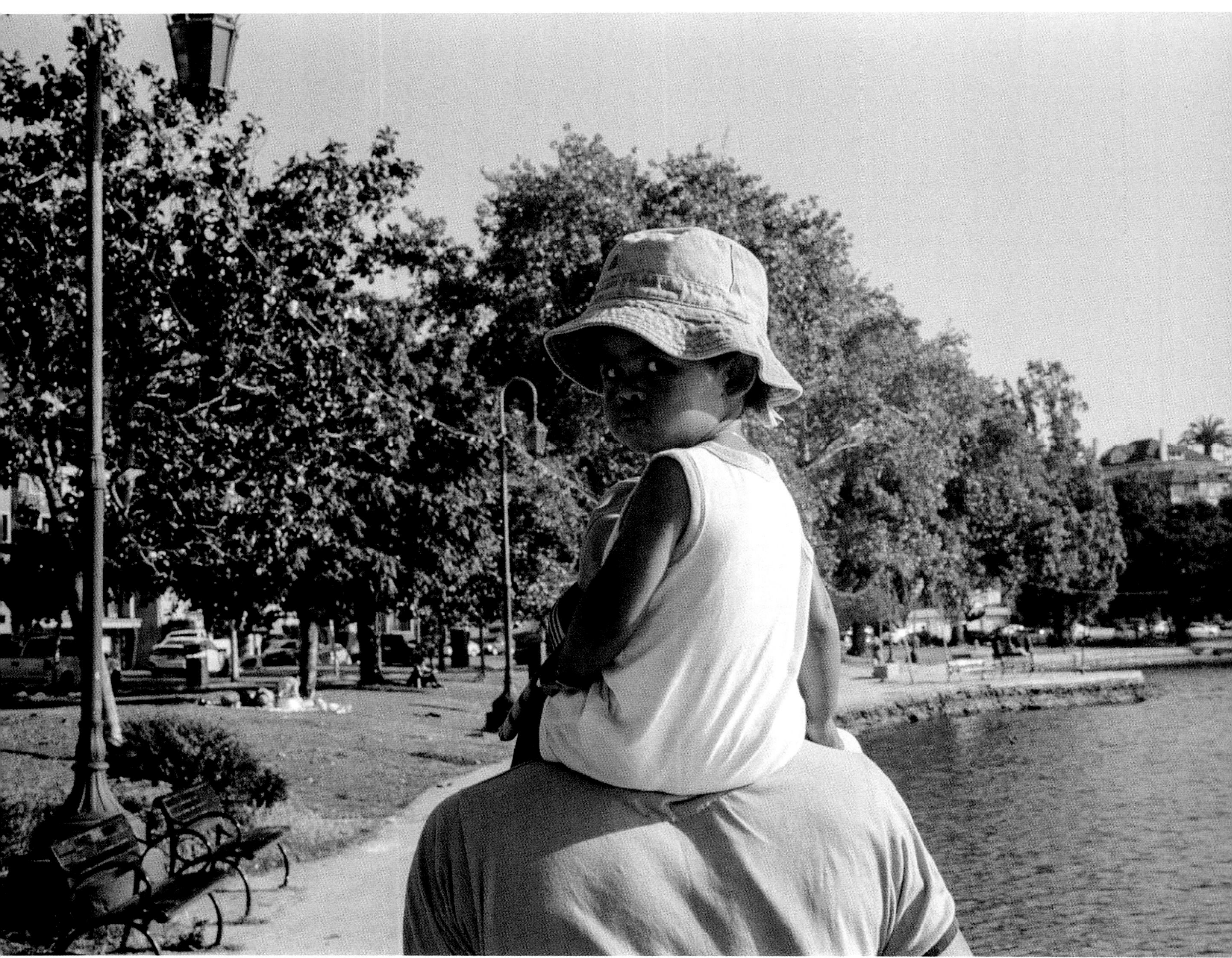

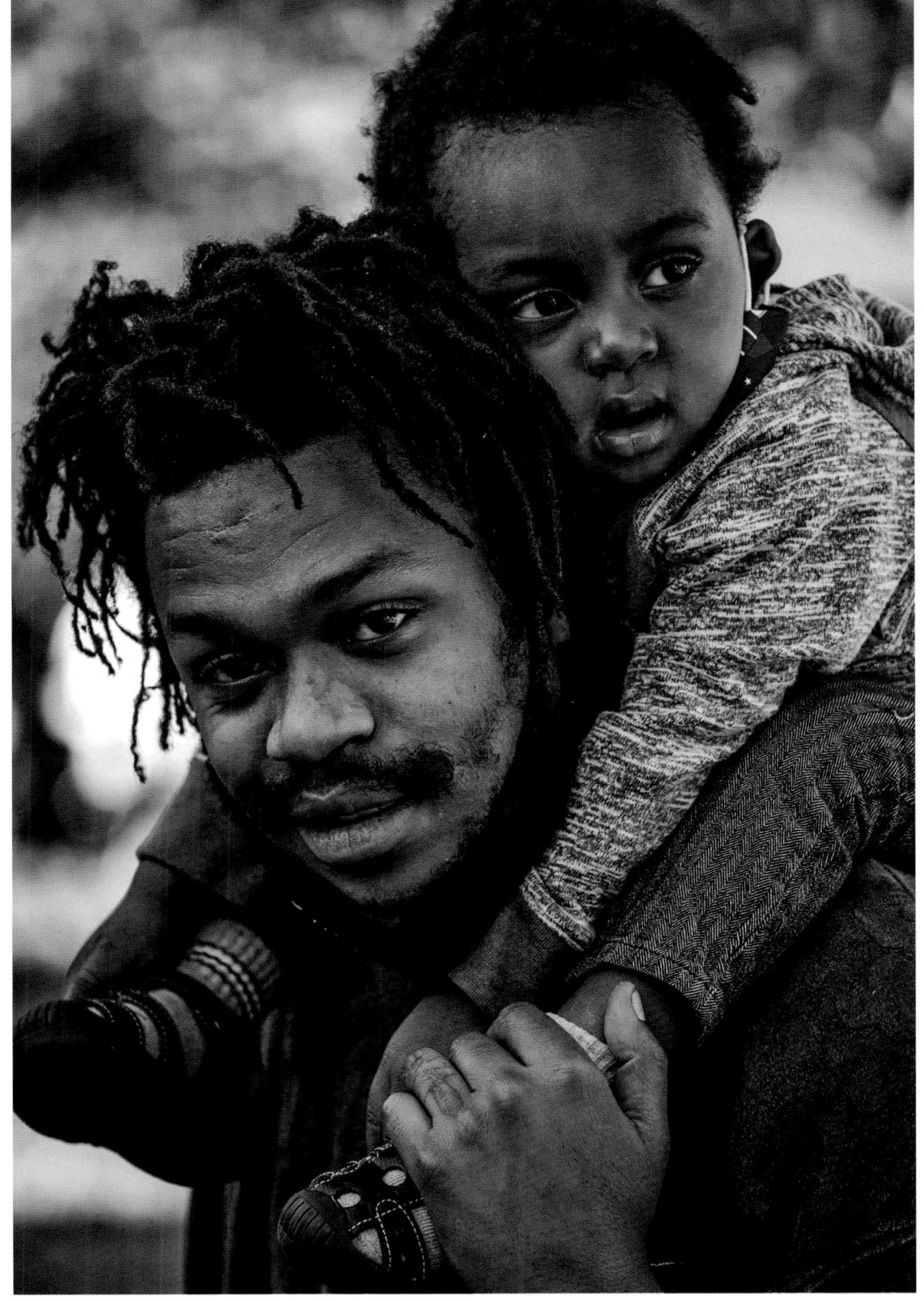

On top of the world

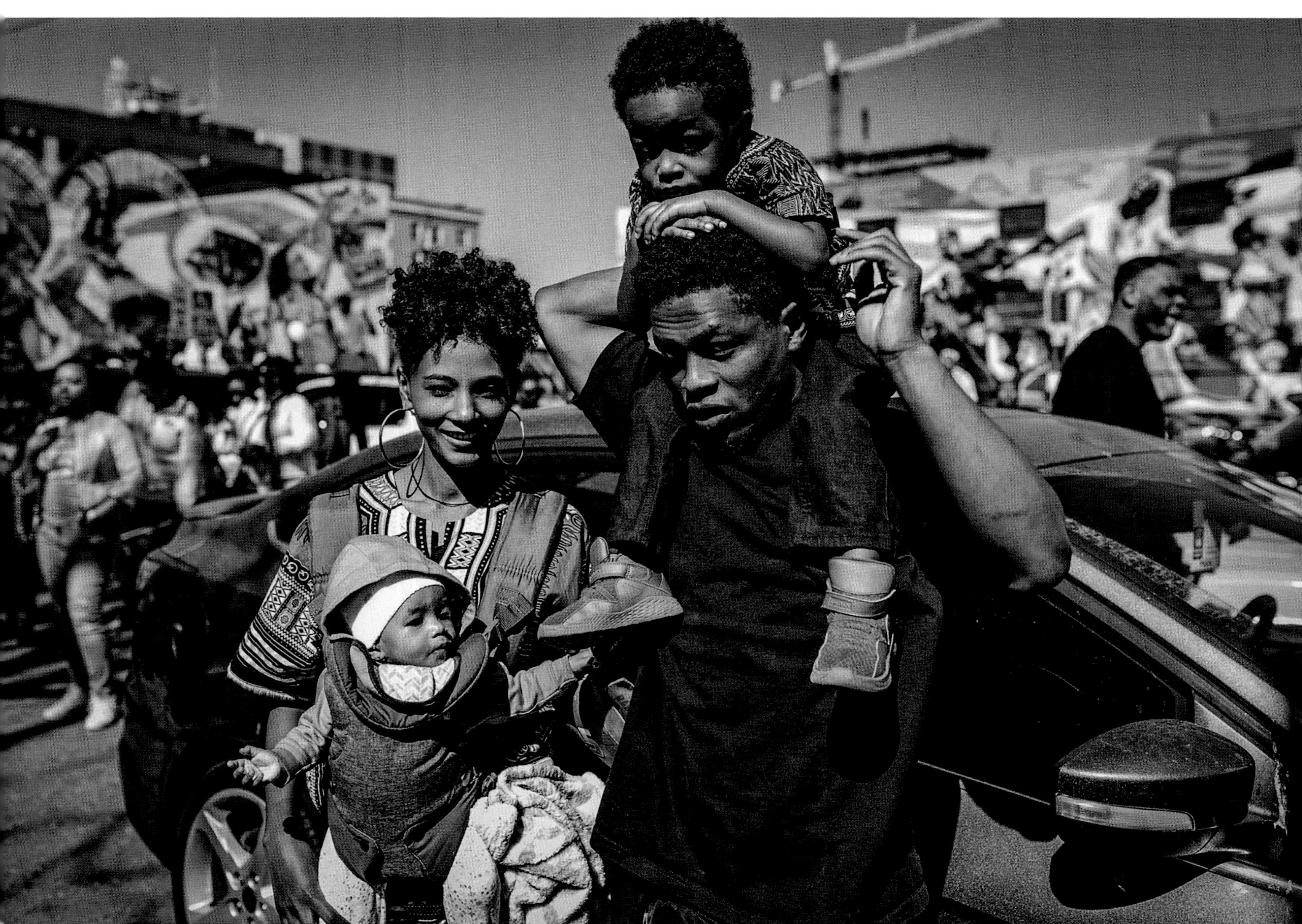

A watchful eye from father to son

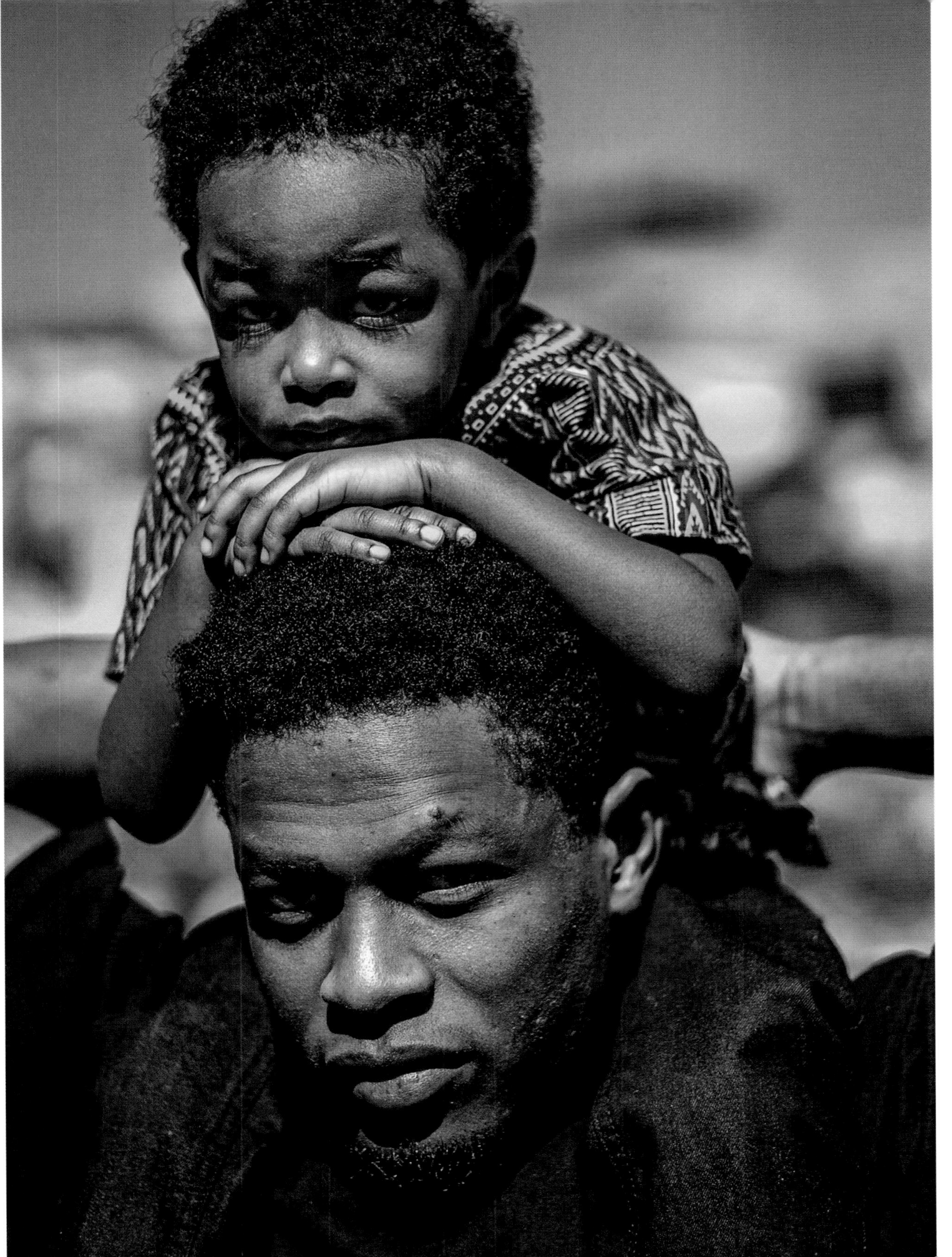

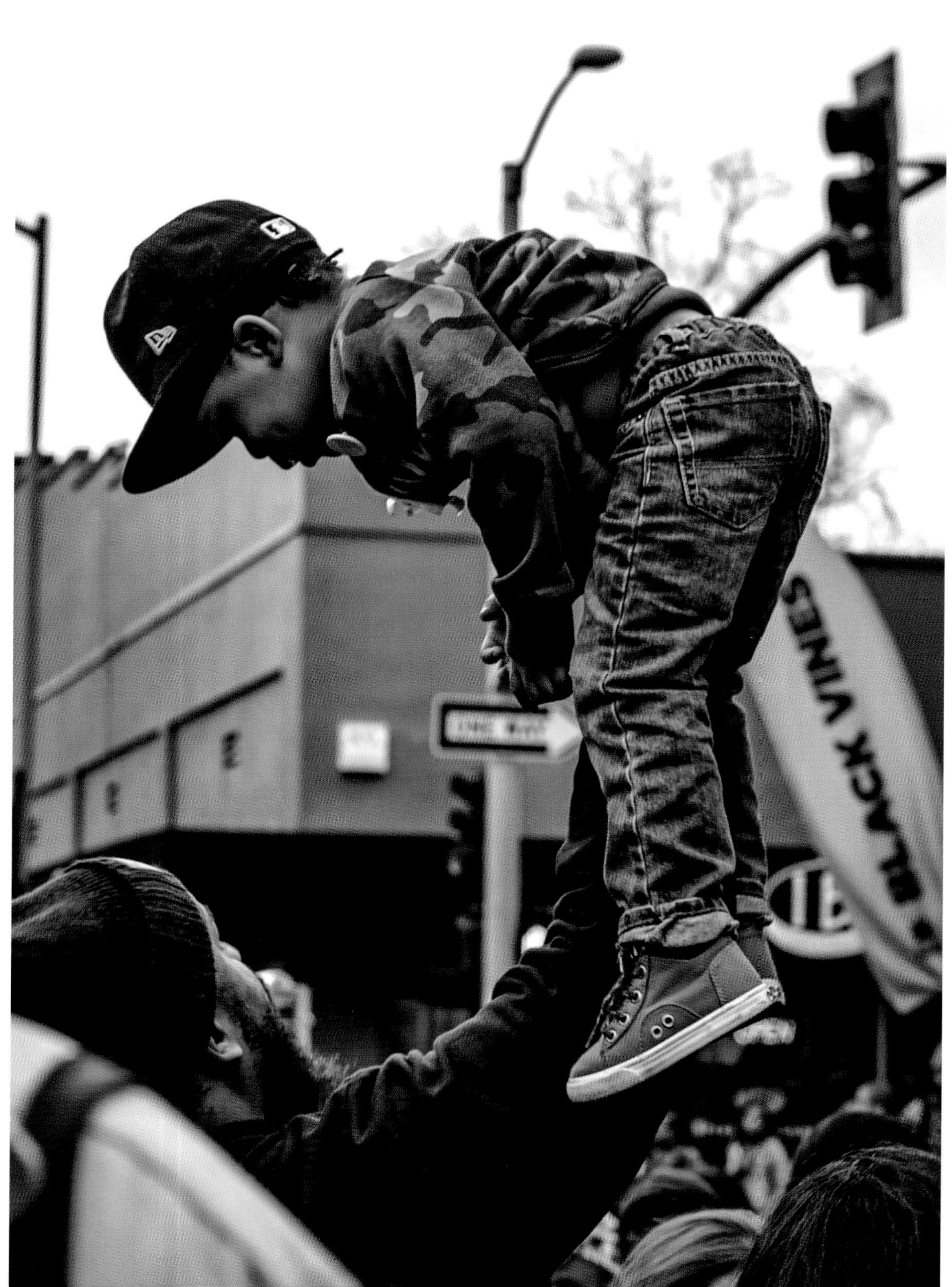

BRANDON RUFFIN

These moments should last forever.

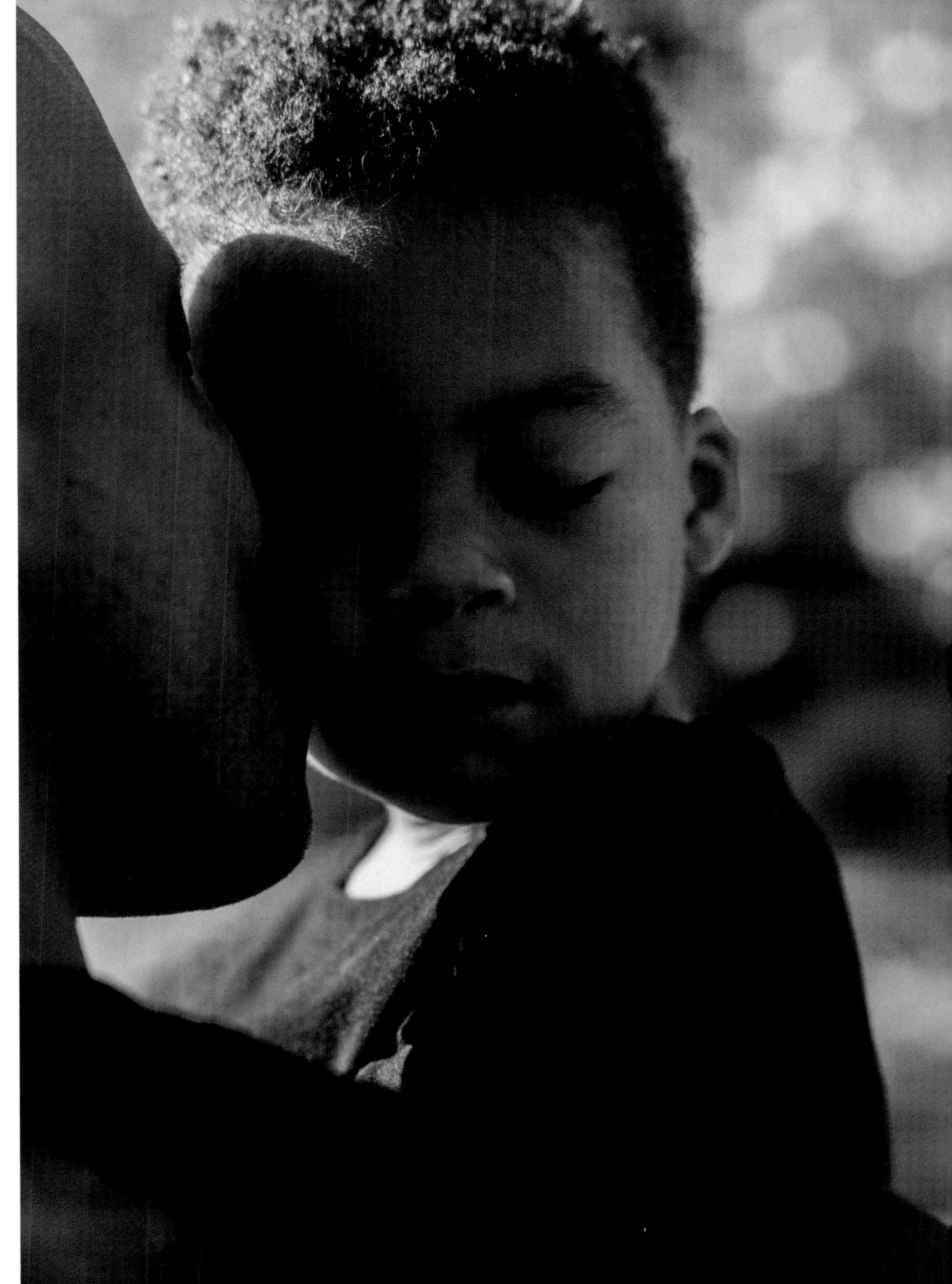

EXCITEMENT & ANTICIPATION

AMIR NASSER

I remember the moment I found out I was going to be a father. Fear, excitement, joy, angst, purpose, and triumph all rushed through my mind. My wife, Fabienne Antoine-Nasser, and I were married in September 2019, and only a few months had passed before she showed me the pregnancy test. The new year was fresh on our minds. We moved into a new place that was perfect for our first child: a two-bedroom apartment with a room for our daughter. What we didn't know was that the pandemic would derail all our immediate plans.

Luckily I got to hear my daughter's heartbeat on the ultrasound before I was no longer allowed to attend the appointments. My in-laws were only a thirty-minute drive away, but they couldn't see their pregnant daughter. My parents were even closer, and we all kept to ourselves. The apartment became a prison. We tried our best, but beyond me leaving the apartment to pick up food every once in a while, we both decided it was safer for us to stay away from people as much as possible.

The birth was terrifying. Two weeks before, I had spoken to my best friend, Sean Dallas, a father of three beautiful Black boys. He told me I would be an amazing father. He was excited to meet my daughter, and I was excited to meet his sons. Unfortunately I never heard from him again. On the day I took my wife to the hospital, he was murdered in a road rage incident, leaving his three sons behind. I wasn't allowed to leave the hospital, or at least I don't remember being allowed to leave, once we got inside. It was just my wife and me. We danced and talked to the nurses when they came by; we FaceTimed with family. Although I was excited about being a father, I felt an unbelievable pressure to protect my wife. I had read about Black women and childbirth, and I did not want to lose the love of my life because of neglect or miscommunication. Sparing the details

> ". . . MY DAUGHTER WAS BORN. MY WIFE WAS SAFE AND RECOVERING. AND MY LIFE WAS CHANGED FOREVER."

of what felt like the longest five days of my life, my daughter was born. My wife was safe and recovering. And my life was changed forever.

The pandemic was a blessing in disguise. Growing up, I was told that fathers must sacrifice time with their children in order to work hard to provide for their families. I never thought I would get the chance to spend every single day with my daughter. I was able to work from home; I would have my daughter in my lap during a meeting without a second thought. Life was *good*. But we knew she would need more exposure to kids and learning environments. After her little brother was born, we moved to Atlanta, enrolled her in a Montessori school, and watched her and her brother blossom into fine young toddlers.

As their father, I am constantly under their watchful eye. They know when I'm tired, they know when I'm happy, they know when I'm sad or angry. They help me with chores and want to know everything I'm doing. If I leave the house, they're distraught, but they trust that I am coming back. They both don't want to go to sleep until they know I'm home or safe. This isn't what I was expecting when it came to being a father.

Maybe it was society. The funny thing about being a Black American in a diverse area is that you start to notice how ridiculous stereotypes can be firsthand. Kids of every race deal with divorce or loss. There I was, a Black boy with a Black father.

Now every Black man I know with kids has this to say: "I could *never* abandon my children." And I'm proud to say I am a part of that club.

TONY MOBLEY

Self-taught photographer passionate about the power of a timeless image to capture the beauty of the everyday

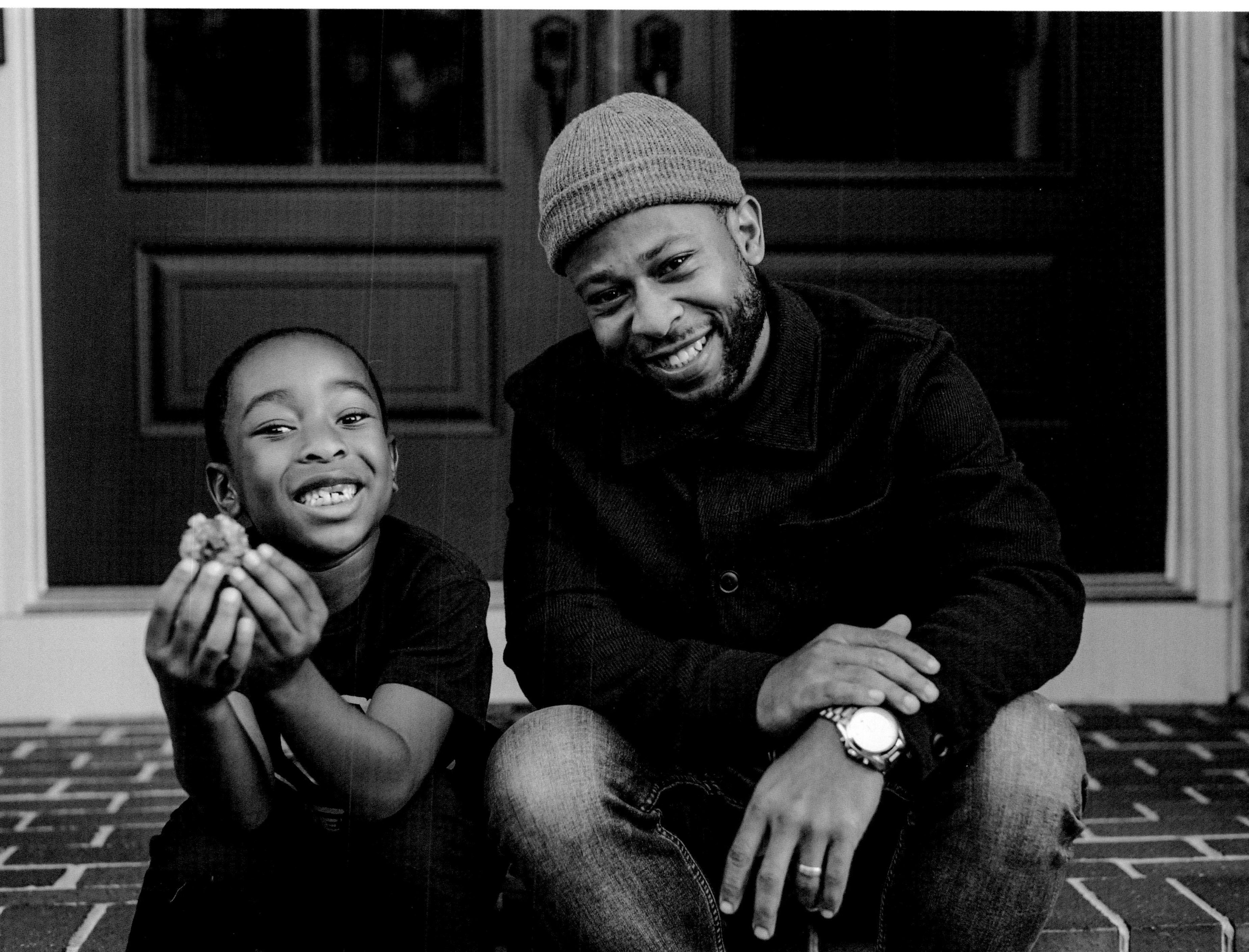

Cameron Brannum and his son, Collin. Like father, like son.

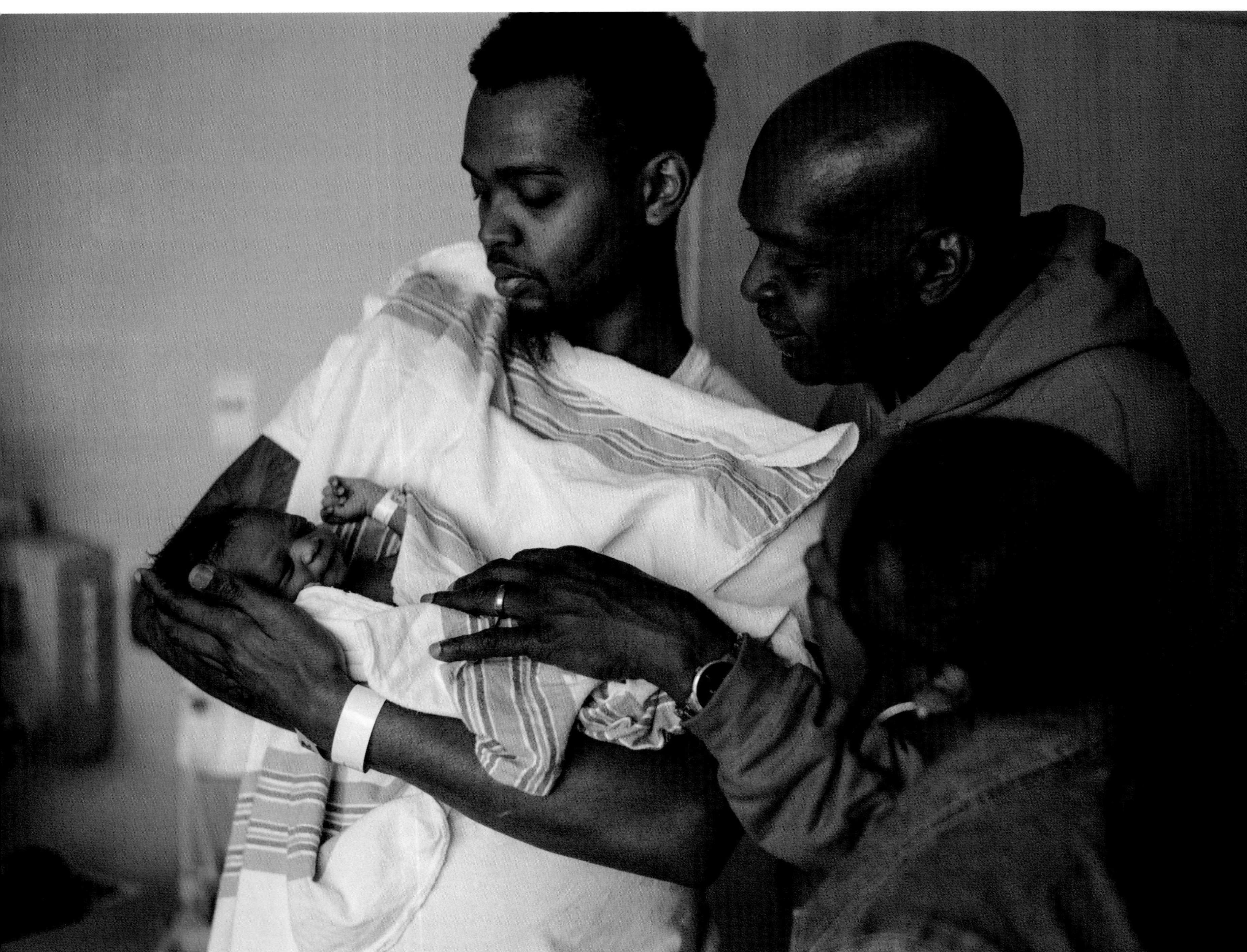

Shariff Levine admiring his new baby boy, Amias Saint, along with proud grandparents Charles and Reneca

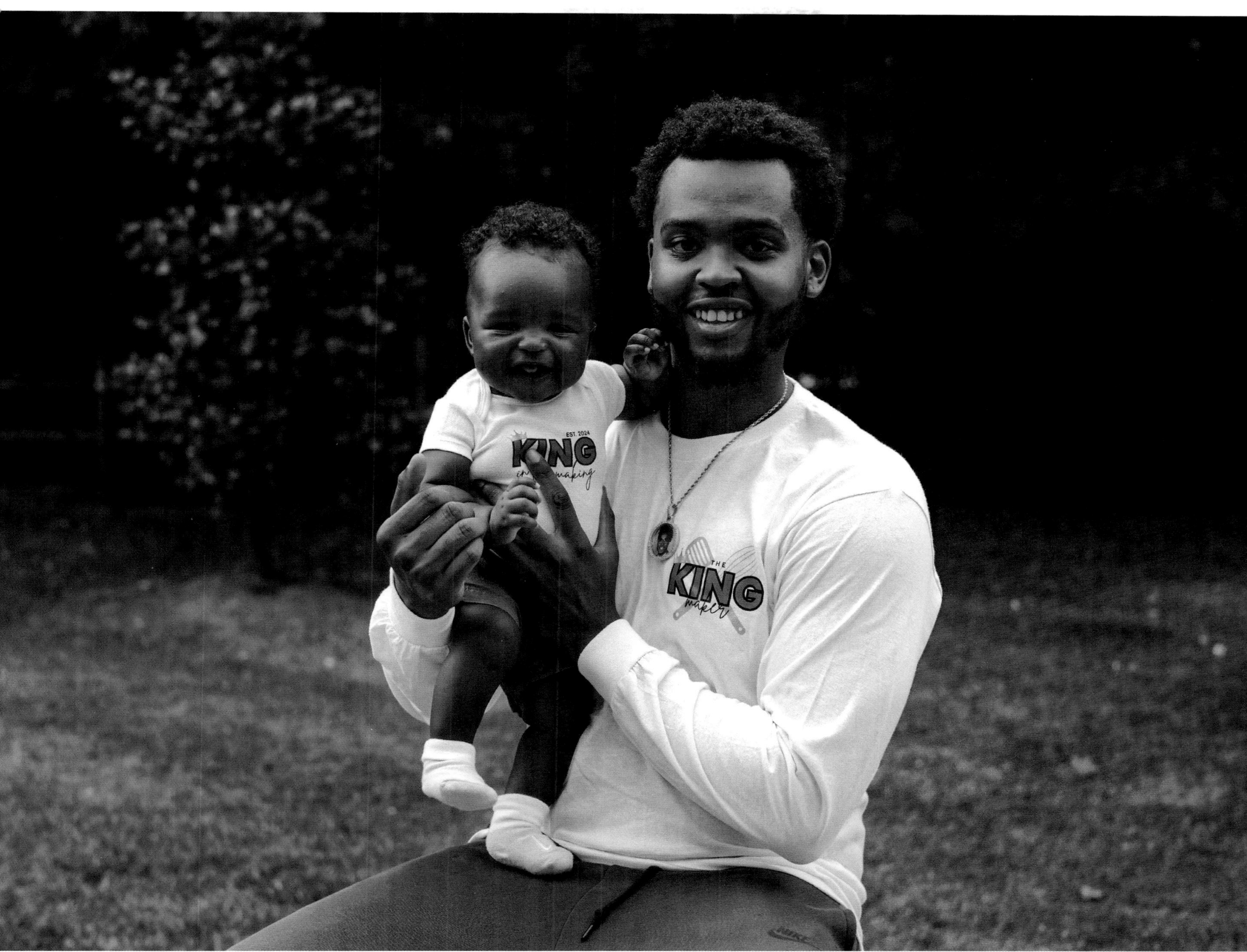

Levine and Amias Saint share a laugh in matching shirts, titled *The King Maker* and *King in the Making*, respectively.

TONY MOBLEY

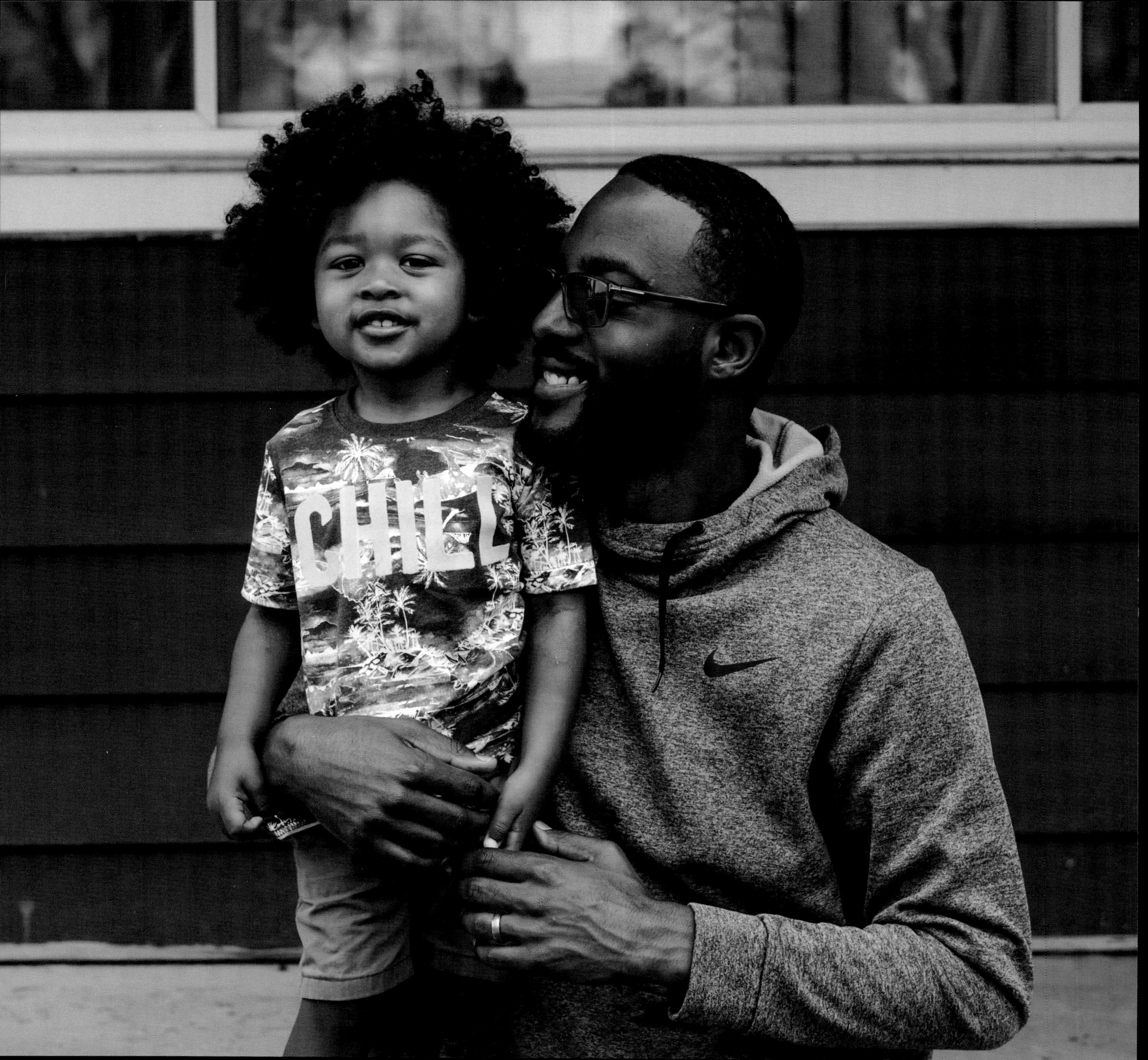
CHILL

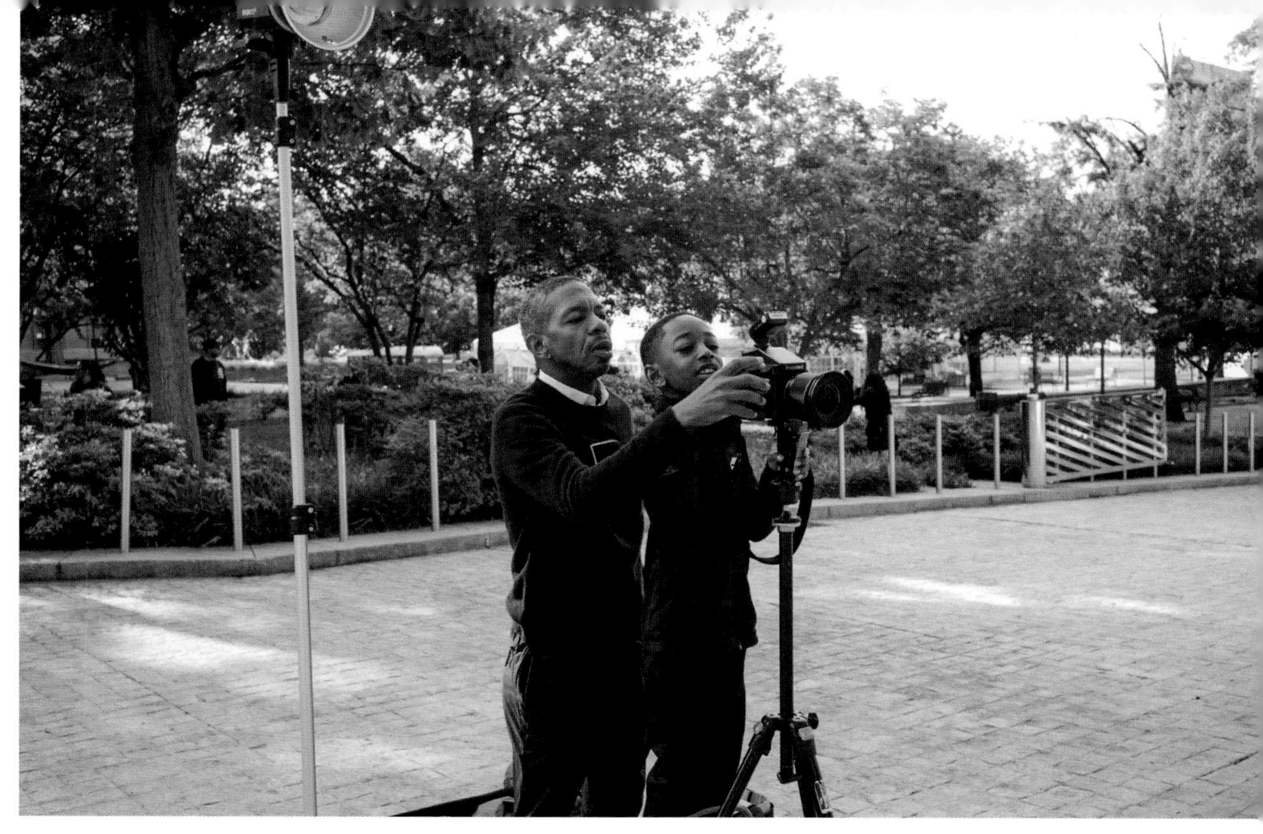

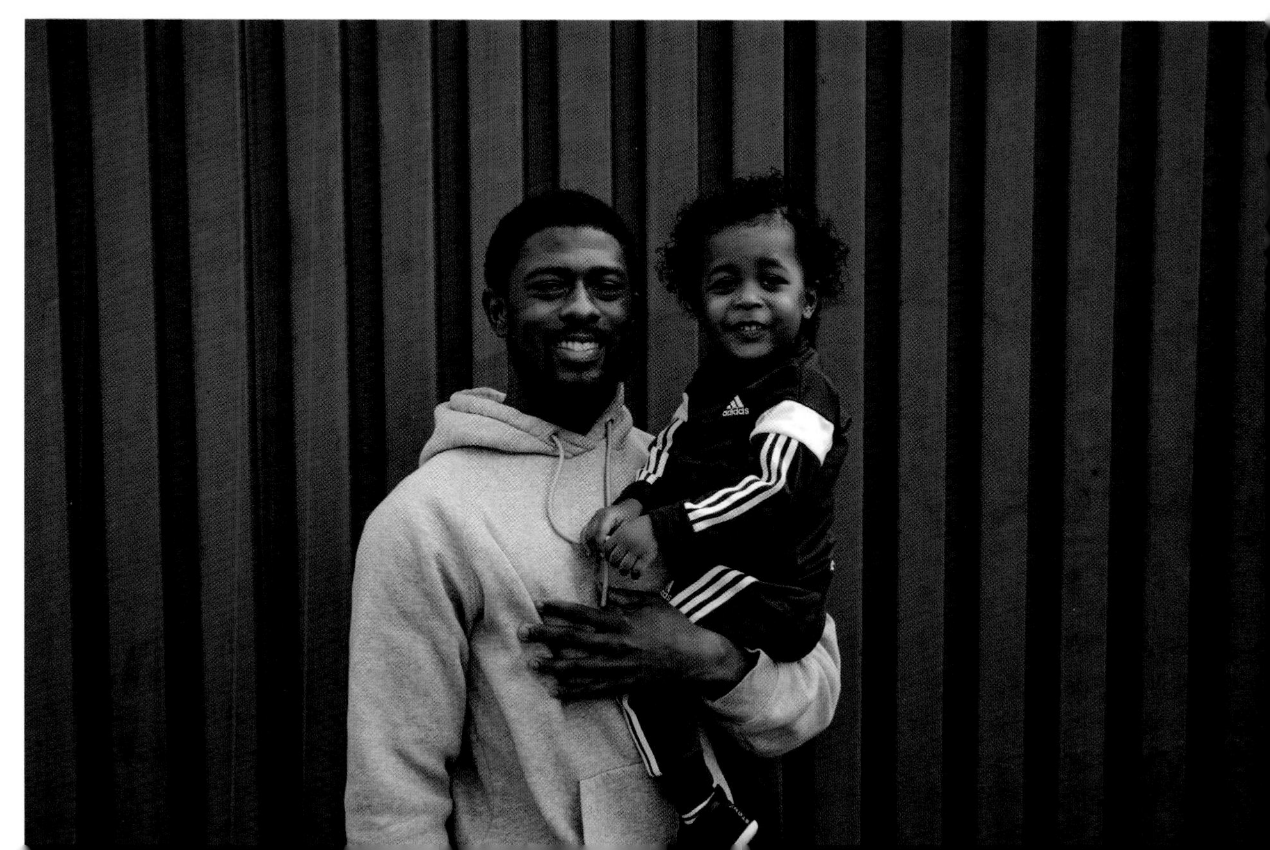

opposite: **Glenn Altman Jr. and his son, Glenn, chill on the front porch of their Detroit home.**

top: **Photographer Derrel R. Todd and his protégé—his son, August—work on location in Washington, DC.**

bottom: **Brandin Dandrige and his son, Khari, smile for the camera, captured in Laurel, Maryland.**

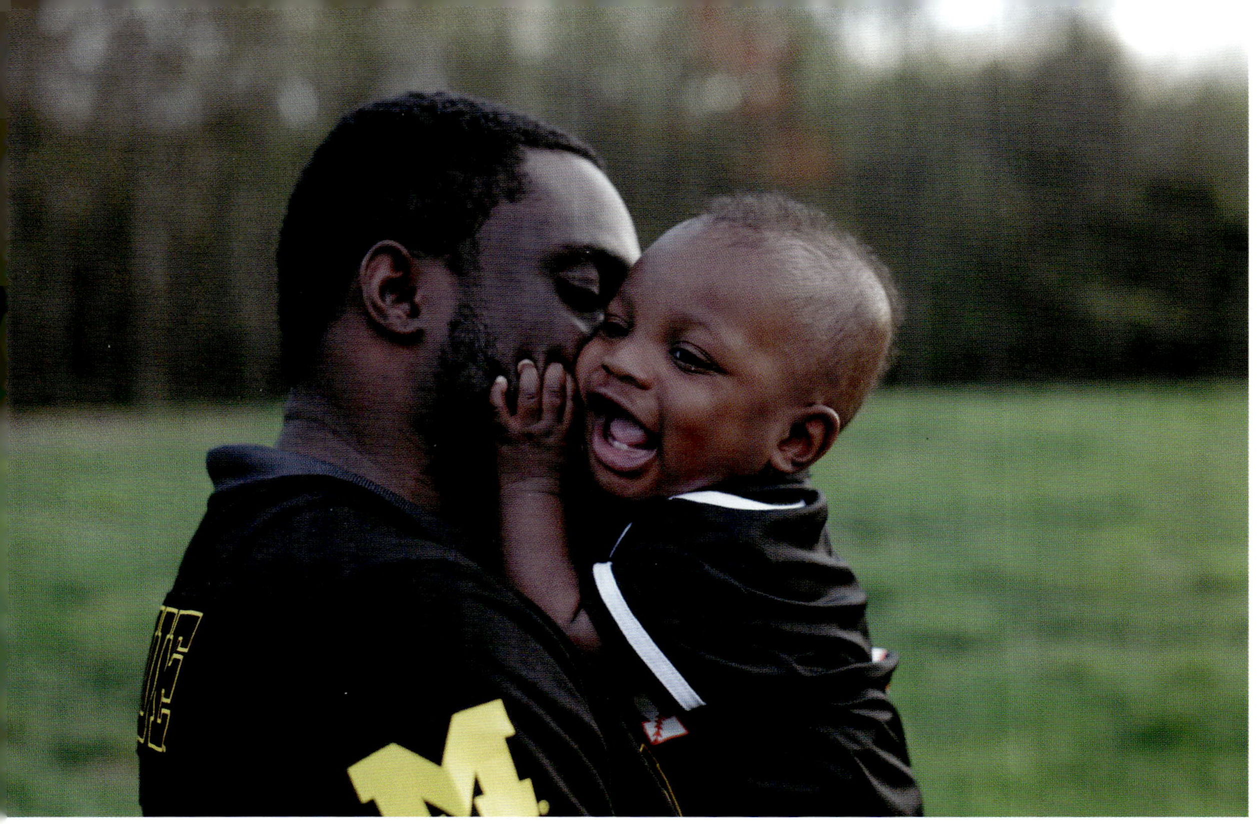

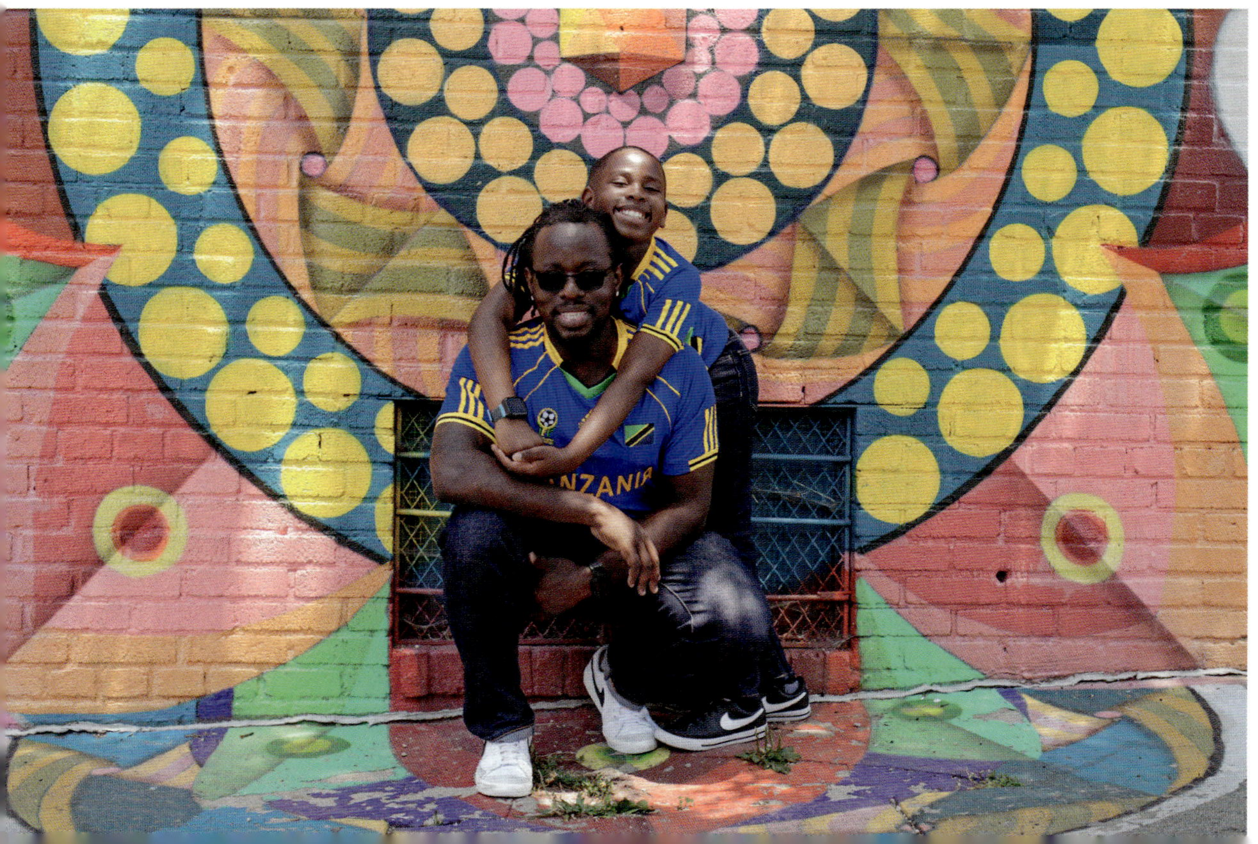

top: **An intimate moment at the park with Deaunte Griffith and his baby boy, Joseph, in Upper Marlboro, Maryland**

bottom: **Jerome Pyuzza and his son, Daniel, representing their home country of Tanzania in front of a neighborhood mural in Washington, DC**

opposite: **Devin Francis and his daughter, Iris, enjoying a sunny day at the US National Arboretum in Washington, DC**

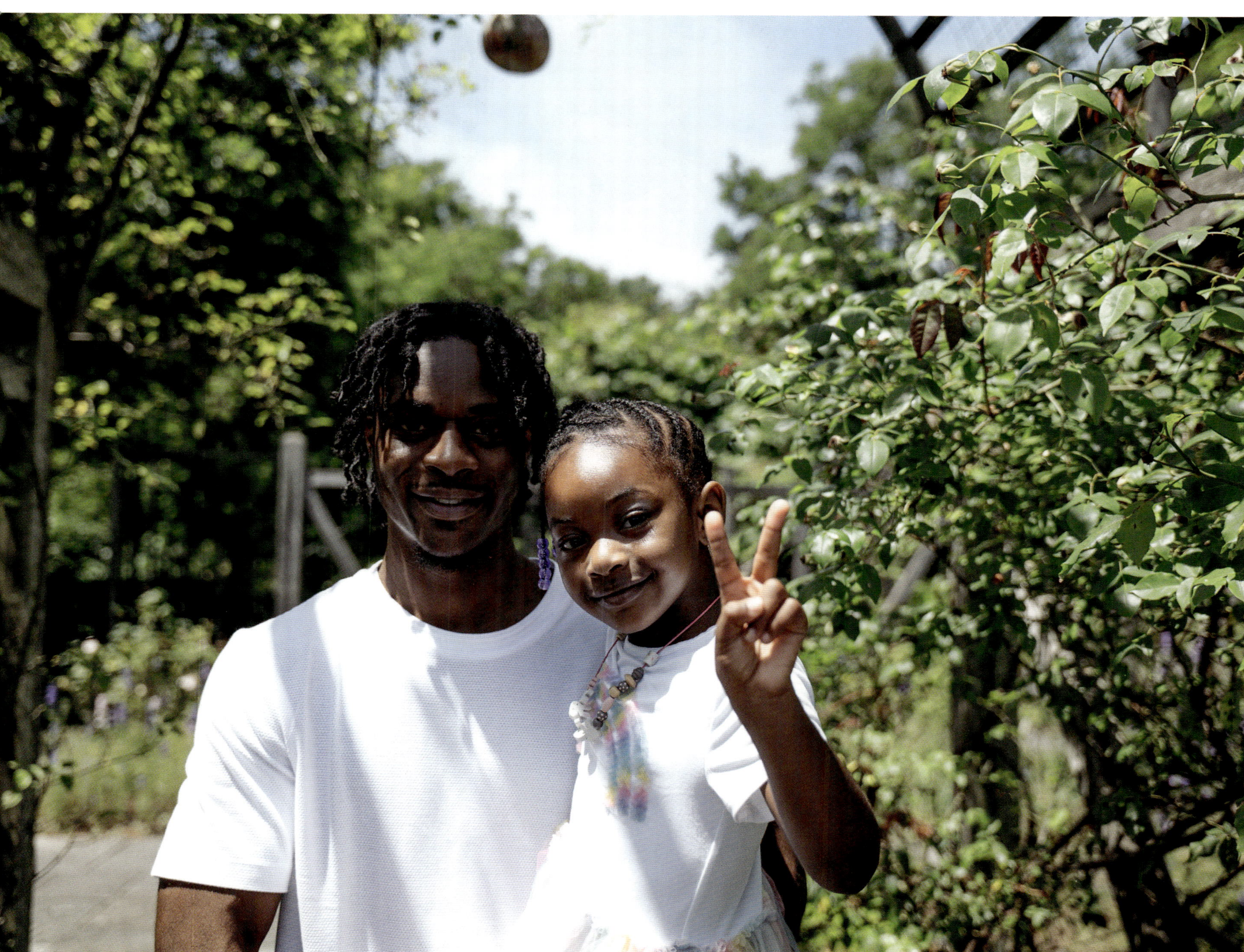

QUINTON PETE

Street photographer devoted to the craft of capturing the heart and soul of untold stories in honor of his late father

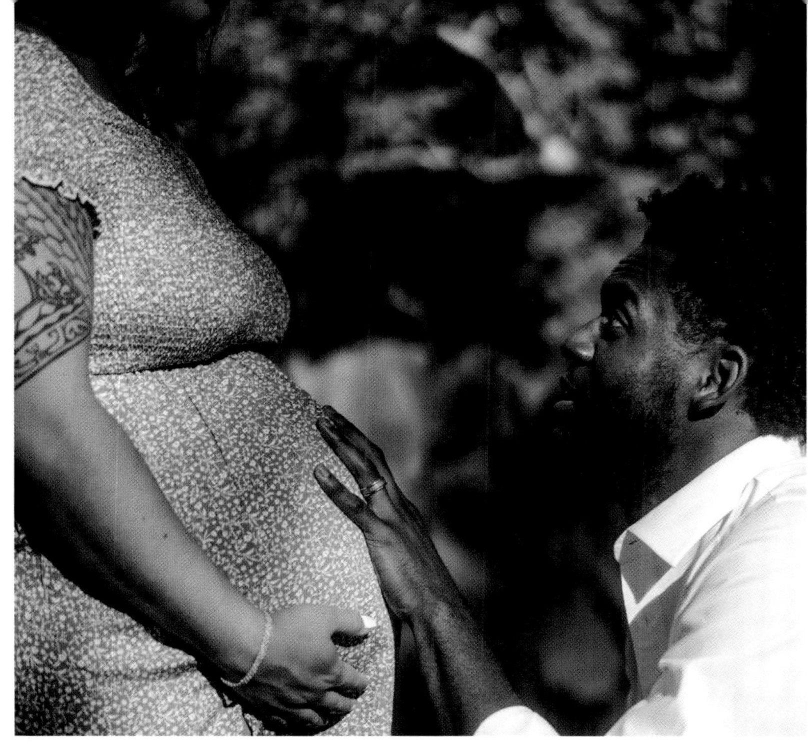

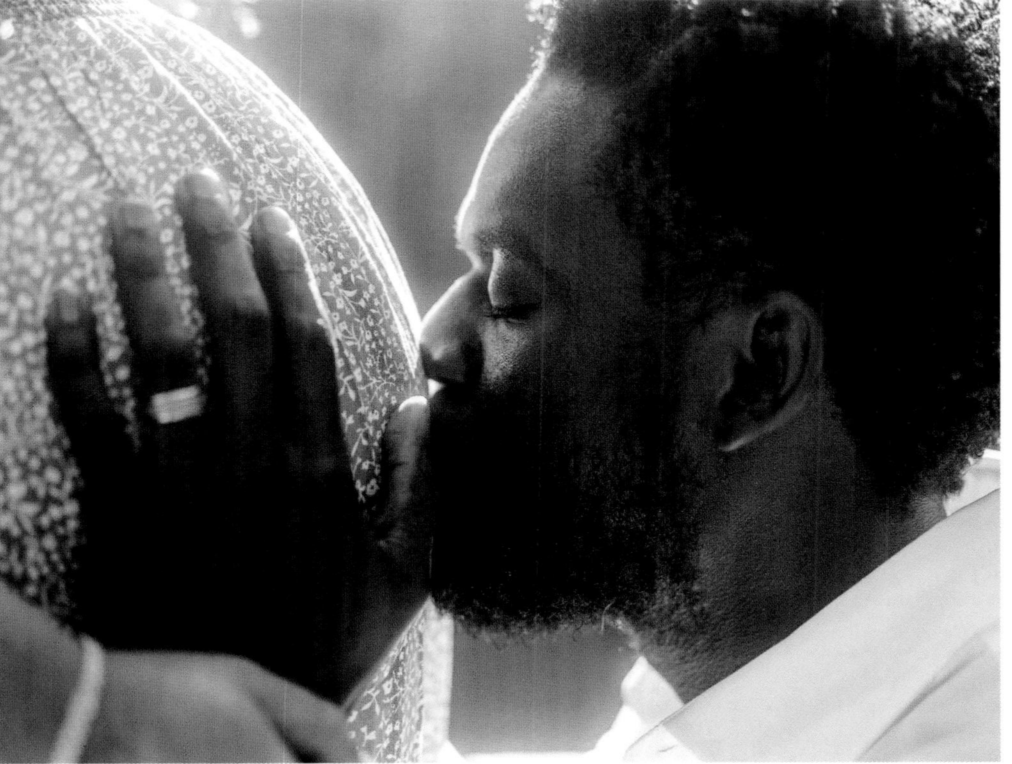

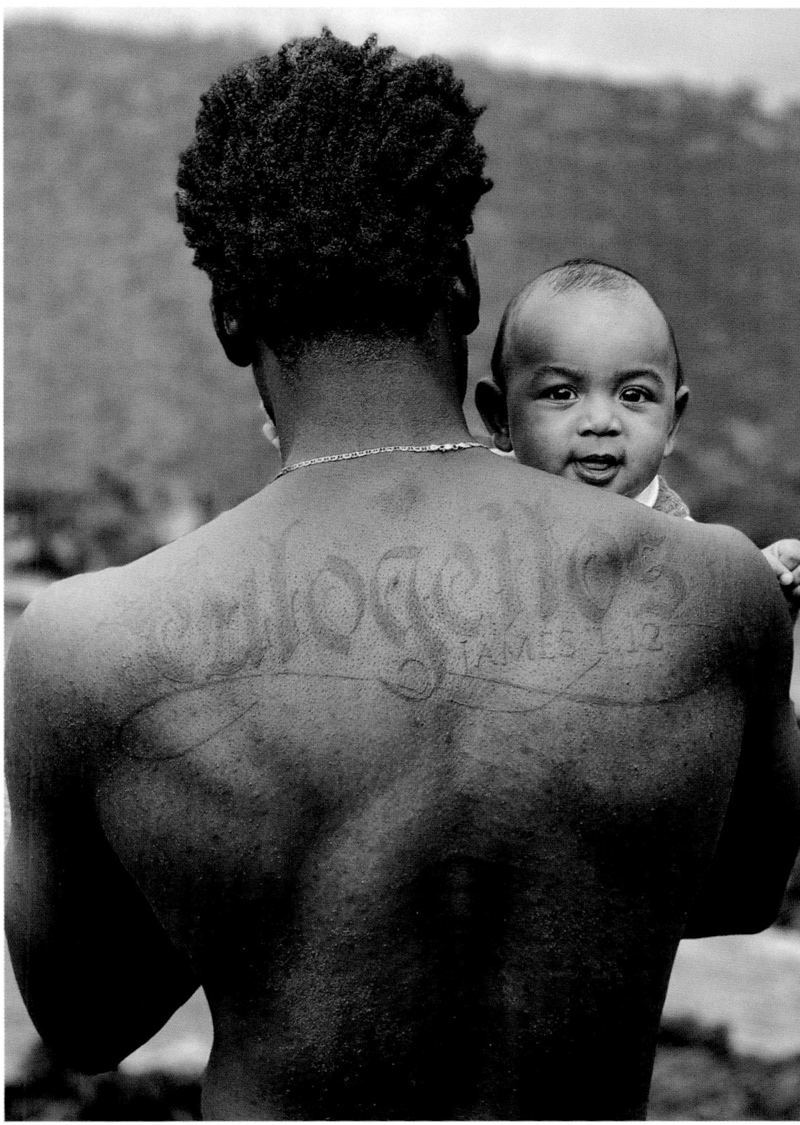

From birth to life, a father in all stages

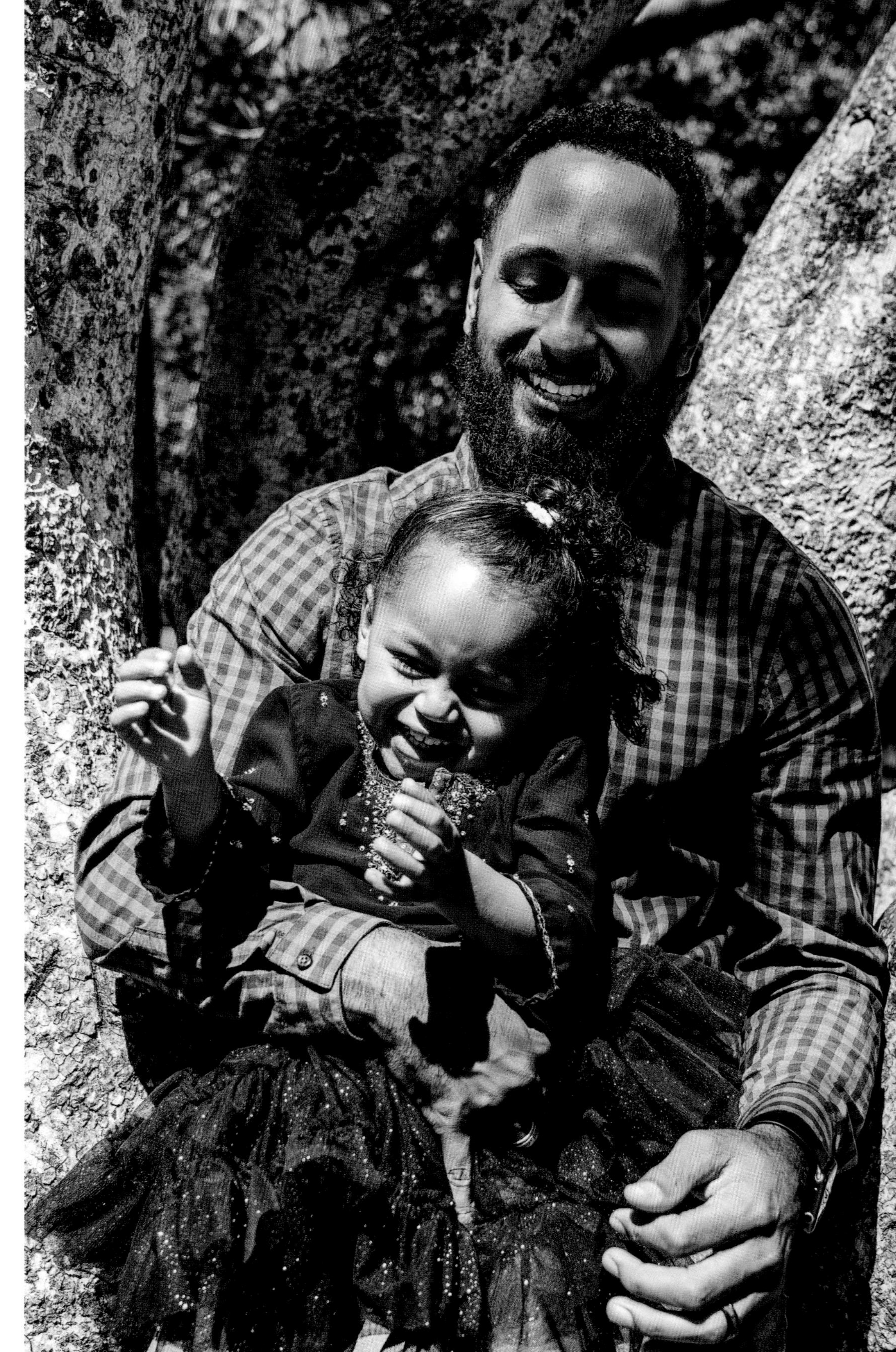

Laughter makes for the best memories.

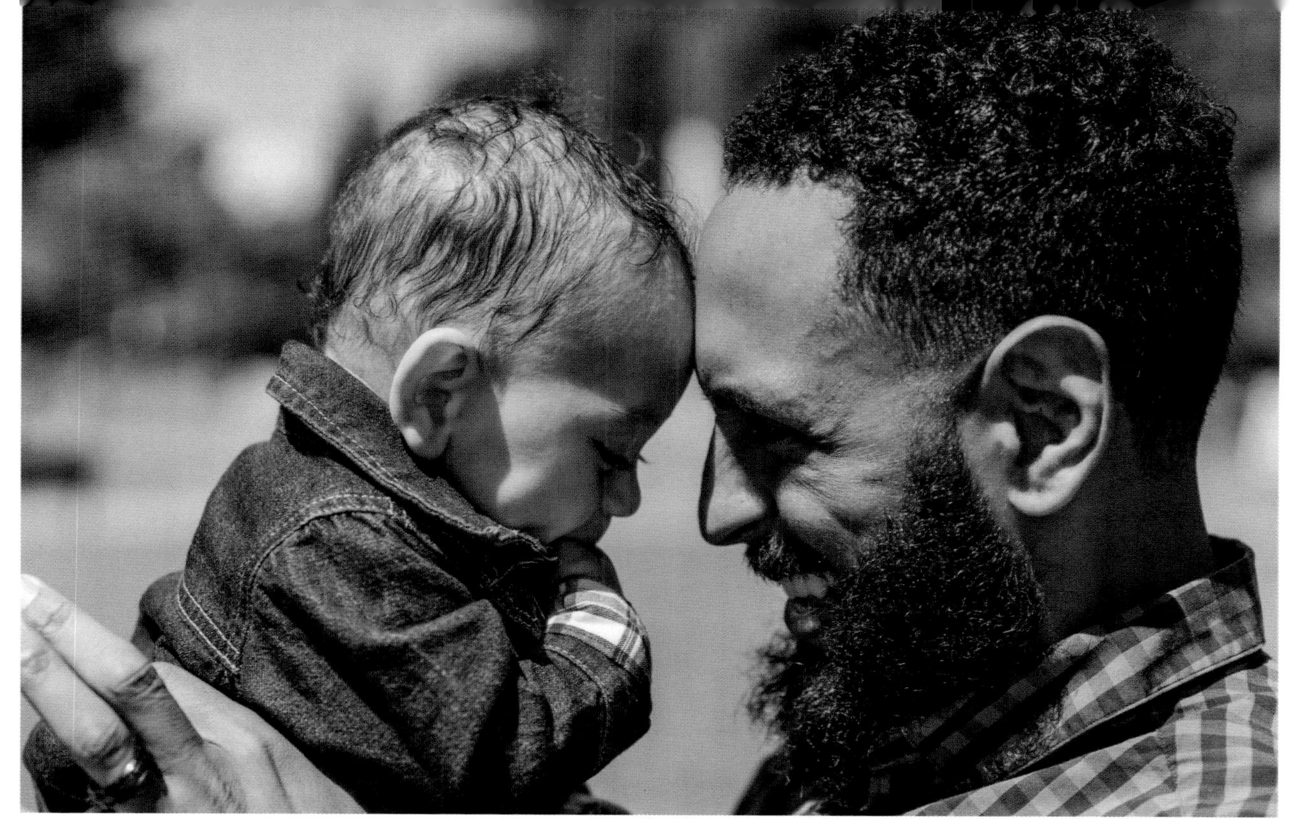

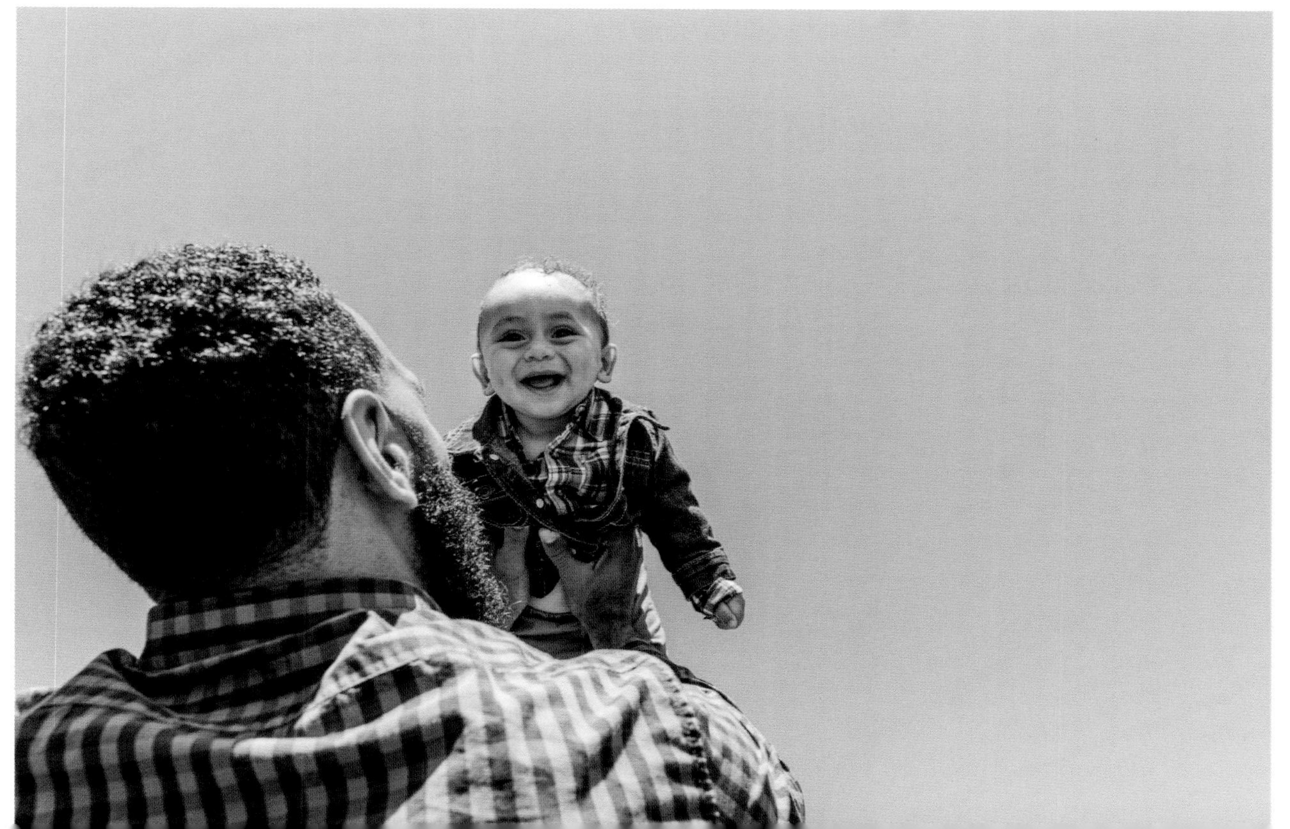

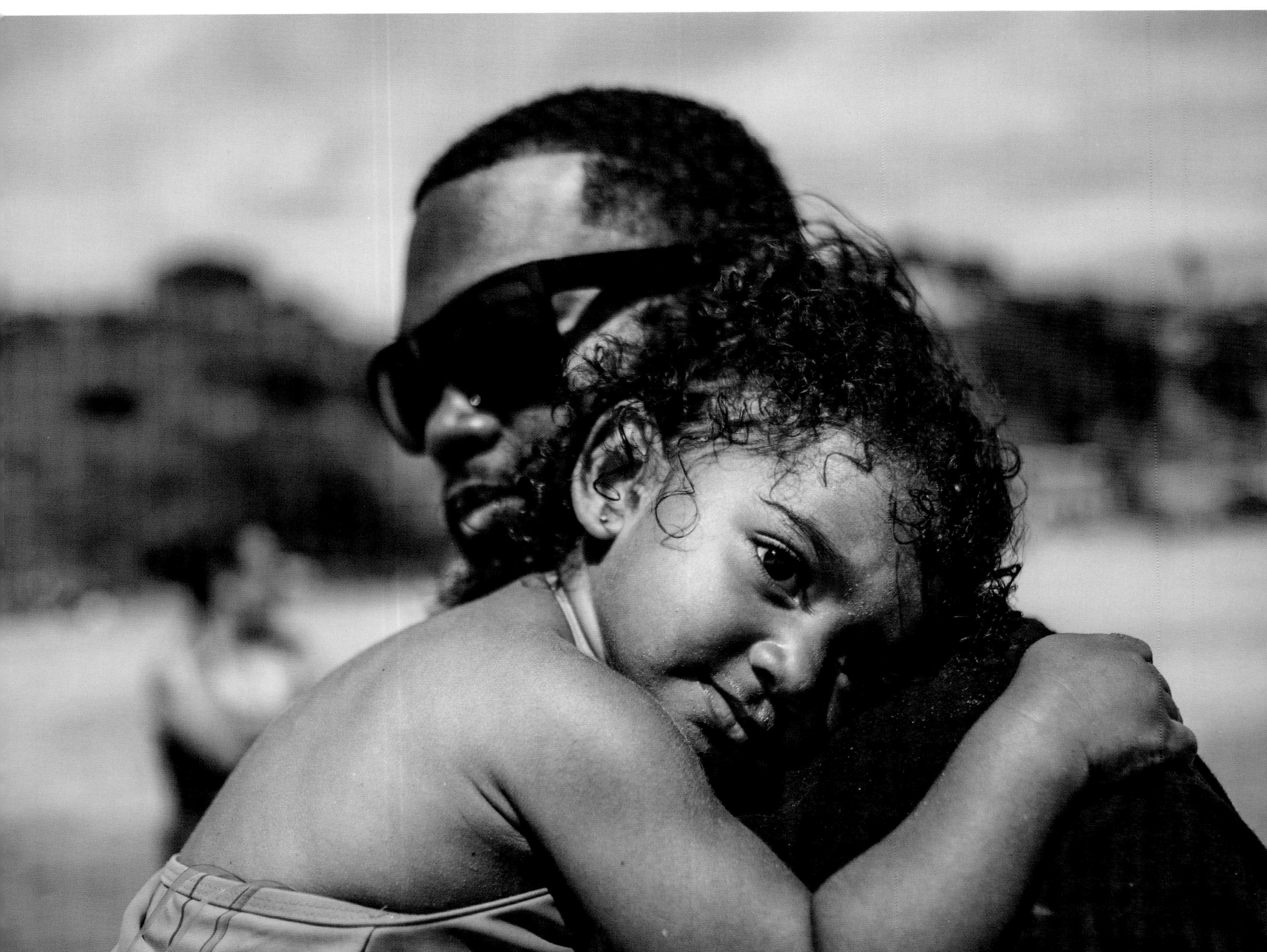

Dad's shoulders, a restful place

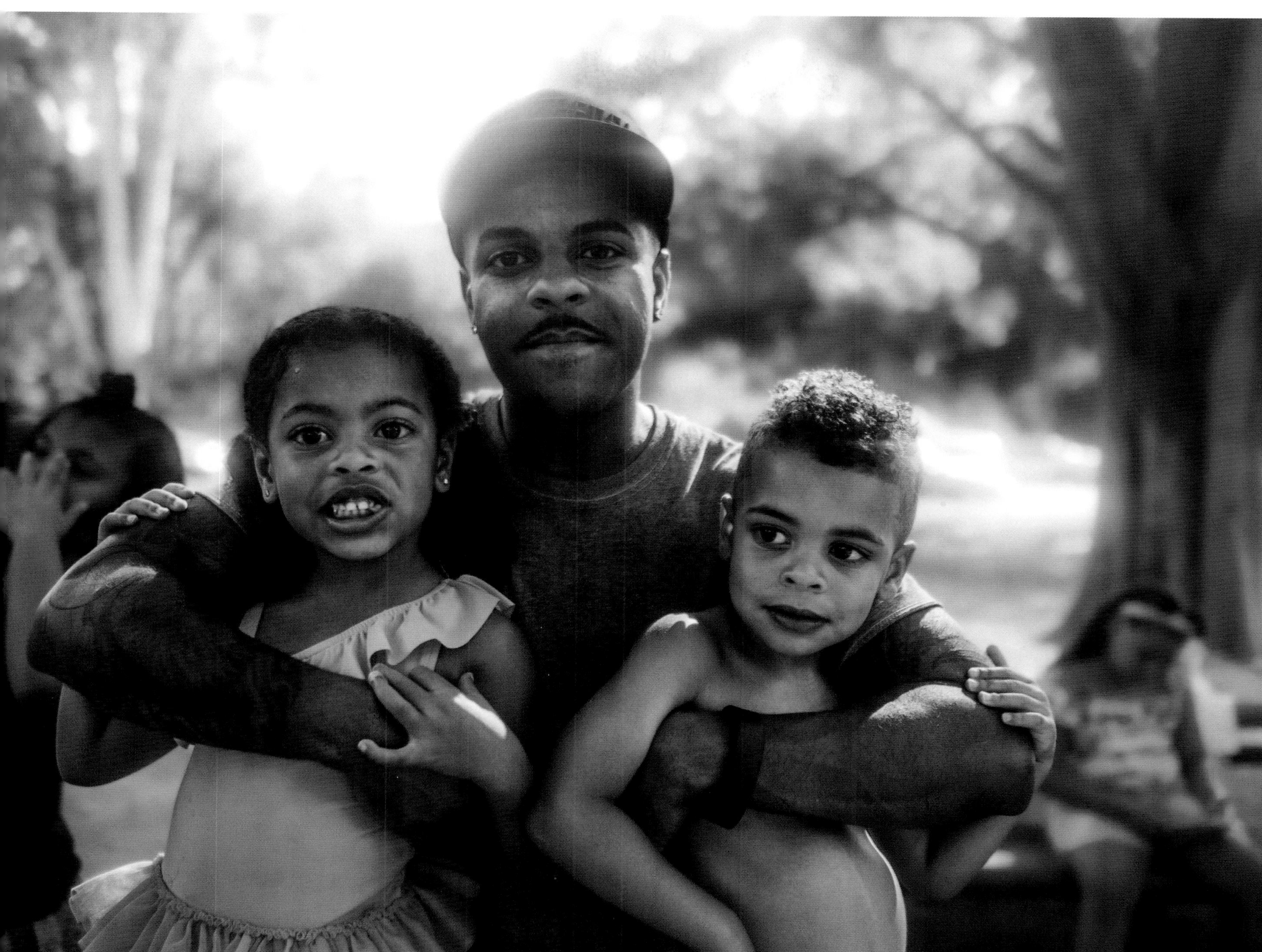

Summertime fun in the sun

REGINALD CUNNINGHAM

Photographer of urban style, culture, and portraiture with a gift for capturing subjects at their most comfortable and joyful

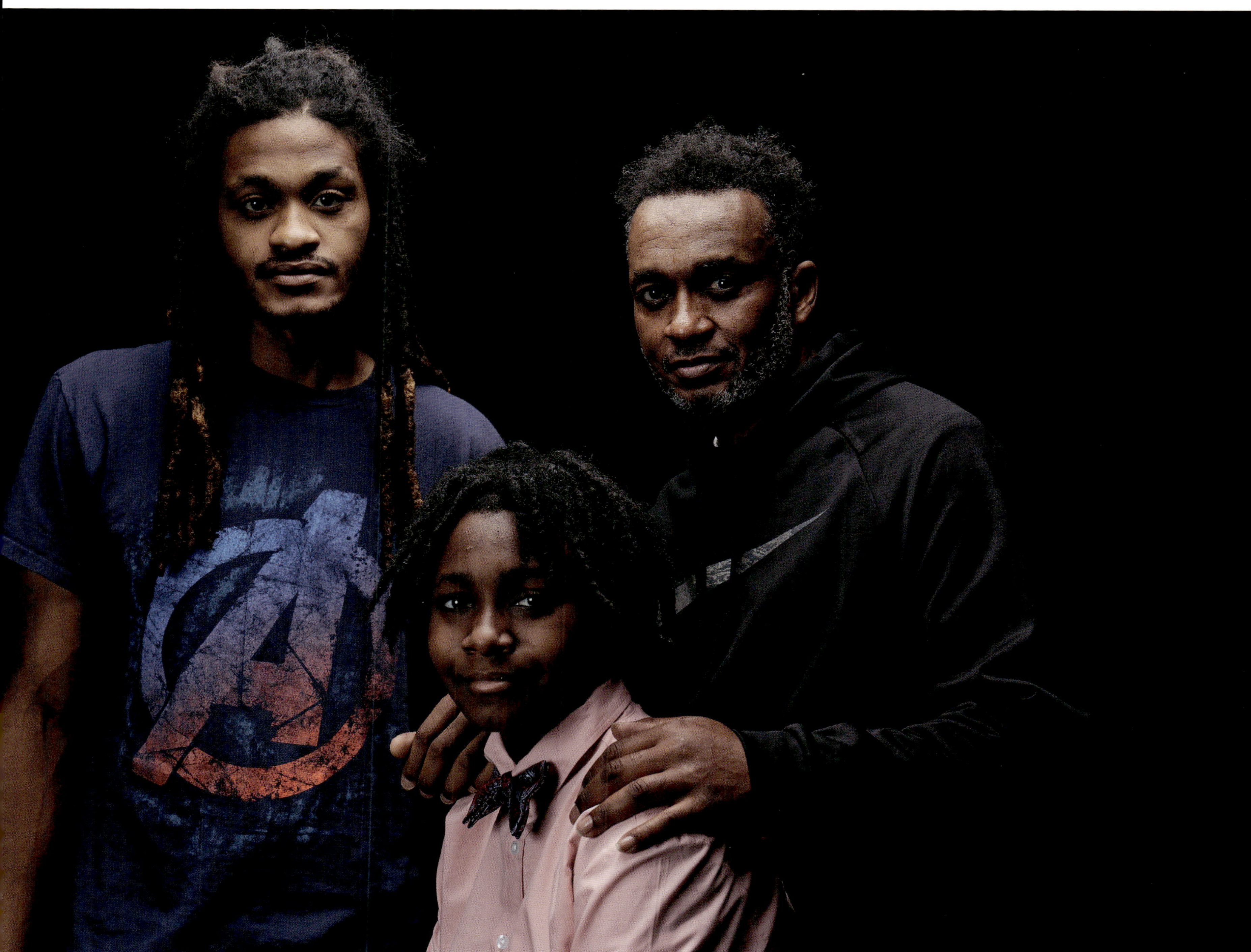

above/pages 66–69: **Raising young men**

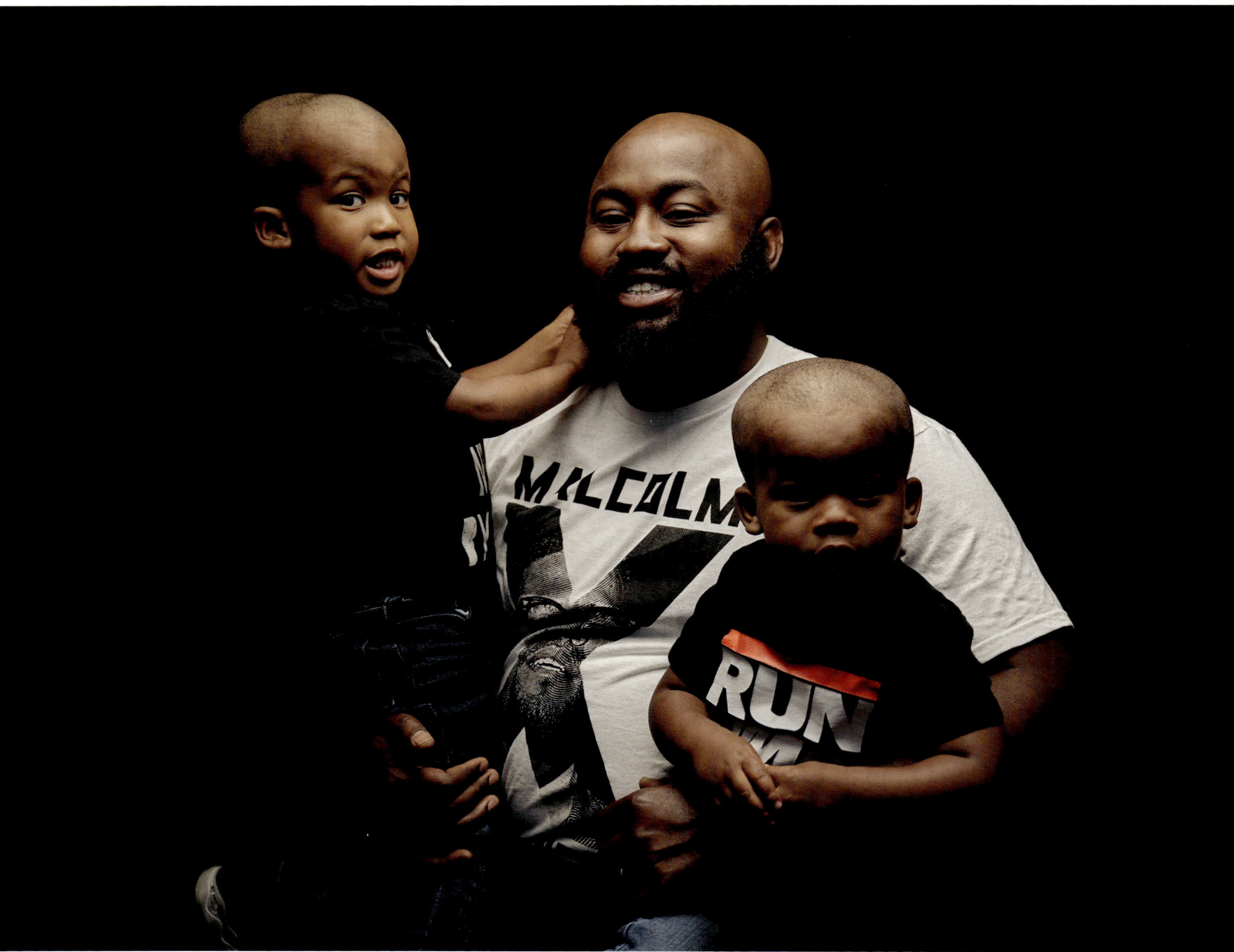
MALCOLM
RUN

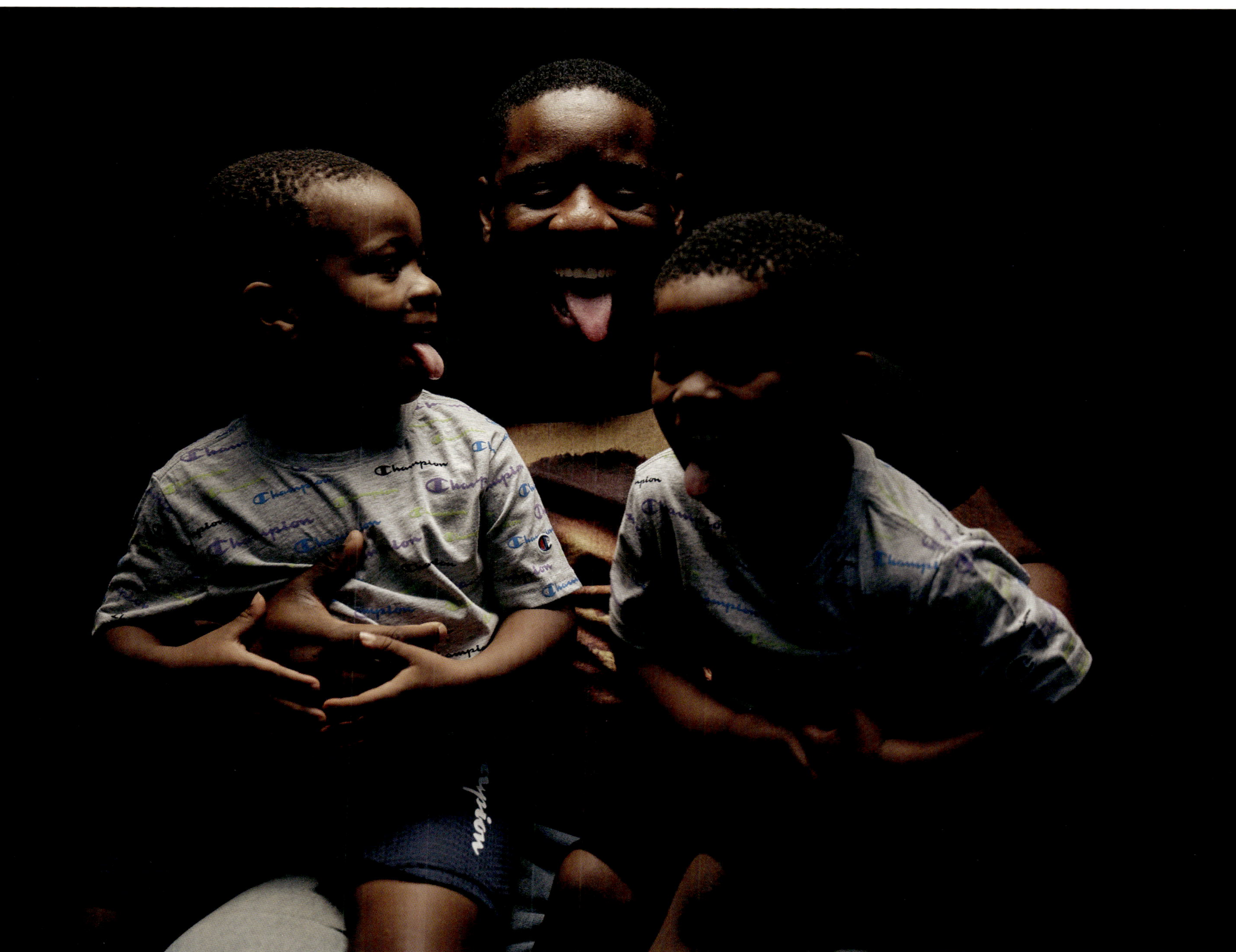
Champion

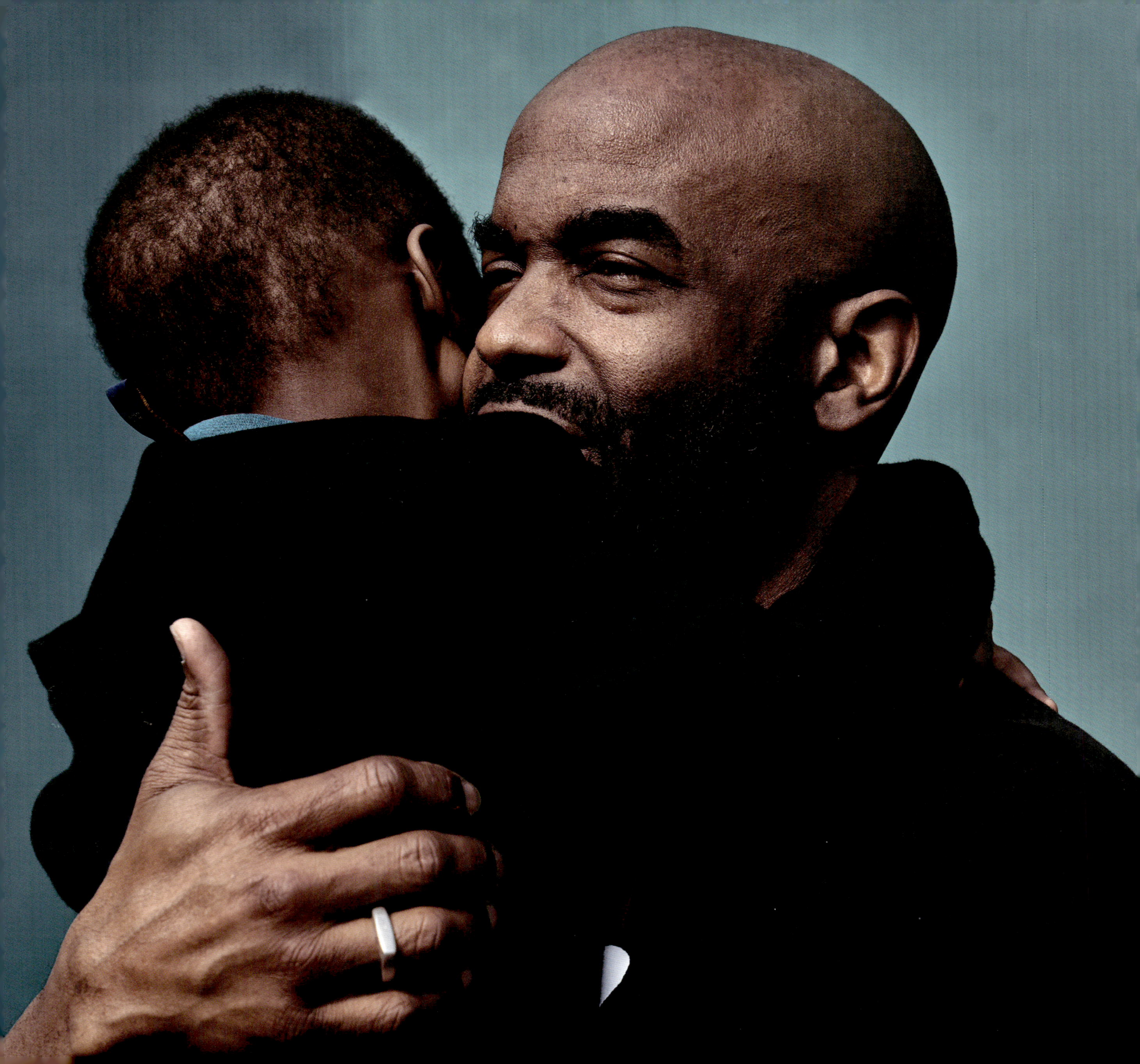

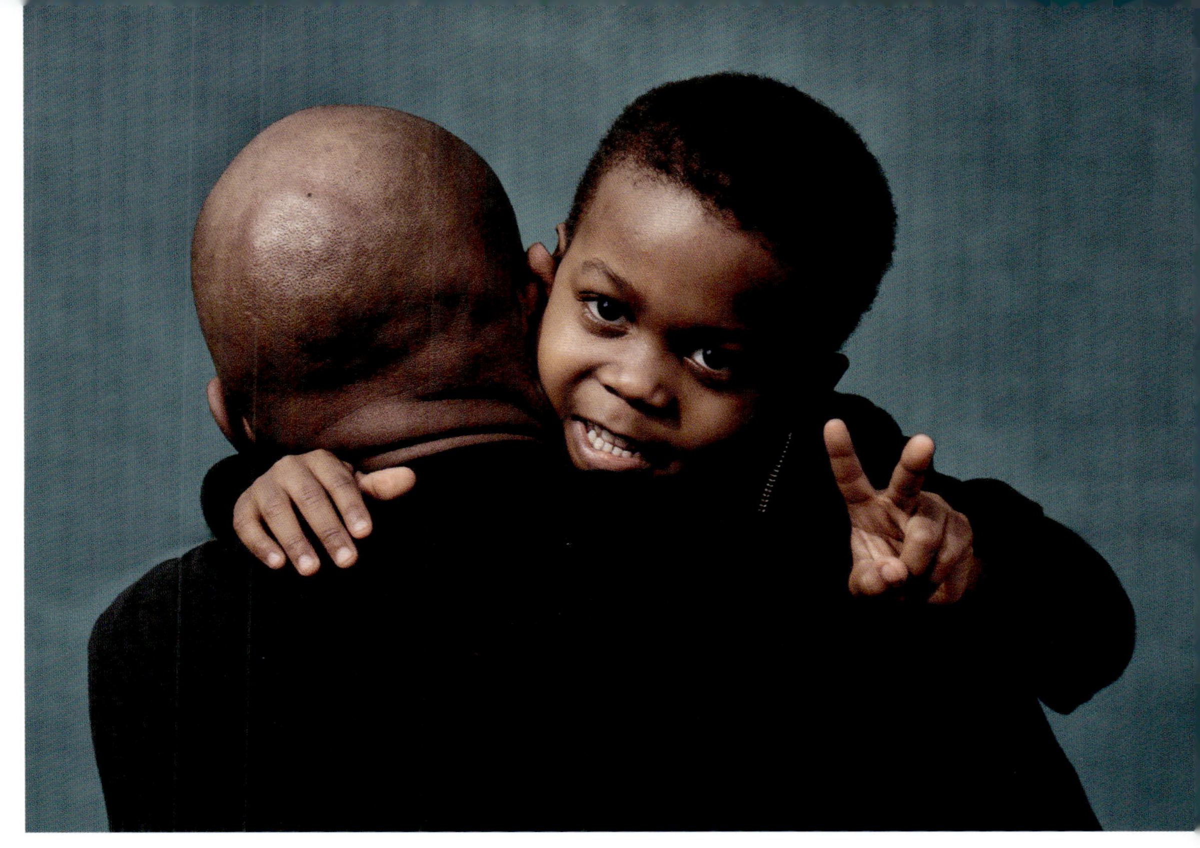

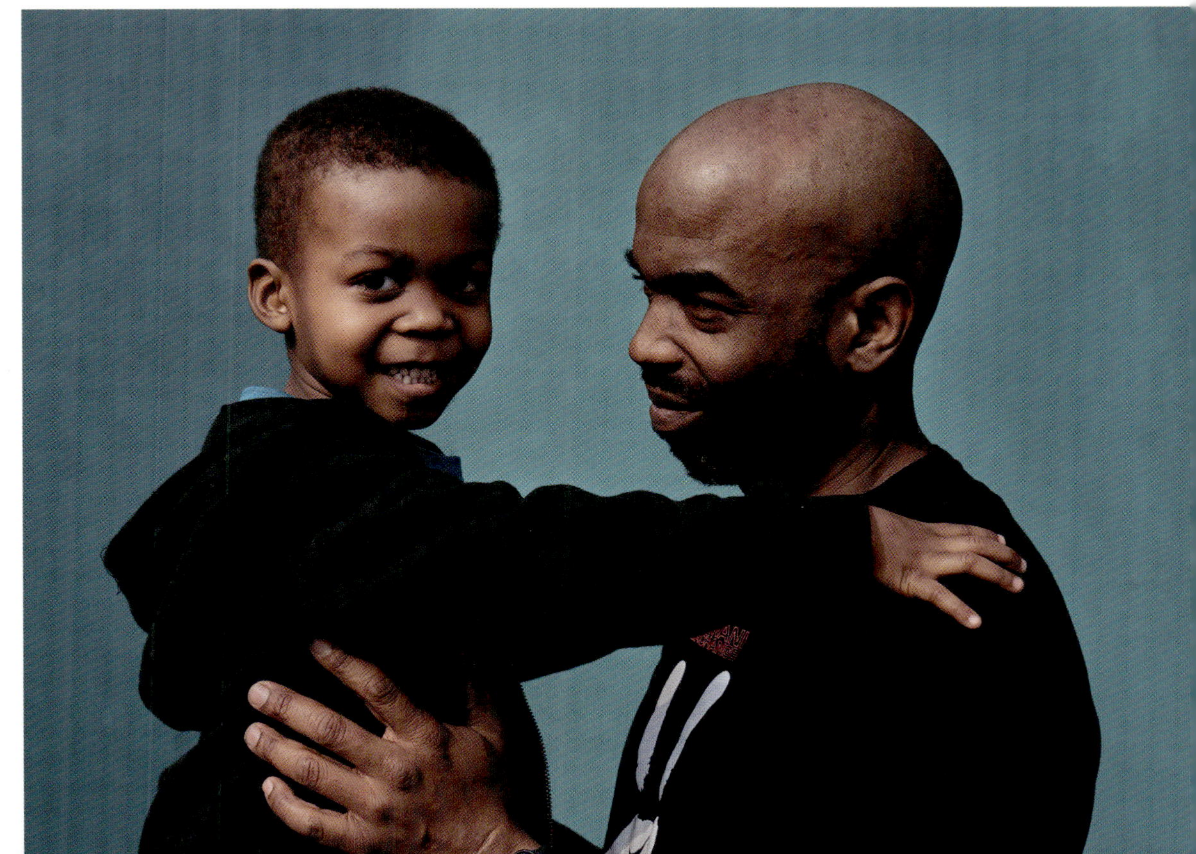

DERREL R. TODD

Photographer and cinematographer dedicated to capturing visual heirlooms that will last a lifetime

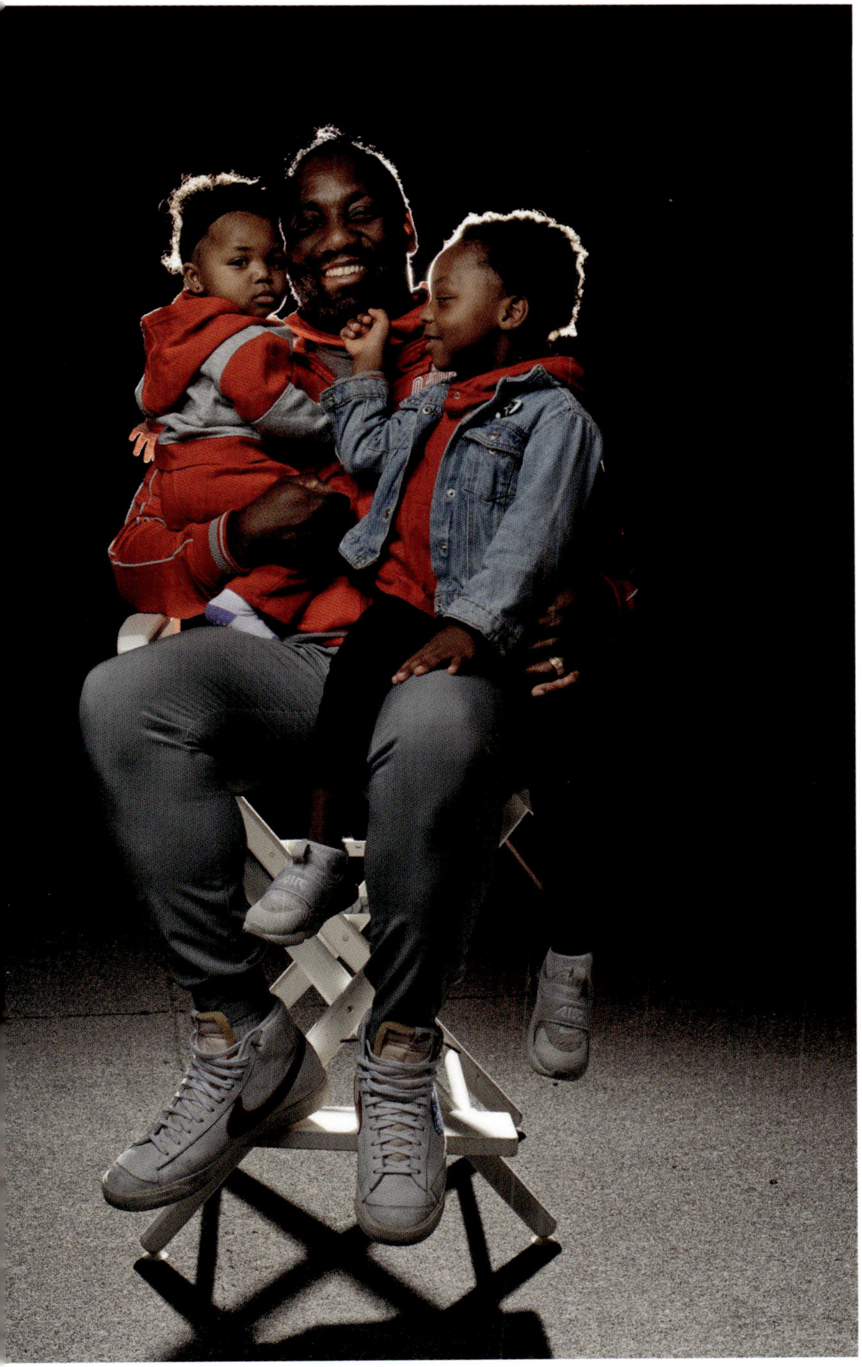

A family that laughs together

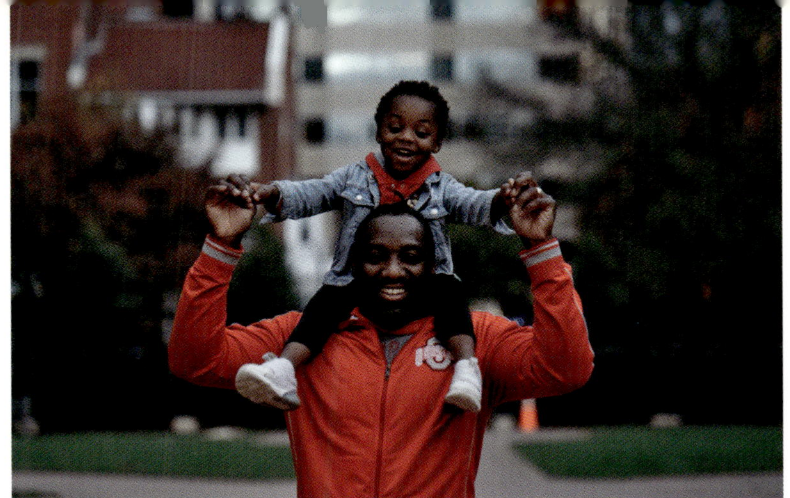

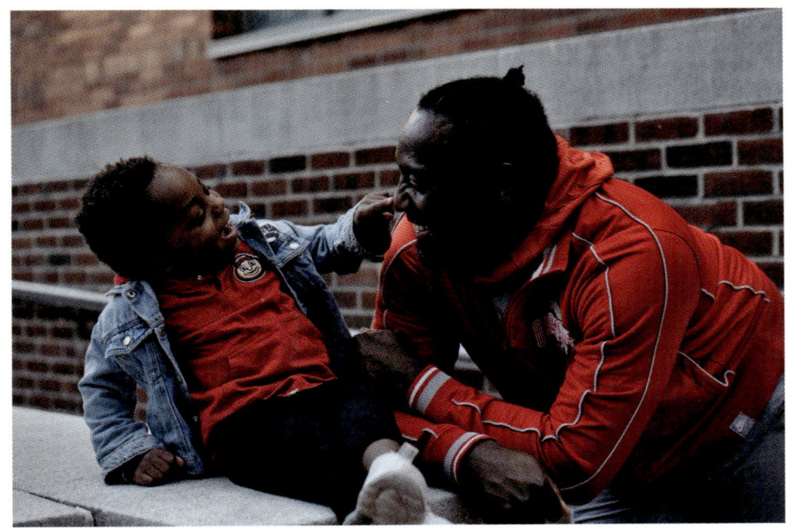

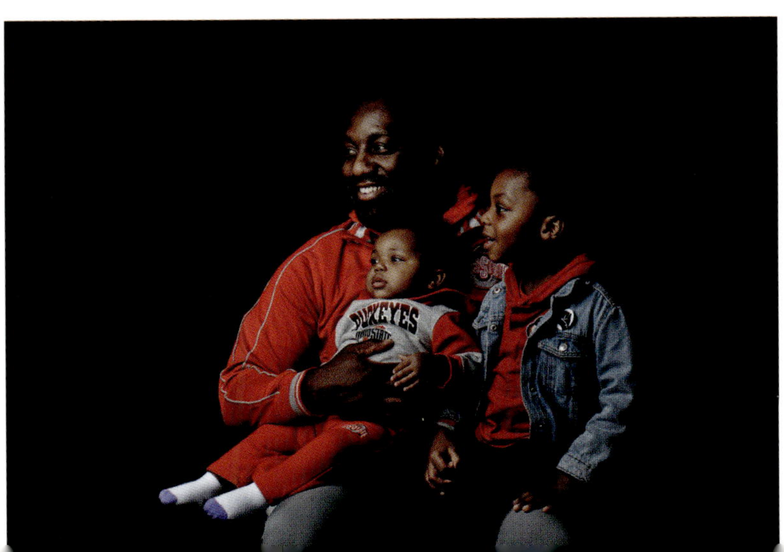

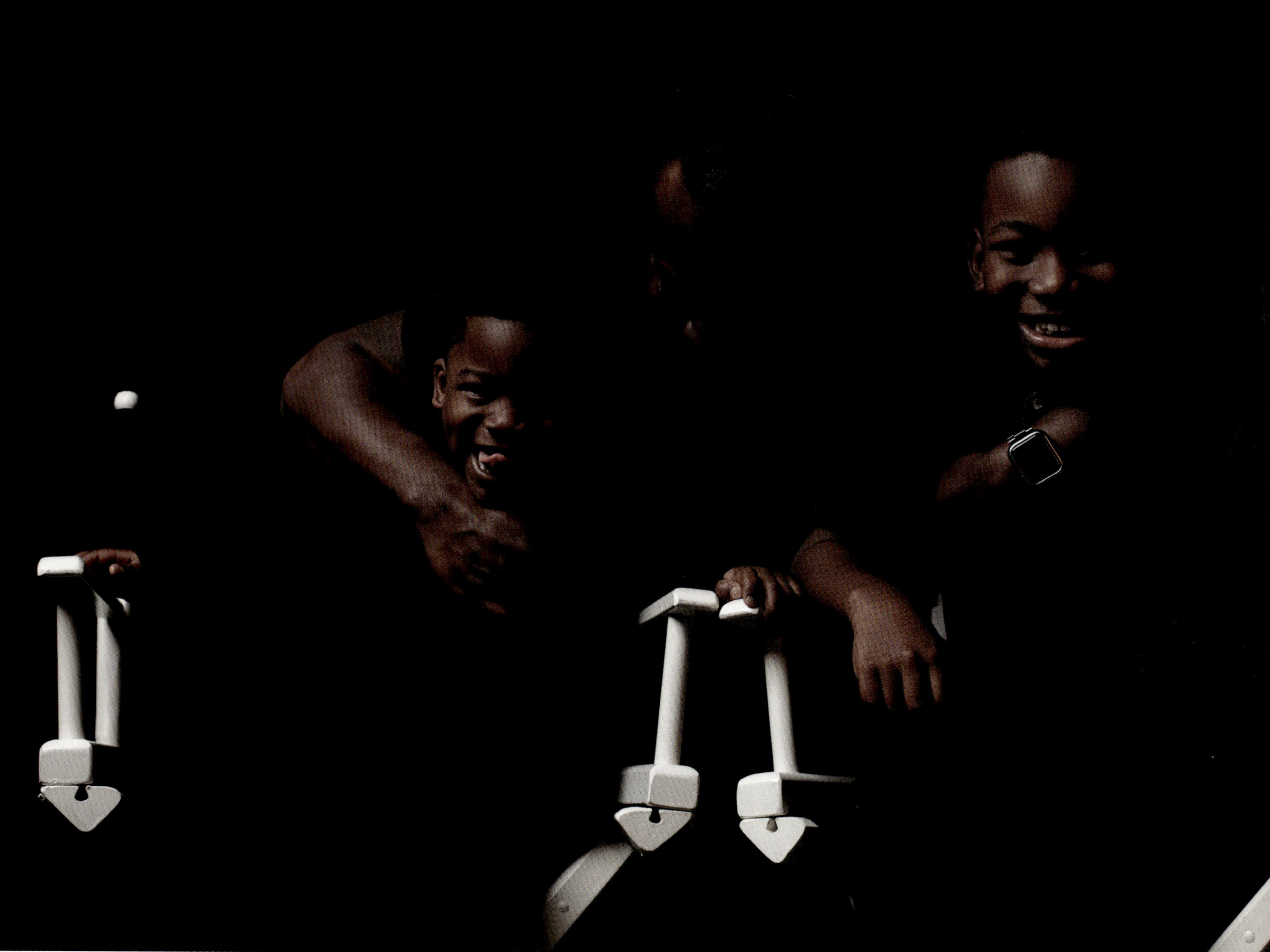

Manhood starts with brotherhood.

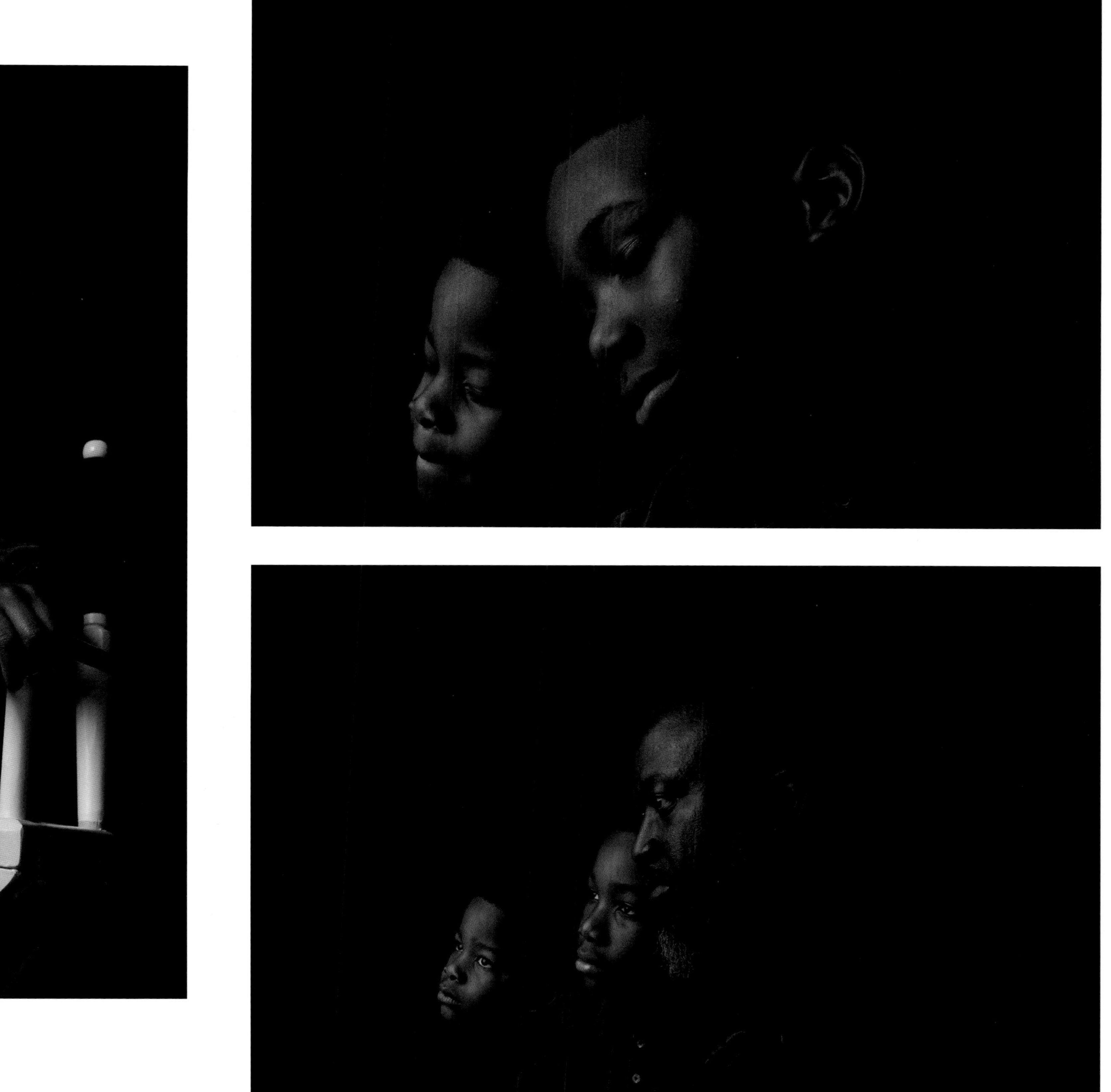

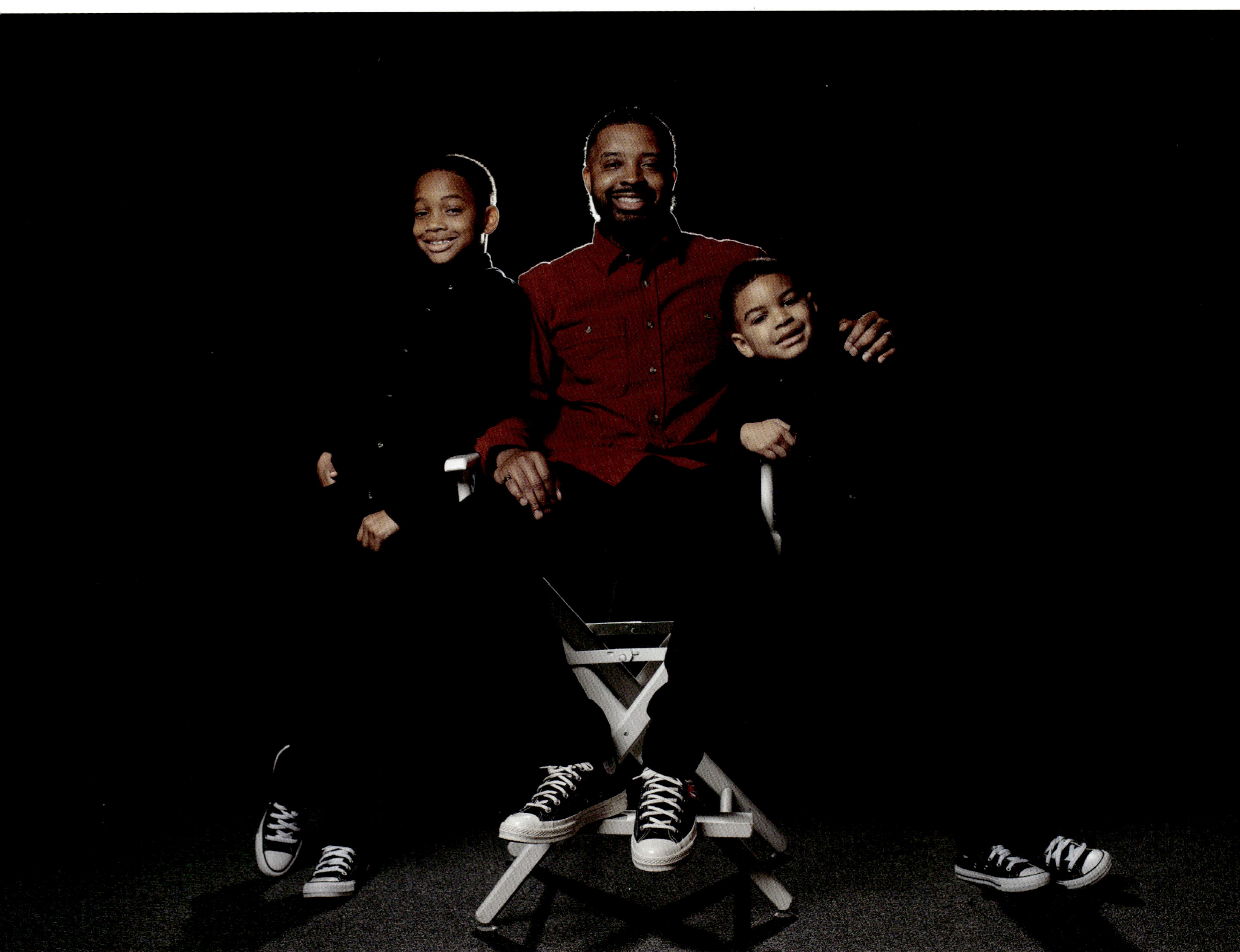

Dads are often our first role models.

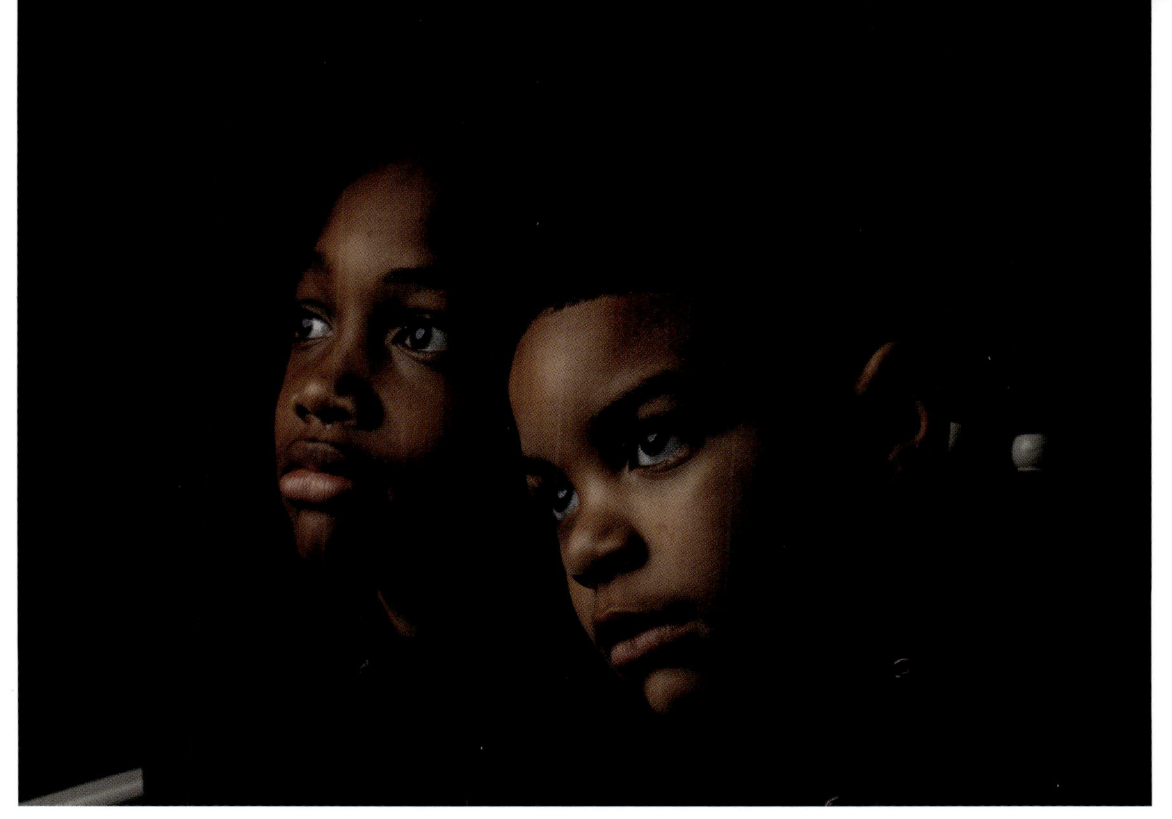

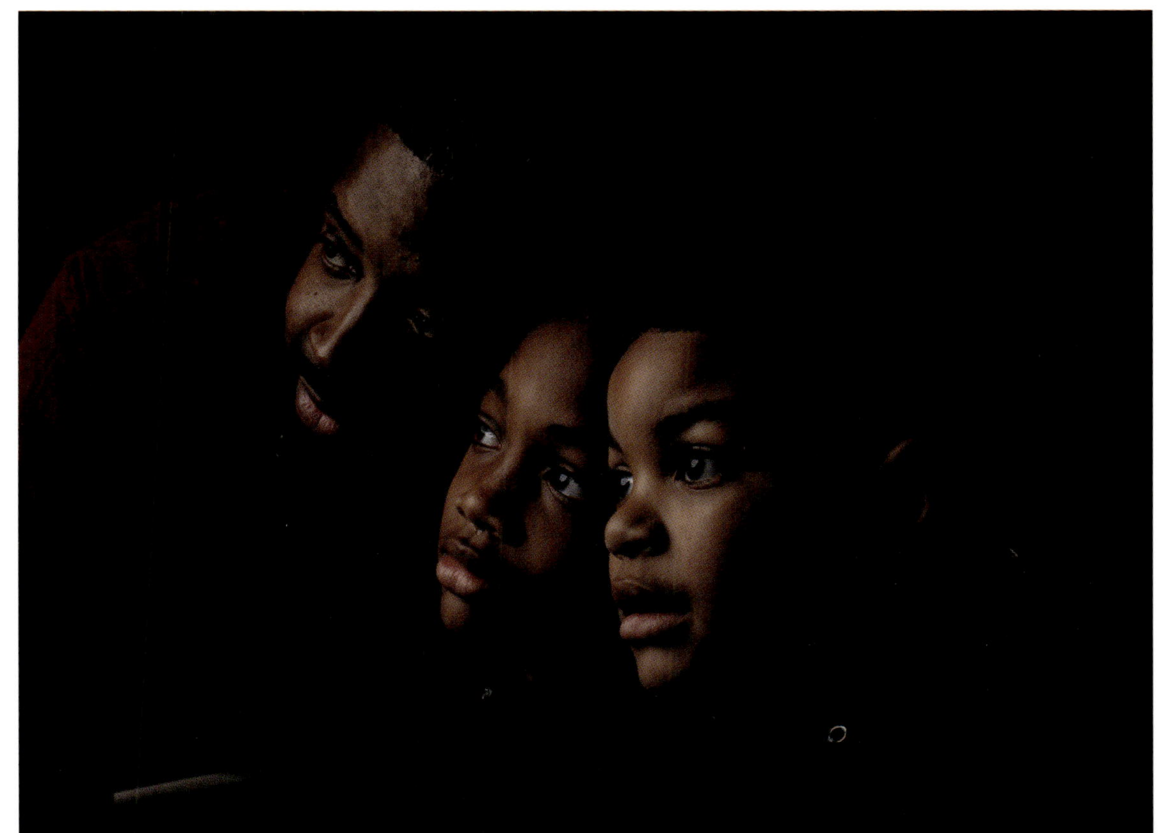

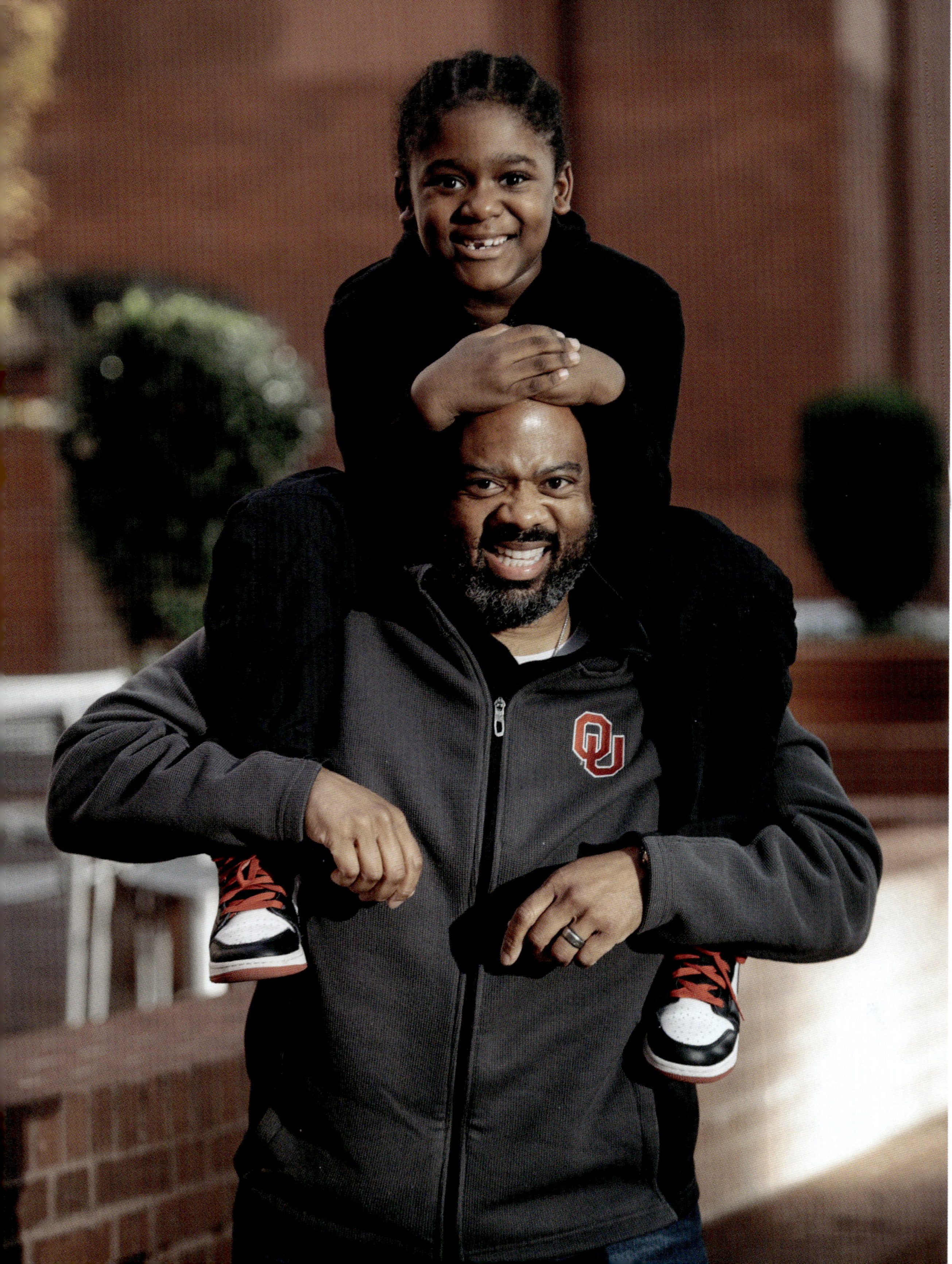

We learn from watching.

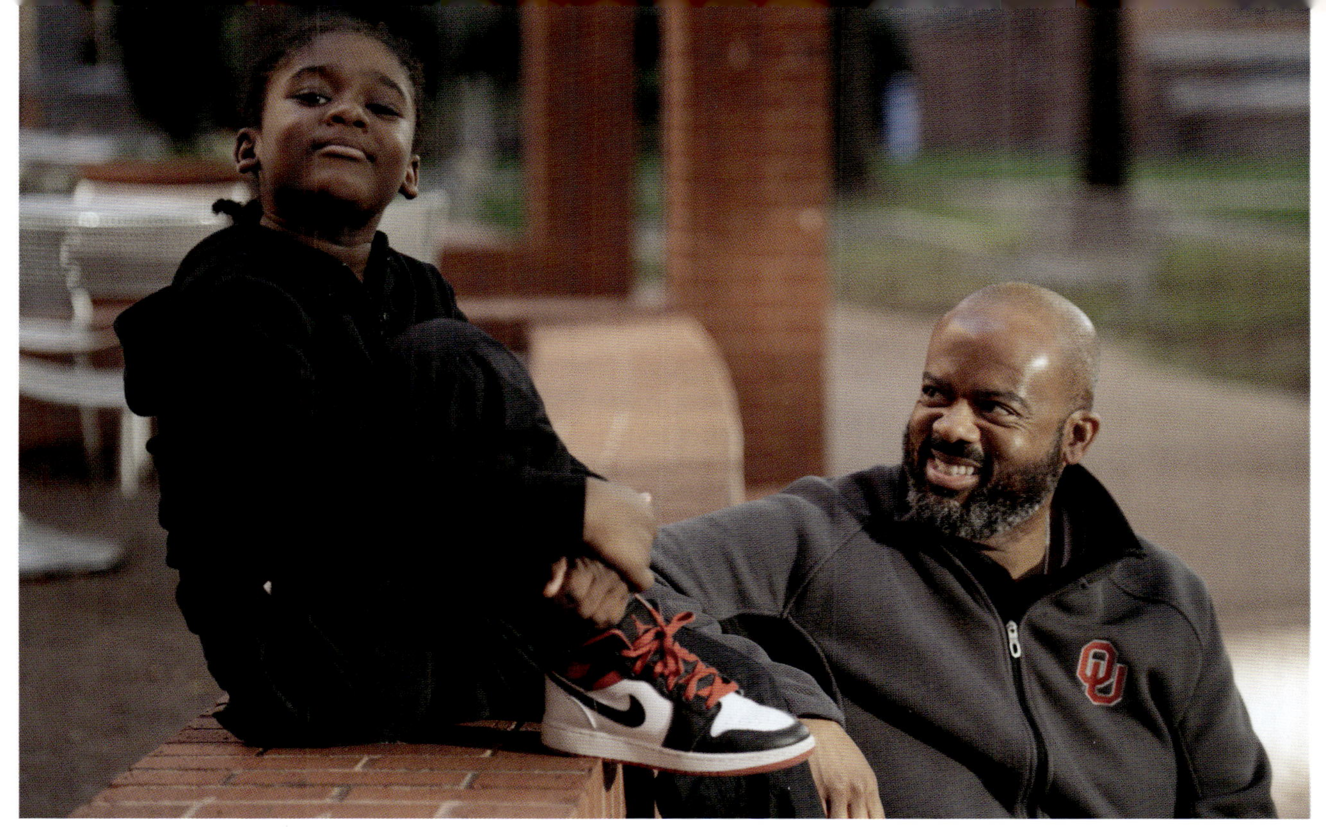
OU

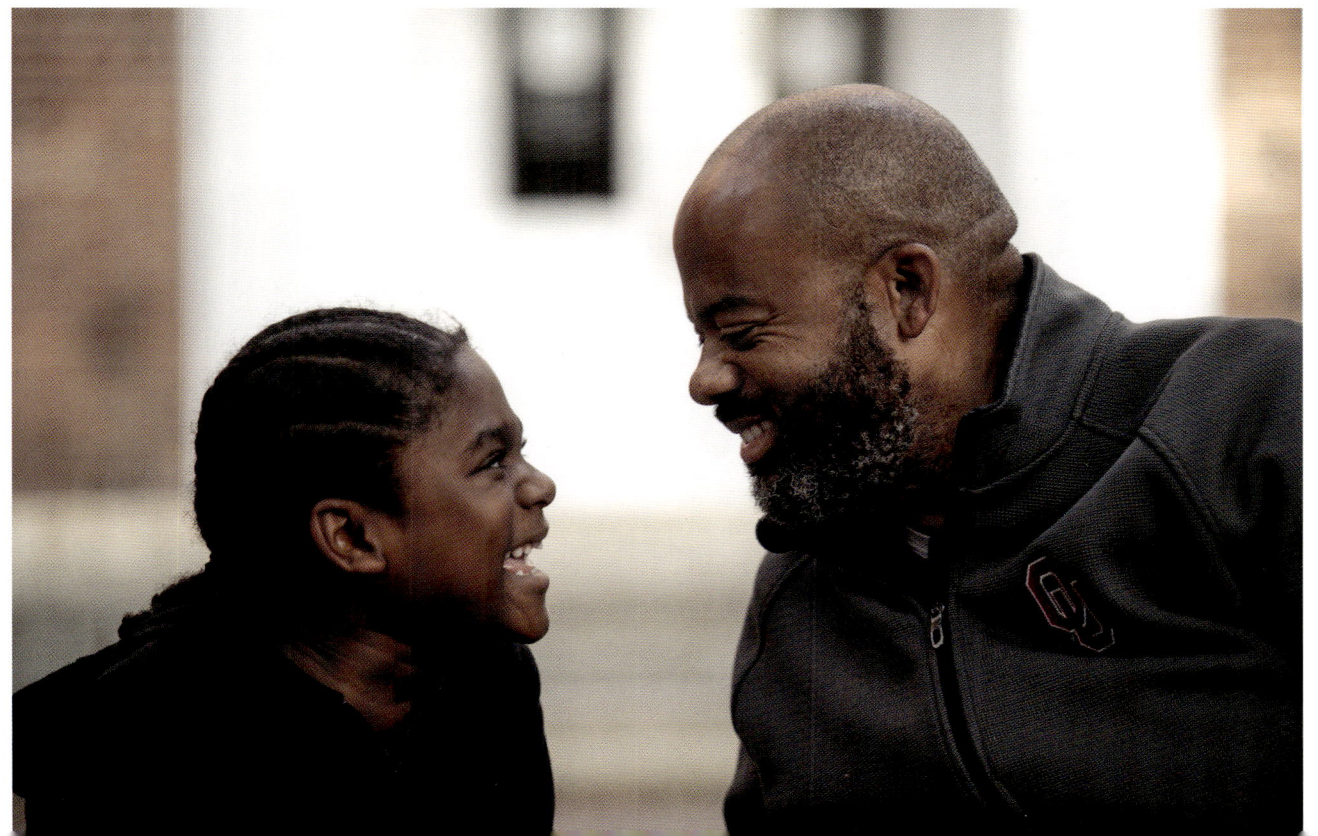

FATHERHOOD IS . . .

LEO ARISTILDE

Fatherhood is a privilege. There's a human who looks at me like I am a deity, and I have the privilege of being a kind, gentle source of love in this beautiful little world of hers. I remember how badly I wished someone would extend patience to me as a kid, and now I have the privilege of providing the safe space I wanted to someone else. I get to learn what she finds funny, how her mind works, what hobbies interest her. And eventually she'll be teaching me a world of things I couldn't imagine arriving at on my own; as her life guide, I wanna be there to root for her forever. That's a privilege.

FATHERHOOD IS A PRIVILEGE.

Every loving dad strives to be a safe space for their child, and some days it requires you to provide safety for your child when your own mind is not a safe place for you. It requires putting the feelings of another ahead of your own because they don't know how to navigate their feelings yet. It requires examining yourself, daily. I started going to therapy once a week months before having a child. I wanted to be a safe space but didn't know what my unhealthy habits were. There have been *many* humbling experiences, but I've always thought about the thirty-year-old version of my kid, and I want to be the safest person on earth for them. Seeing flaws in yourself will test your ego, but it's a worthy price for the safety of your kid. Her needs and feelings change from moment to moment, and showing my child how to navigate them requires leading by example.

FATHERHOOD IS A TEST.

Learning what you know. Learning what you don't know. Learning what is healthy. Learning what is unhealthy. Learning what is valuable. Learning where time was wasted. Learning how to teach. Learning what to teach. Learning what can be taught. Learning how to learn. Learning how to unlearn. Learning how to allow them to experience pain. Learning that one day I won't be here to protect them. Learning that their life is theirs to live and I'm simply a life guide giving everything I have, because there is no way to possibly describe the overwhelming feeling of love that consumes your entire chest when just *thinking* about your kid.

FATHERHOOD IS LEARNING.

Any attentive parent will notice that your child's behavior toward you is one of the purest mirrors of the energy you poured into them. There are few things in this world that feel as good as when your kid abruptly stops and hugs you or randomly assaults you with kisses simply because you've done that to them. Kids mirror what they see. Fatherhood will show you what's on display.

FATHERHOOD IS A MIRROR.

JASON M. JOHNSON

Award-winning photojournalist and author with an eye for the subtle beauty of everyday life

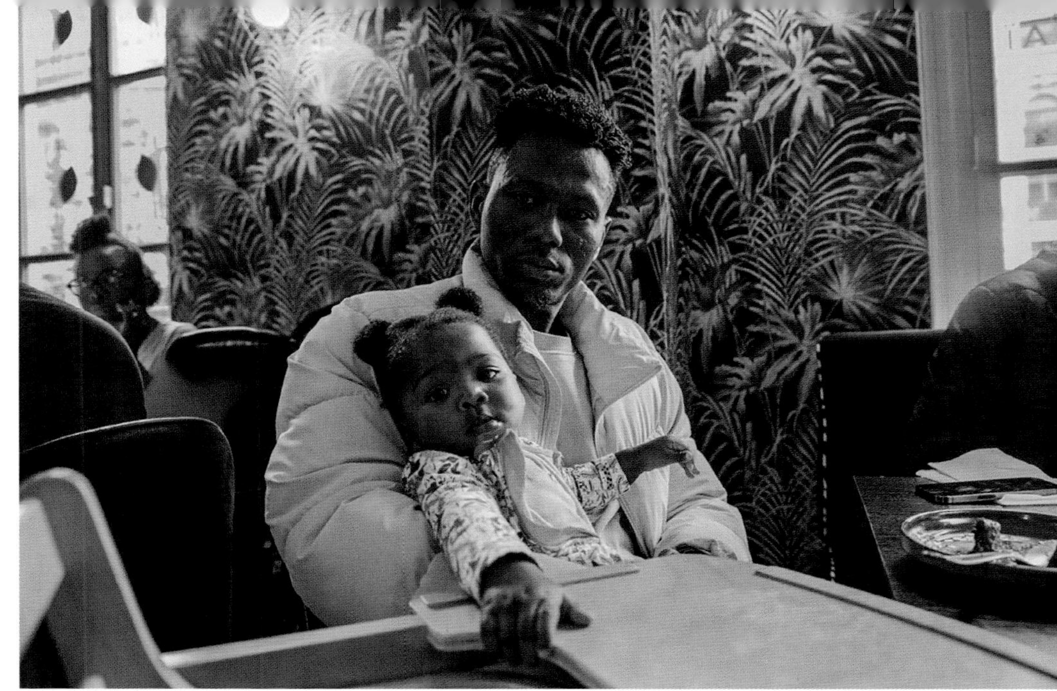

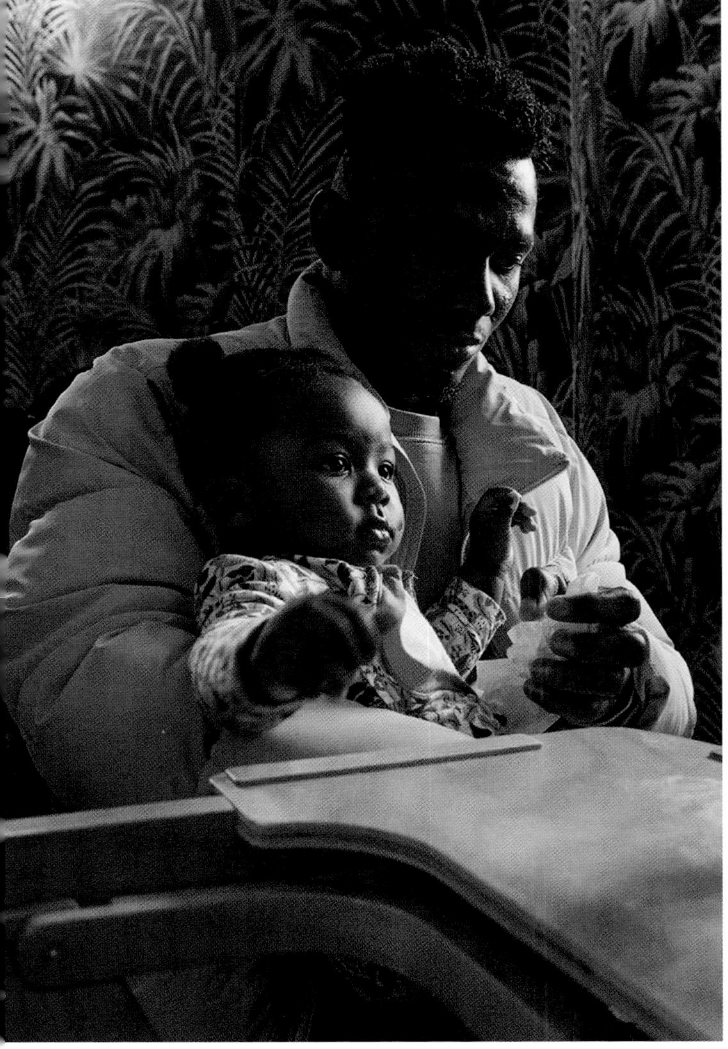

A father and daughter having dinner in Paris, France

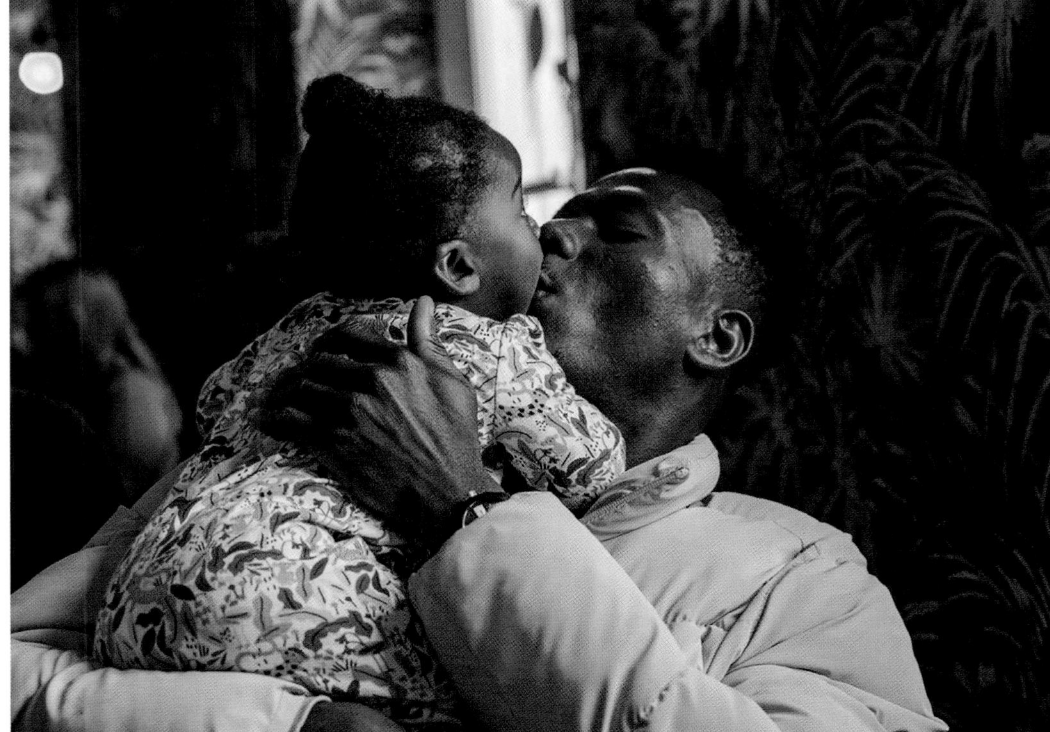

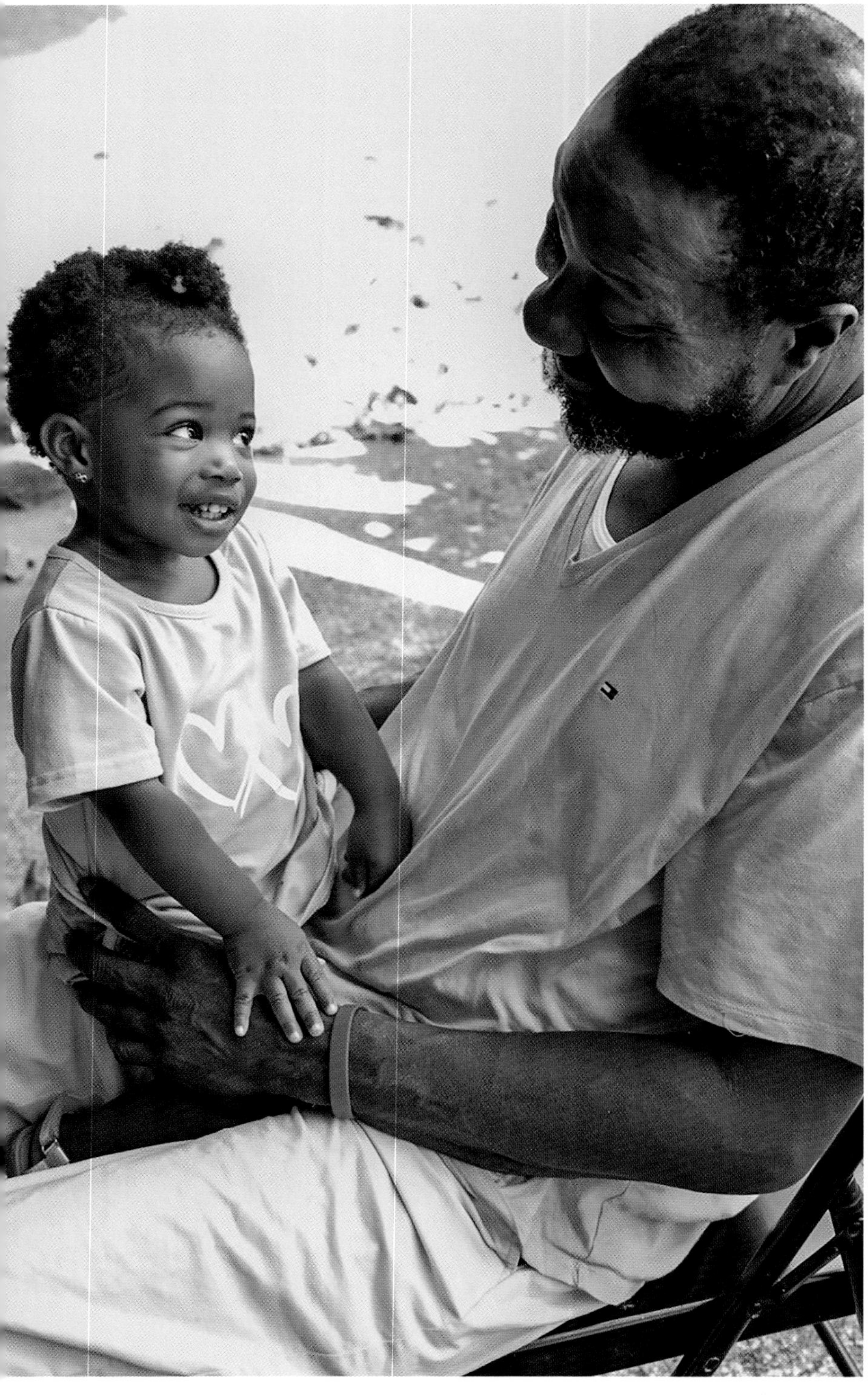

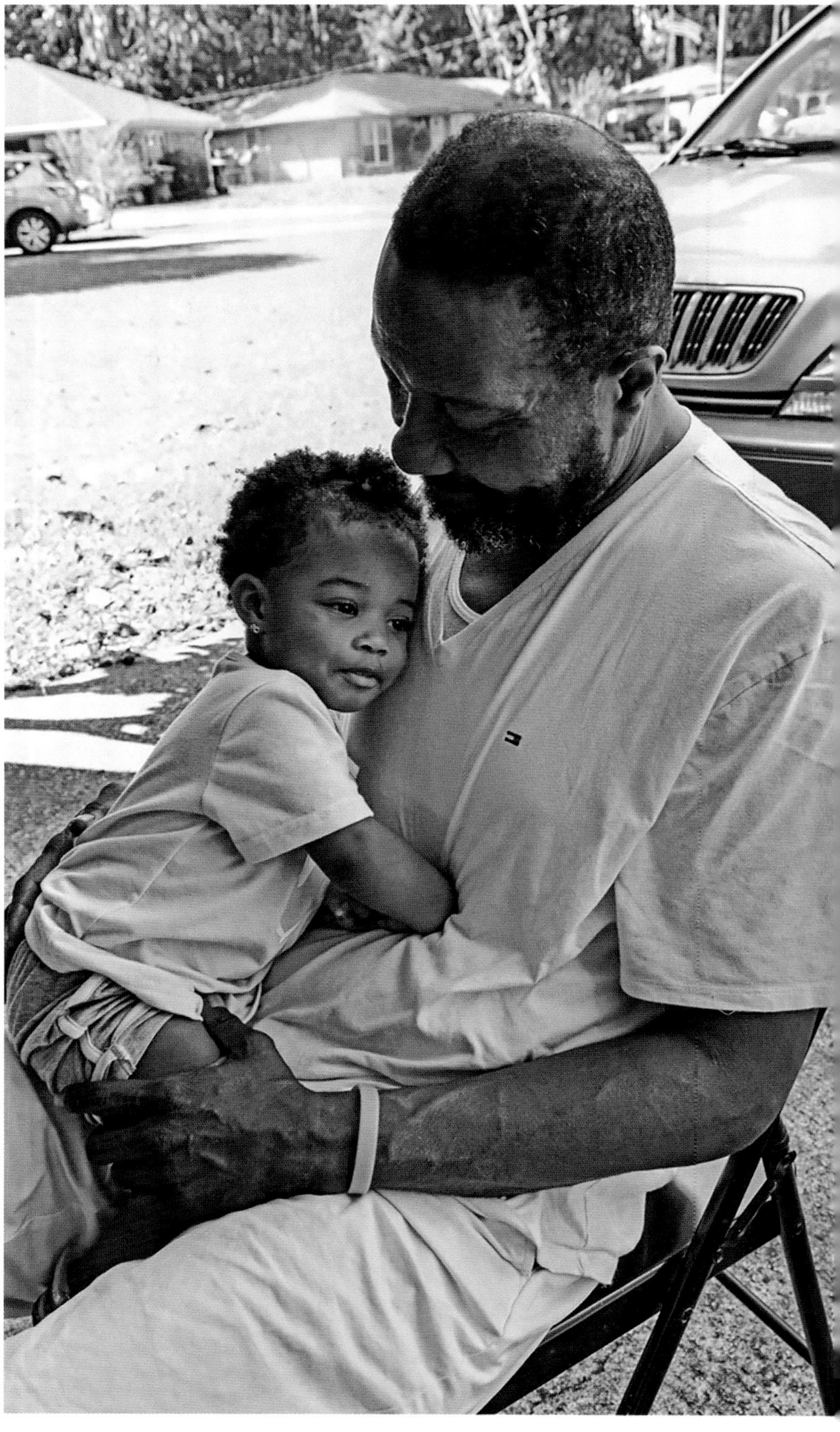

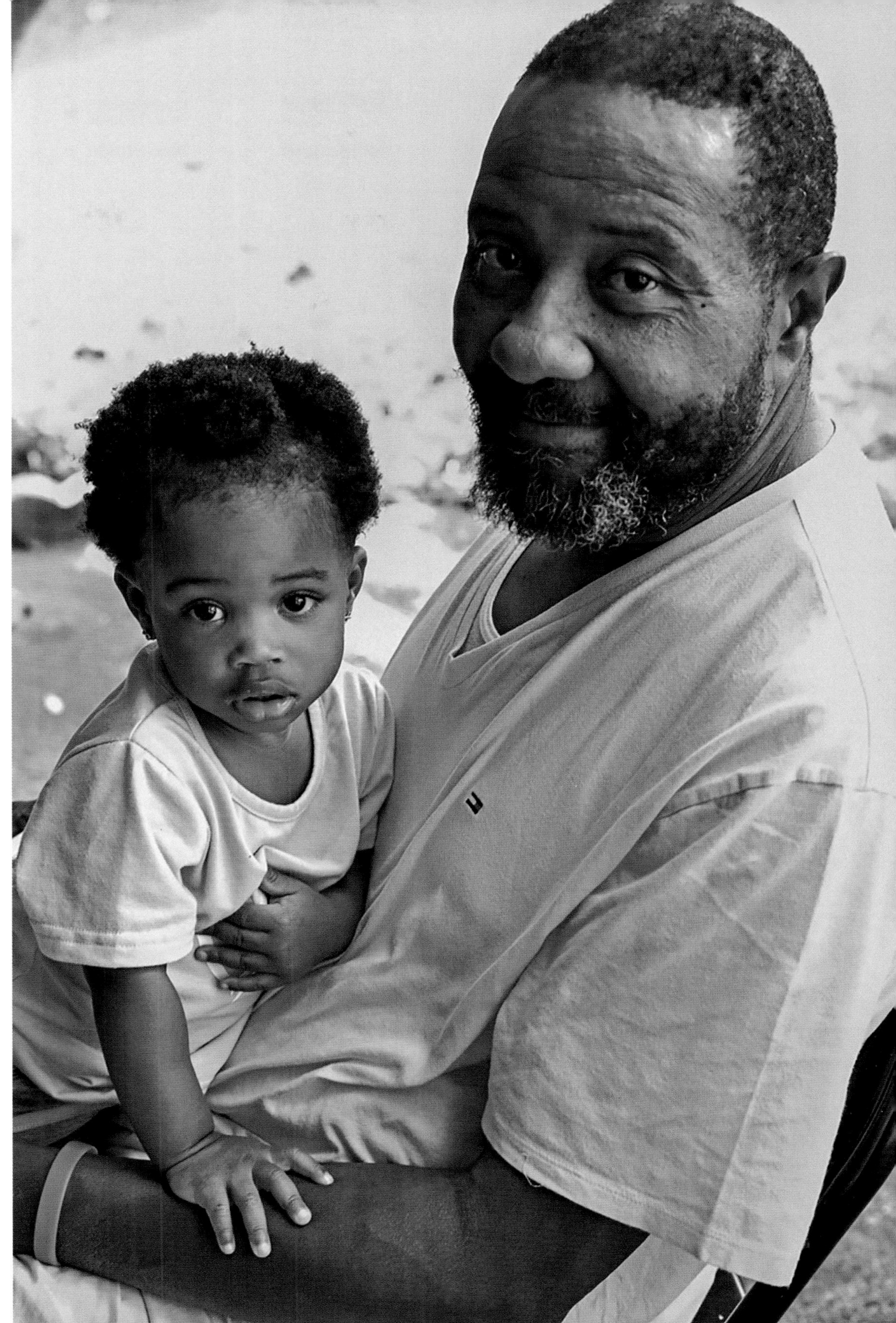

Perry Holmes with his granddaughter Saryah at a cookout in Savannah, Georgia

ANTHONY GEATHERS

Prolific photographer and photojournalist passionate about capturing both the rawness of humanity and the enduring essence of a powerful spirit

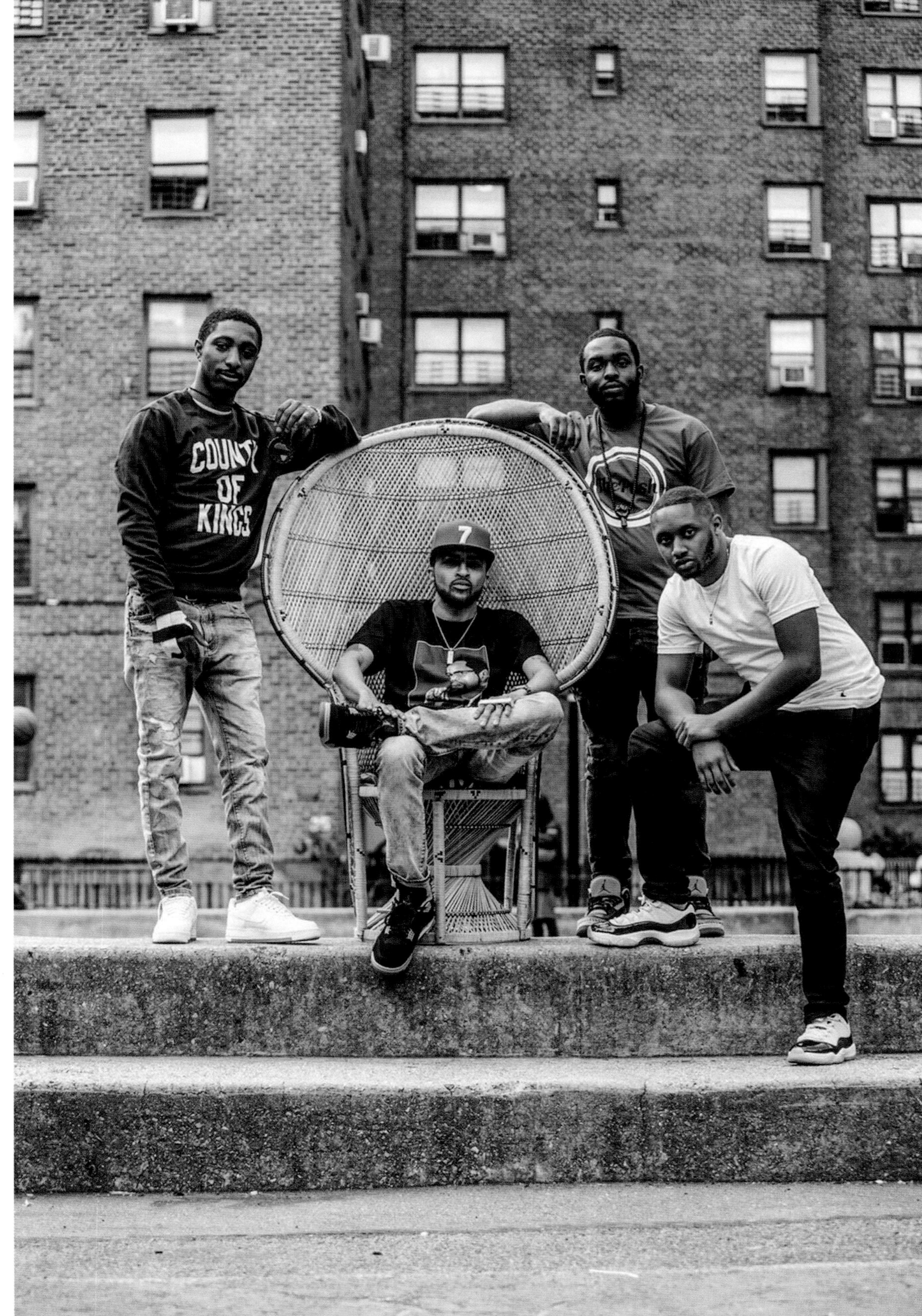

Firefighter Ahmaad Harris (*center*), archivist/historian Brian Valmond (*right*), and friends in Fort Greene, Brooklyn, New York

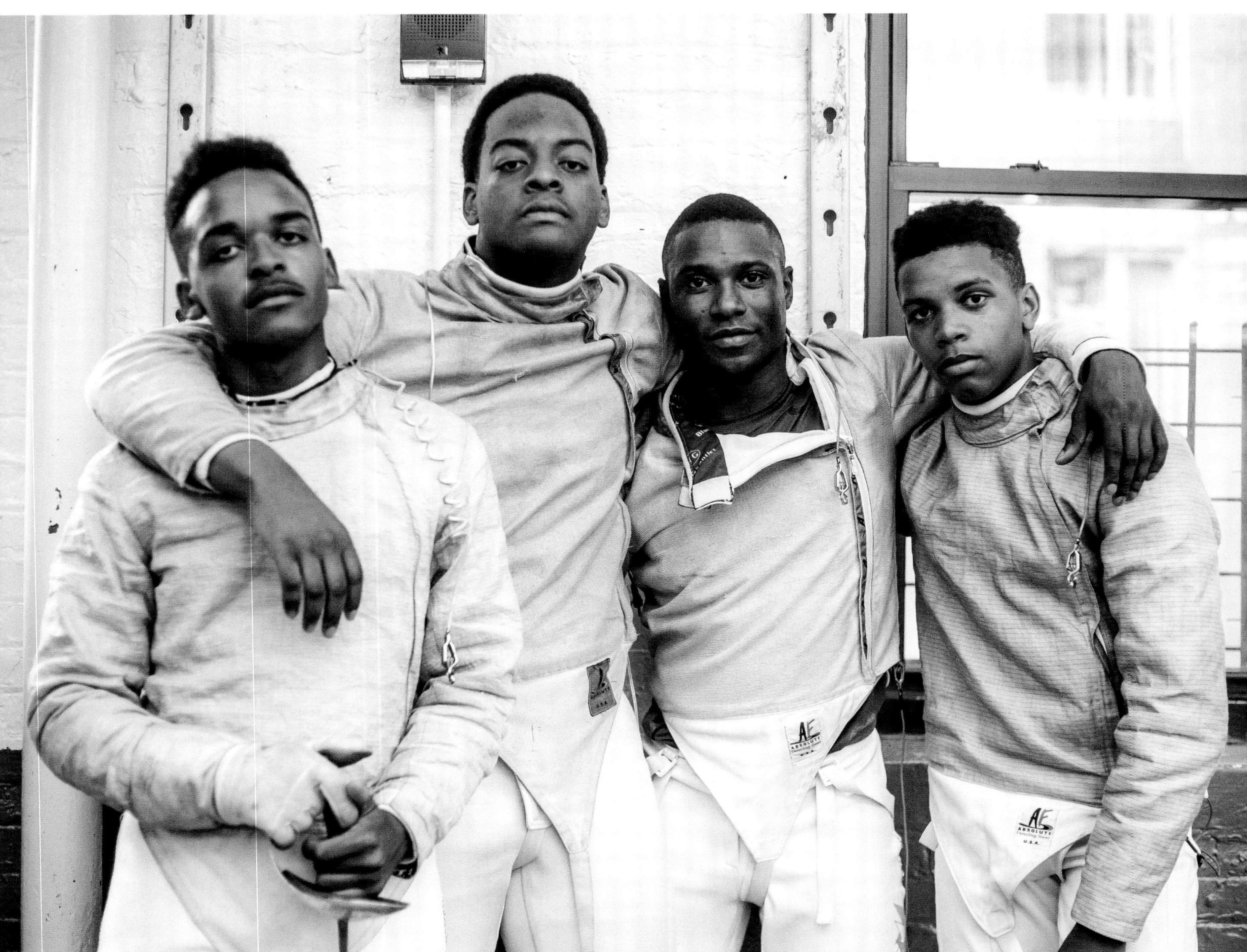

Growing together, teaching one another. Olympian fencer Daryl Homer (*center right*) and his training partners at the Peter Westbrook Foundation Fencing Club in New York.

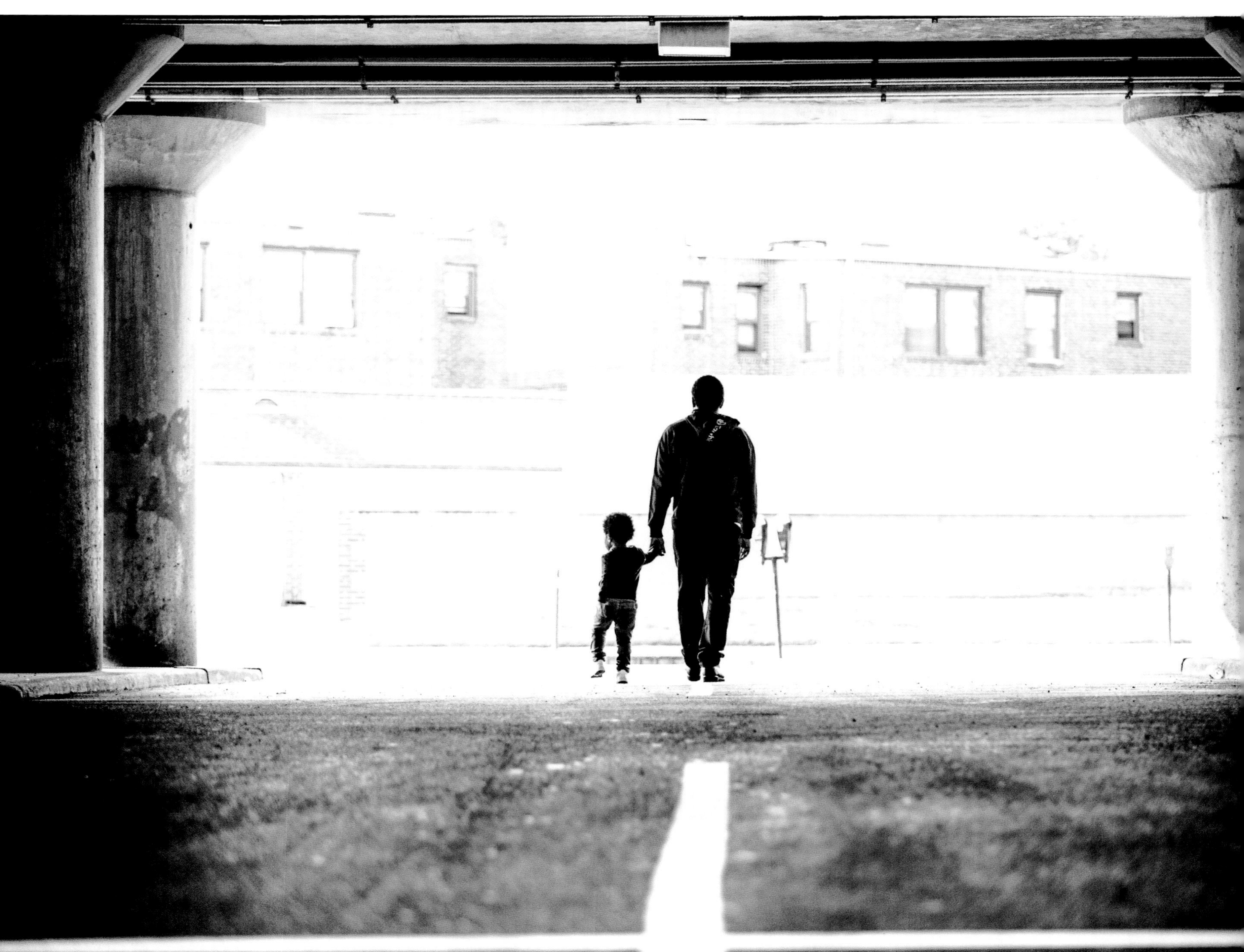

With you, I know no fear. Rapper Lloyd Banks and his son take a walk.

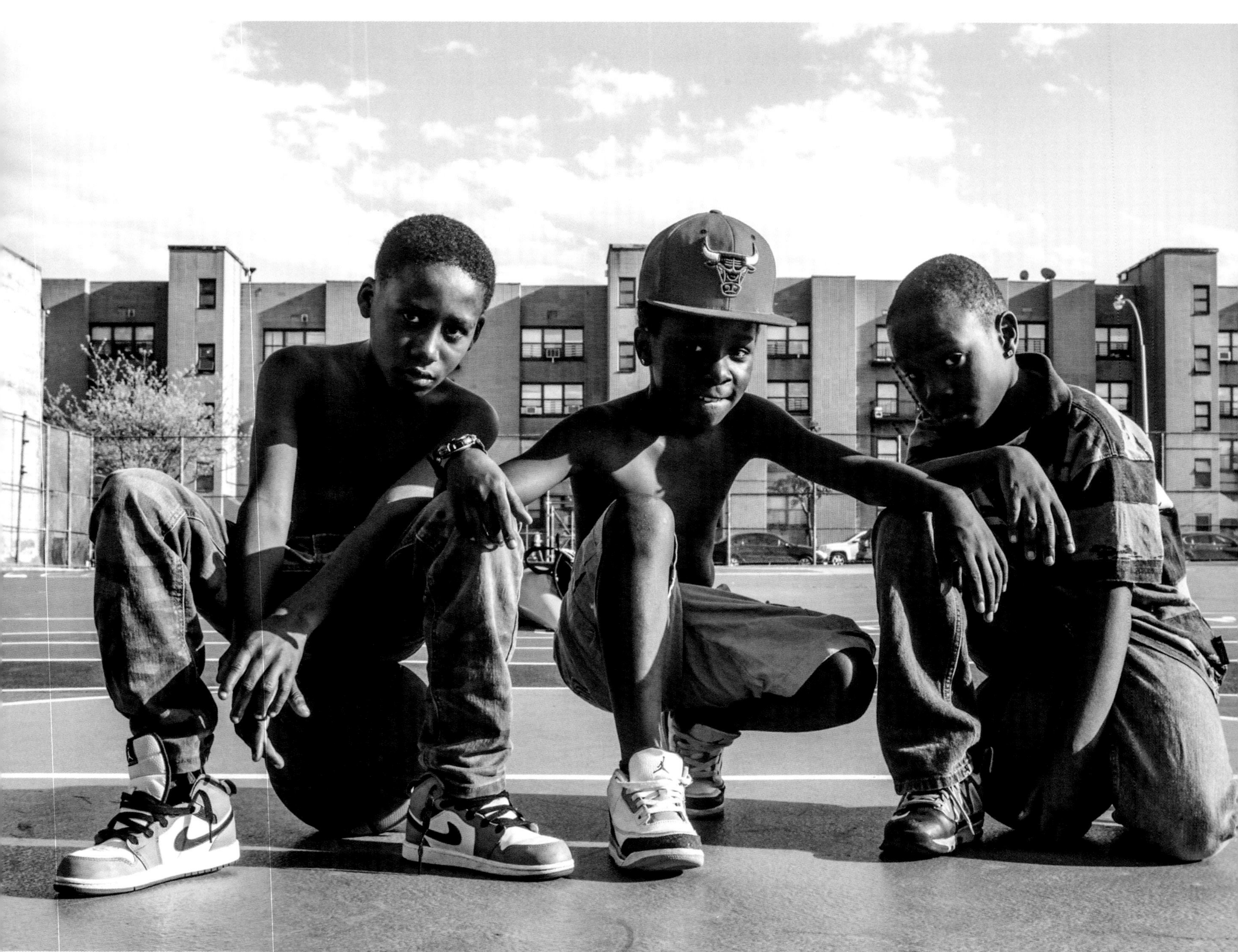

A meetup on the basketball court, Bedford-Stuyvesant, Brooklyn, New York, 2012

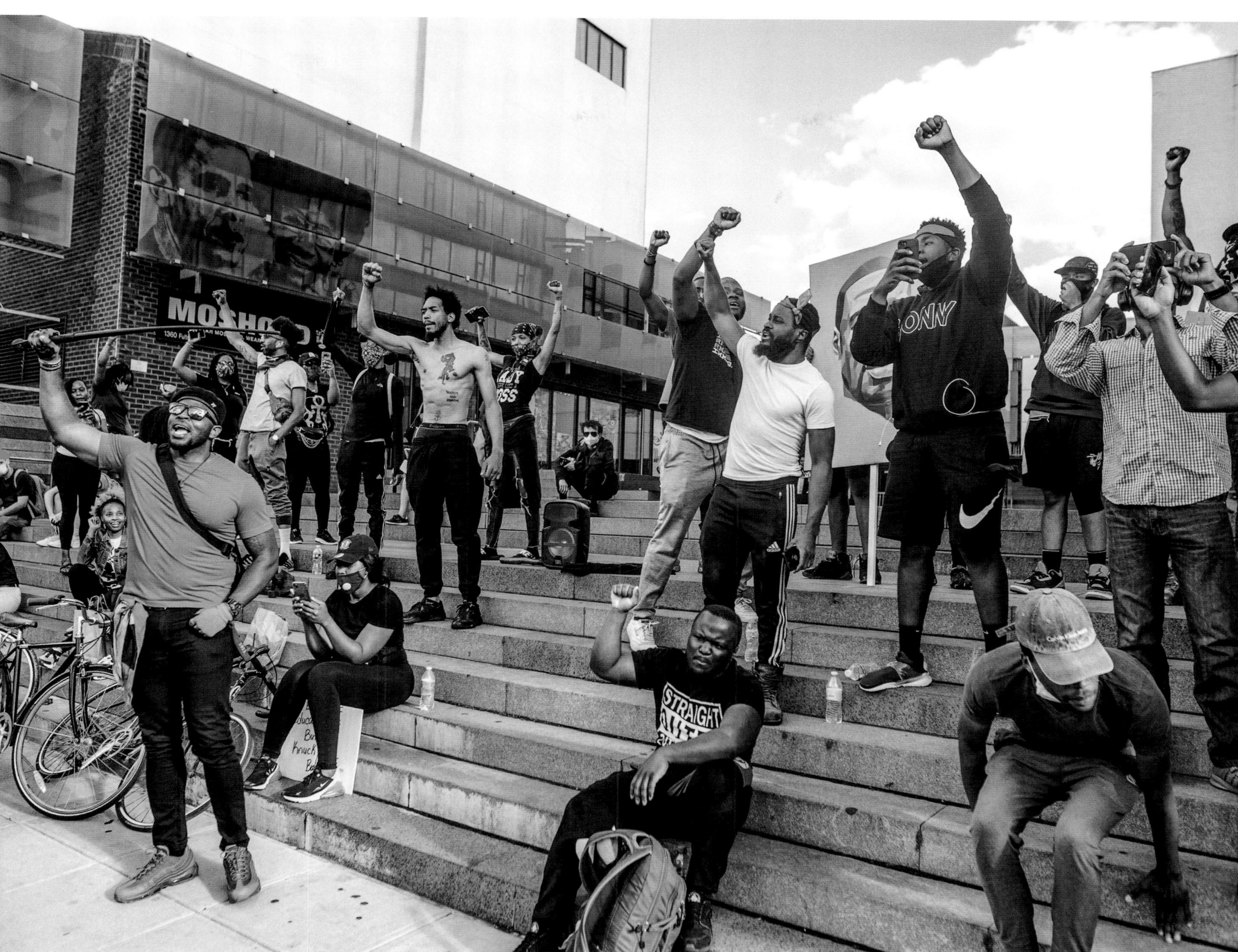

Strength and power. Community members raise their fists in protest to honor the lives of George Floyd and Breonna Taylor at Restoration Plaza, Brooklyn, New York, in 2020.

RUSSELL FREDERICK

Visual activist and self-taught photographer highlighting the narrative of the African diaspora from BedStuy to Sydney

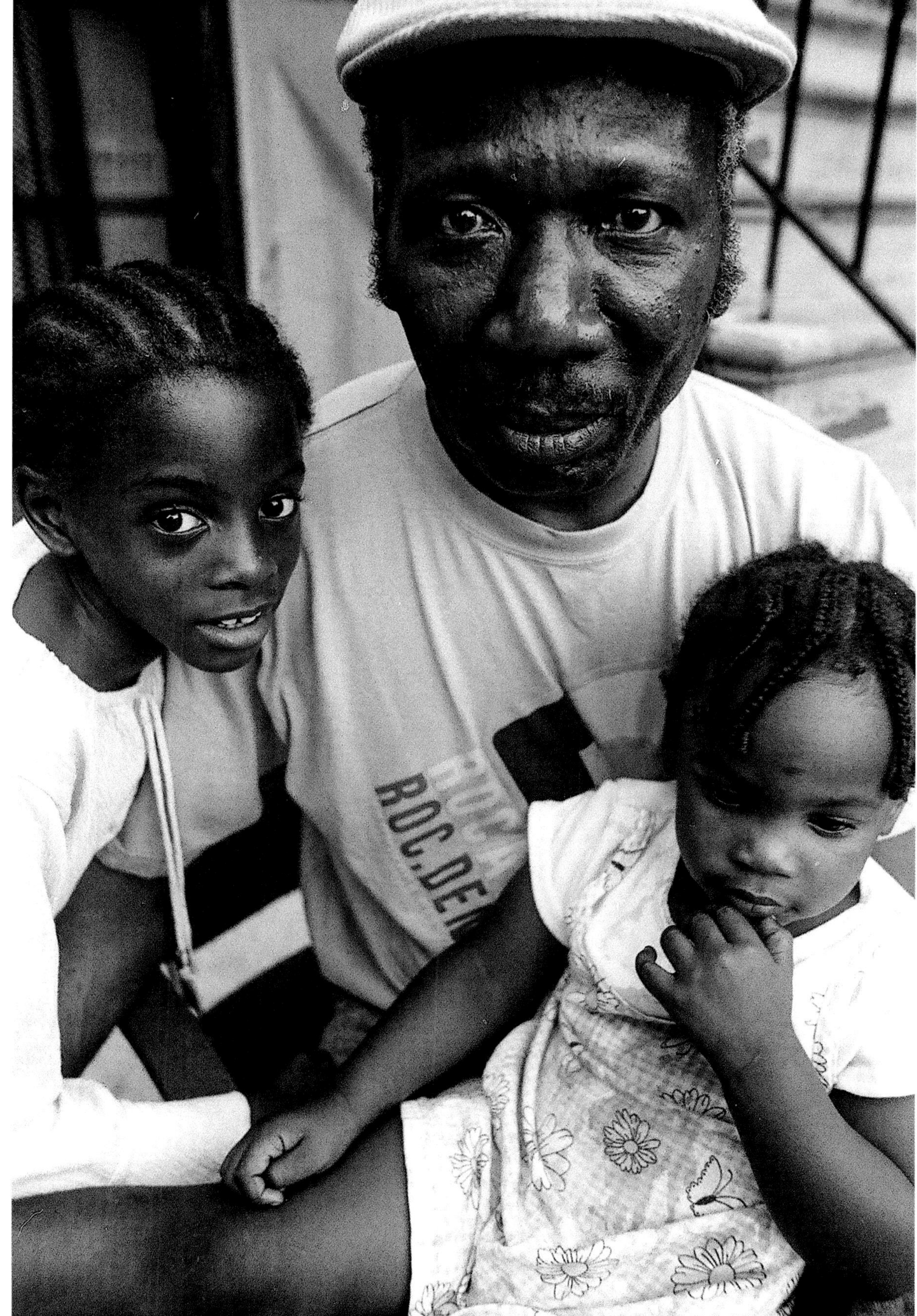

The Babysitter, BedStuy, Brooklyn, 2005

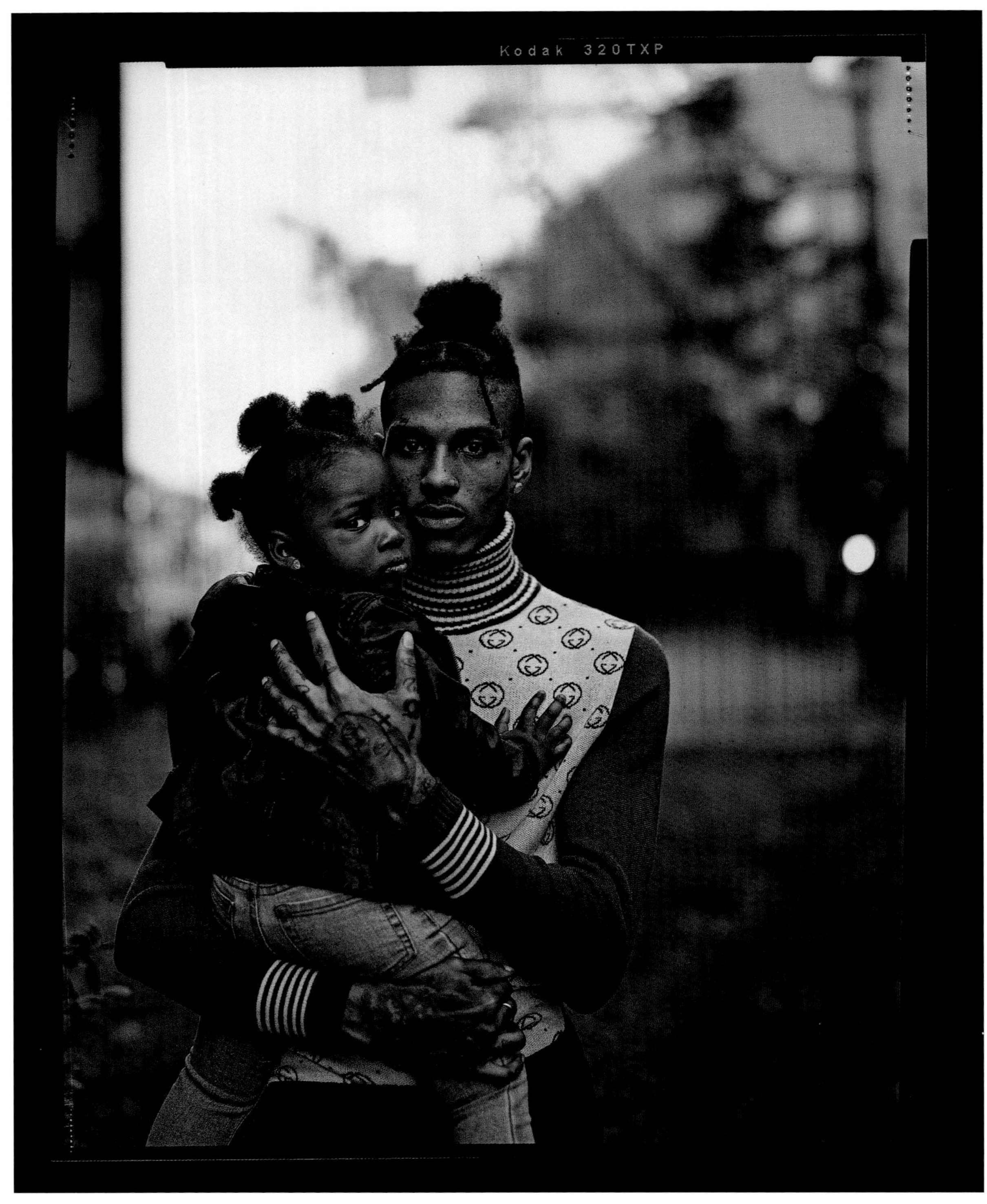

Protect & Provide, Harlem, New York, 2018

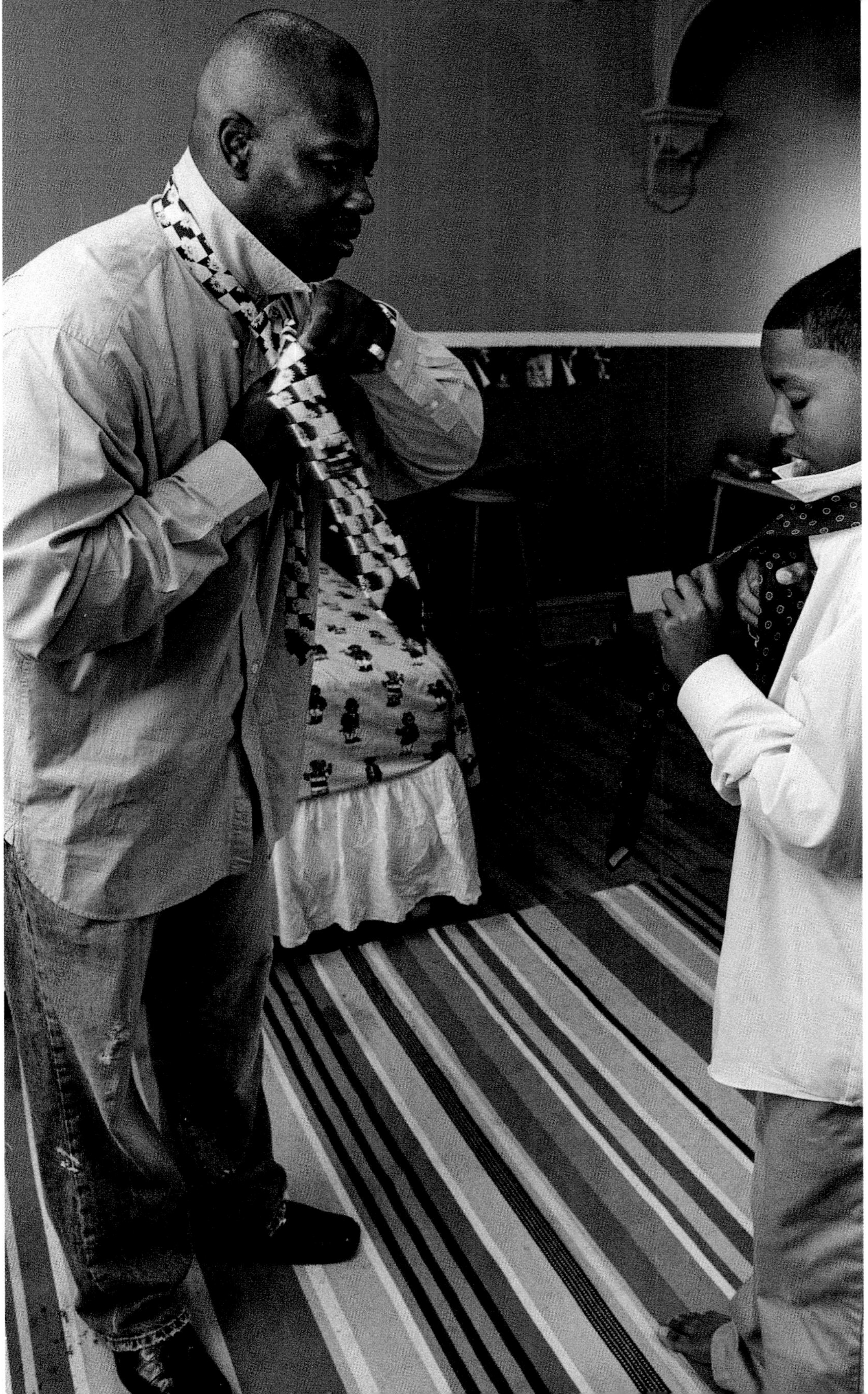

**The First Time,
BedStuy,
Brooklyn,
2005**

MICHAEL YOUNG

New York street photographer passionate about creating images of life that celebrate his love of light and shadow

left: **A moment with Daddy, Bronx, New York, 2016**

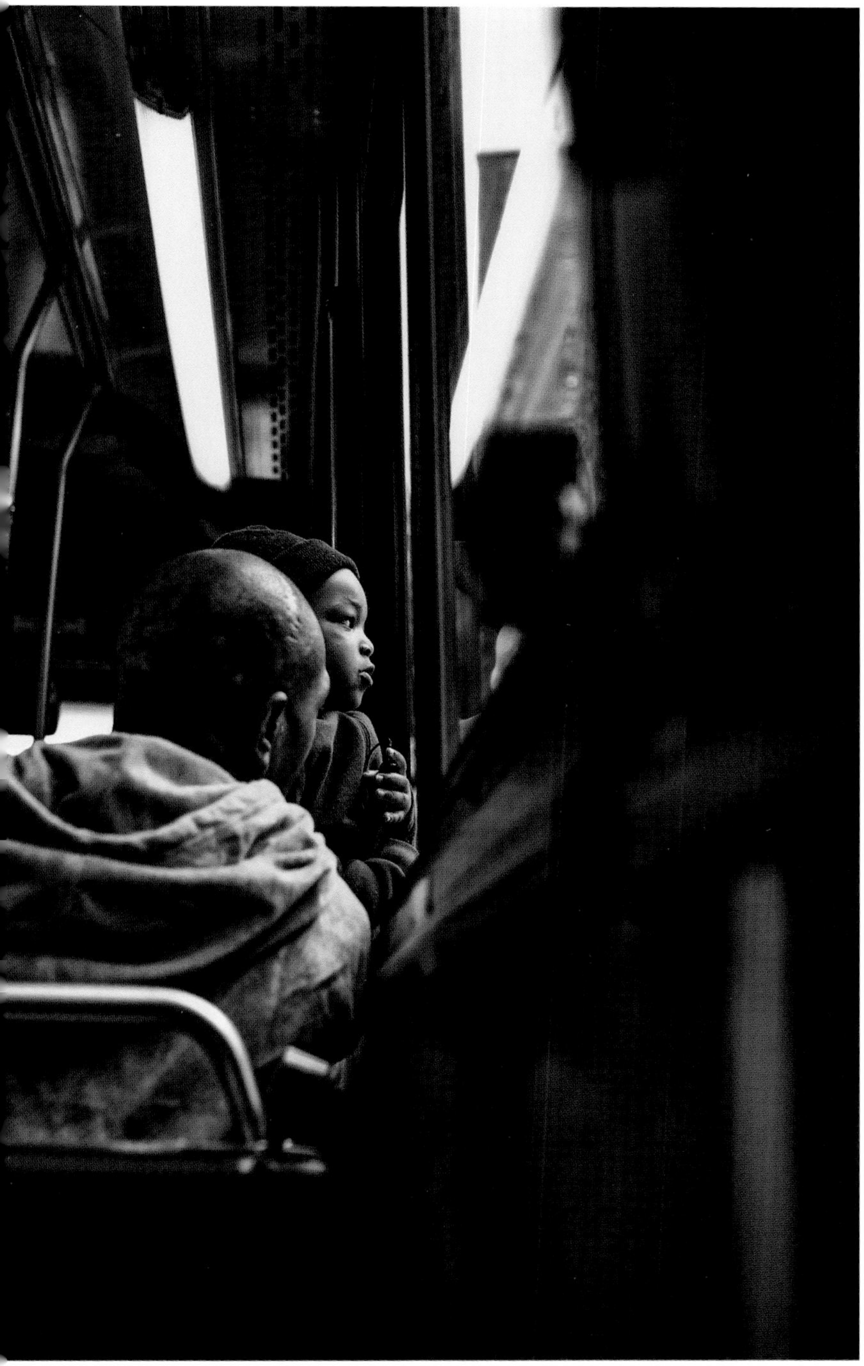

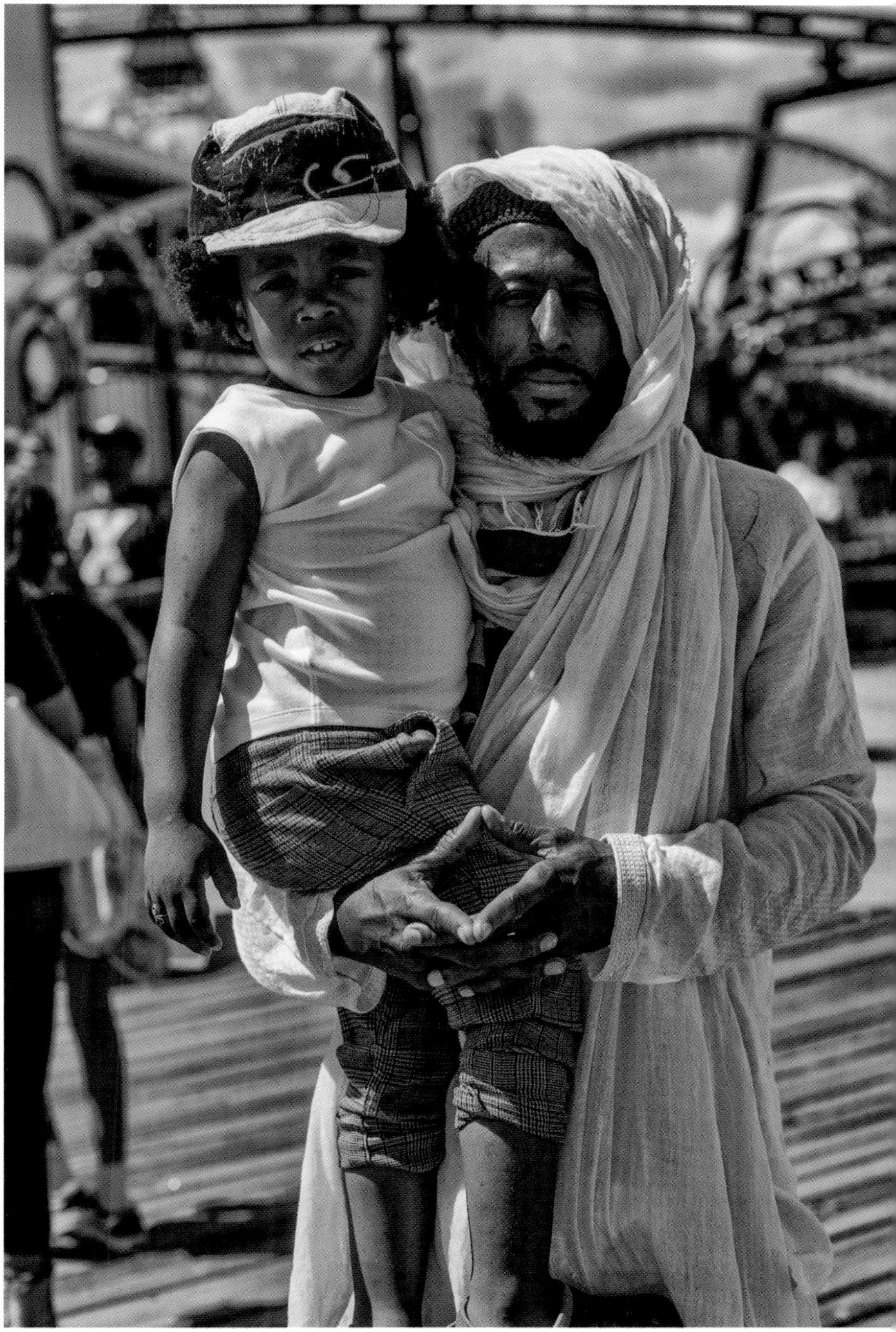

right: **Legacy Middle Passage, Coney Island, New York, 2024**

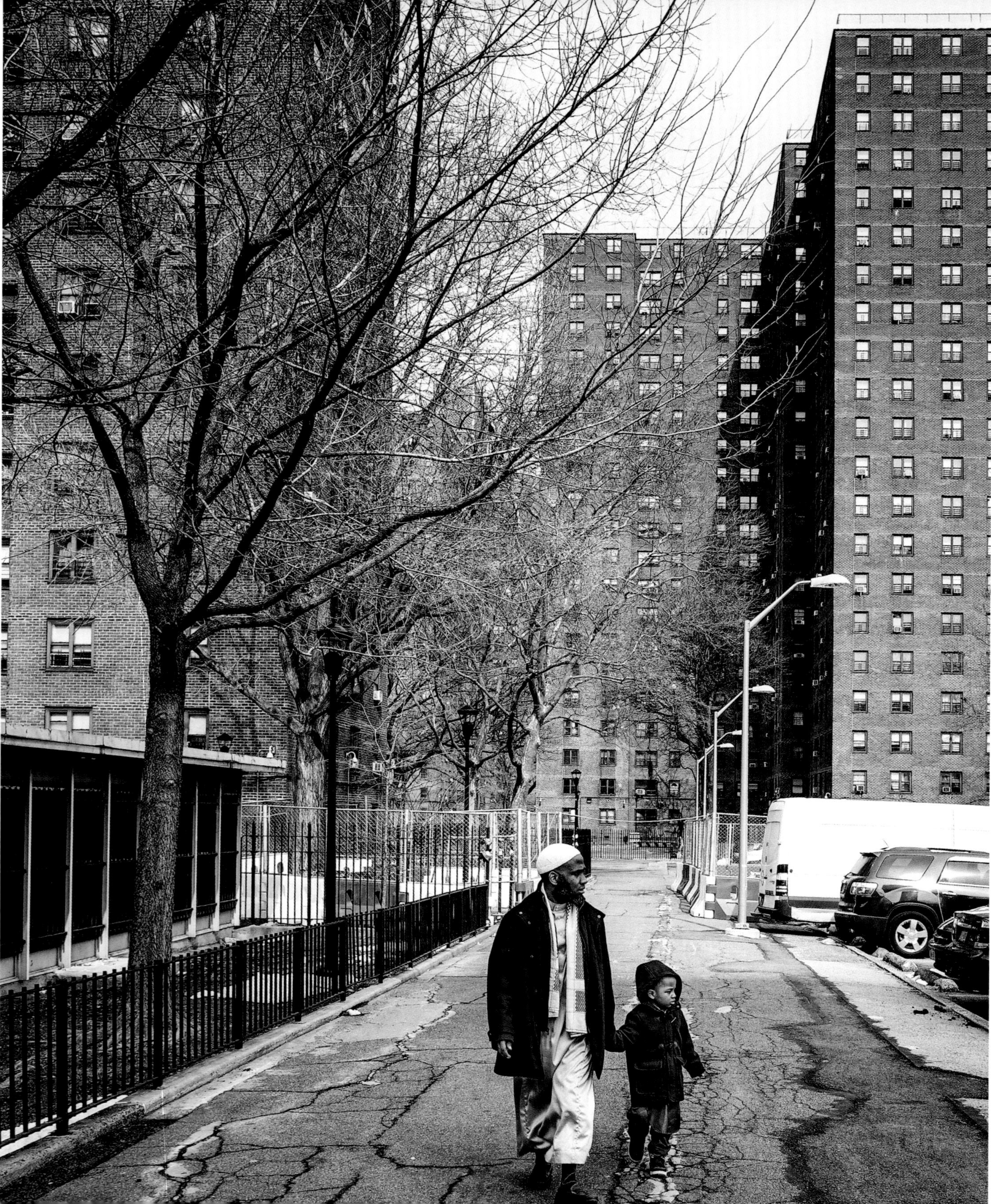

top: **Daddy duty, Bronx, New York, 2016**

bottom, right: **Daddy's girls, Bronx, New York, 2023**

bottom, left: **Safe in His Arms, Bronx, New York, 2018**

opposite: **Father and son, Claremont Village, Bronx, New York, 2019**

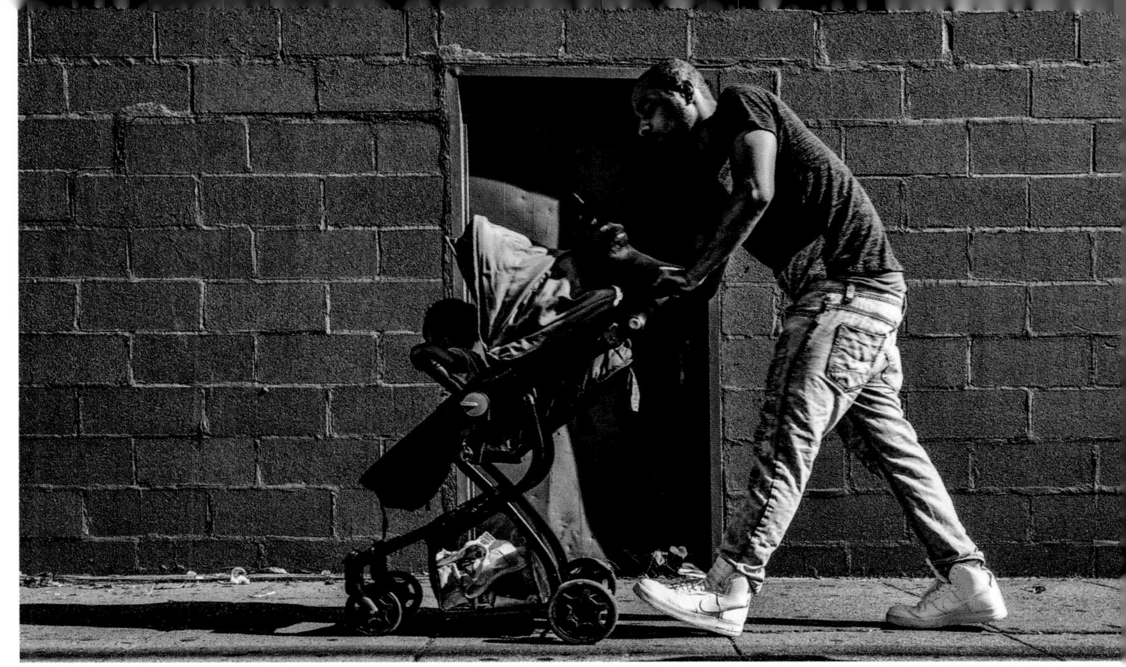

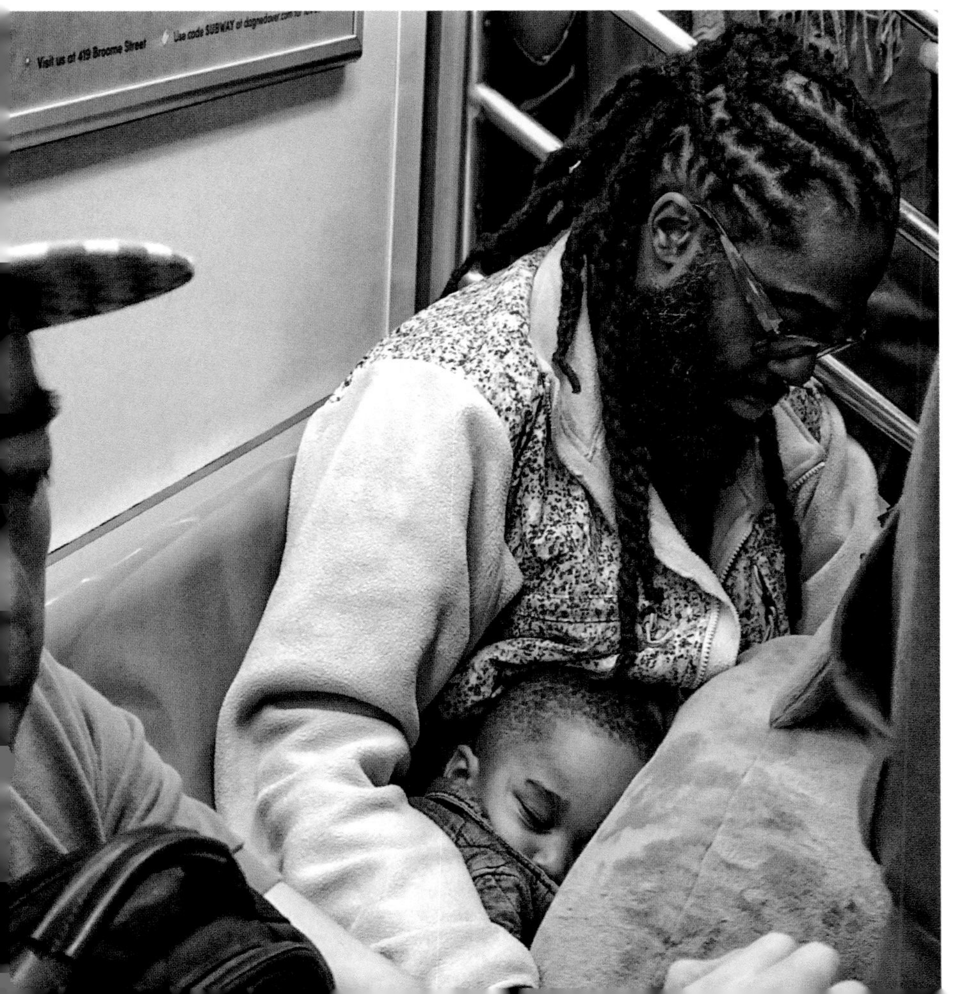

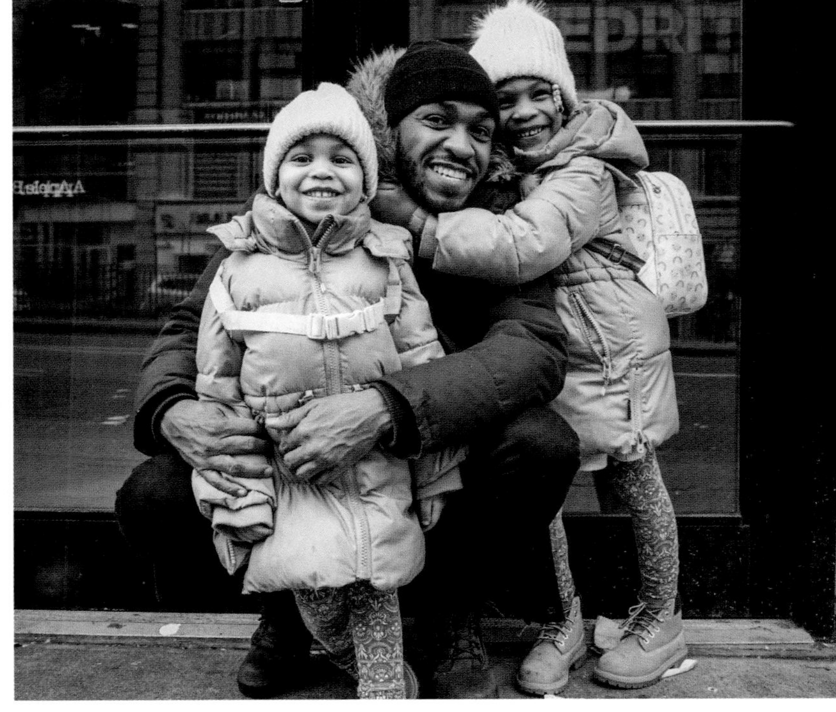

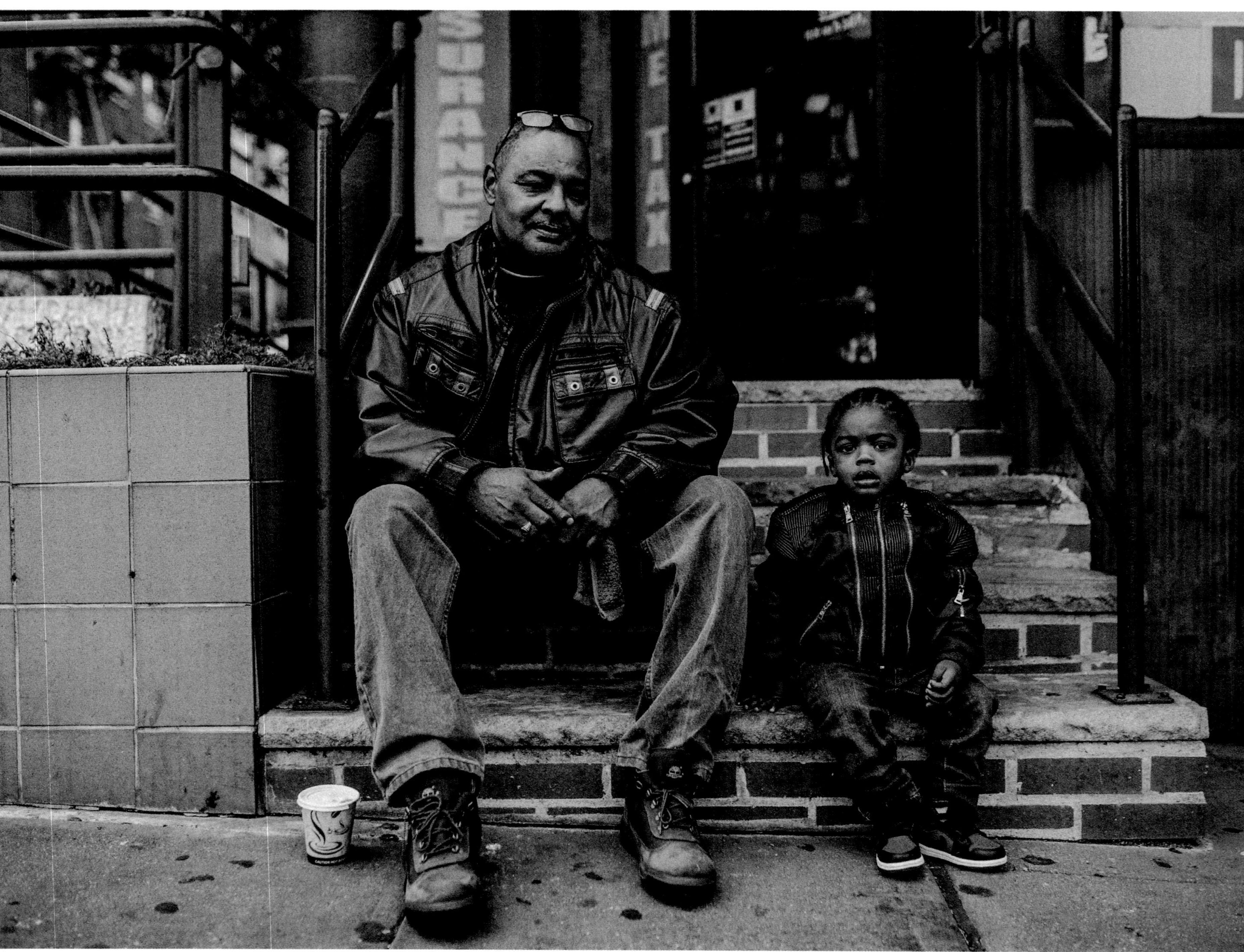

Generations, Bronx, New York, 2018

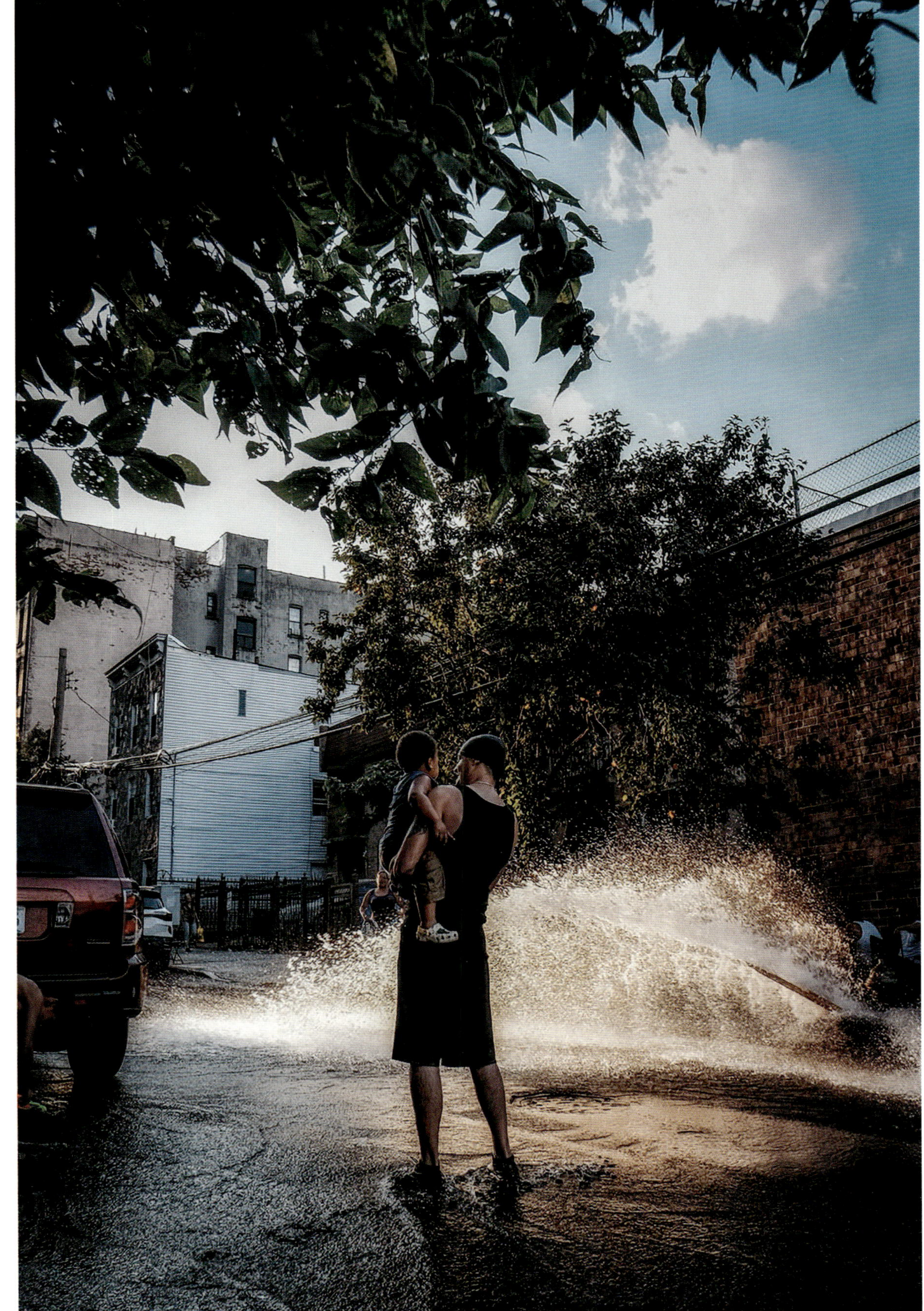

Papi, Bronx,
New York,
2023

KHARY MASON

Detroit native and multidisciplinary artist using photography to explore advocacy through imagery and protect the next generation of artists

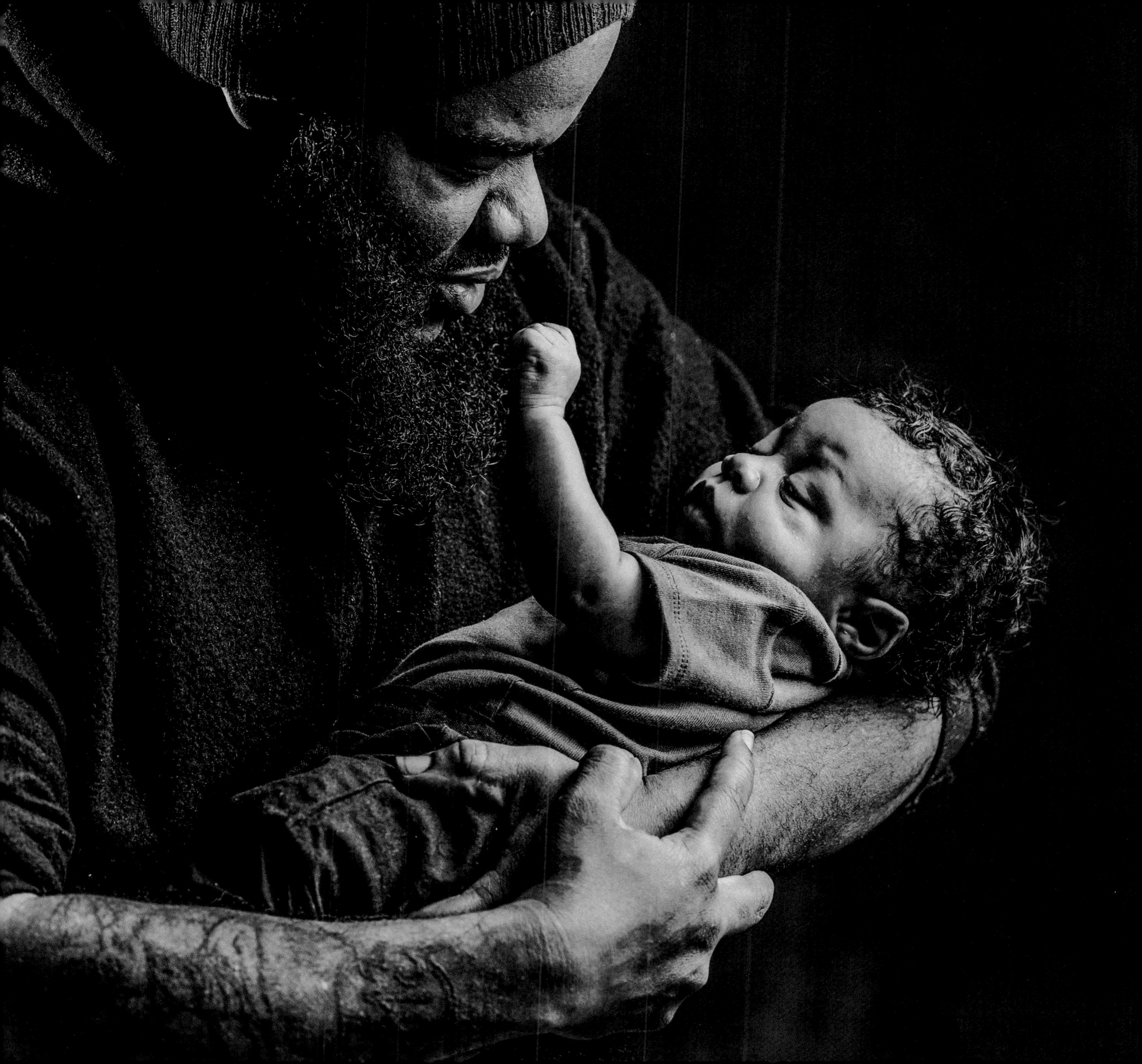

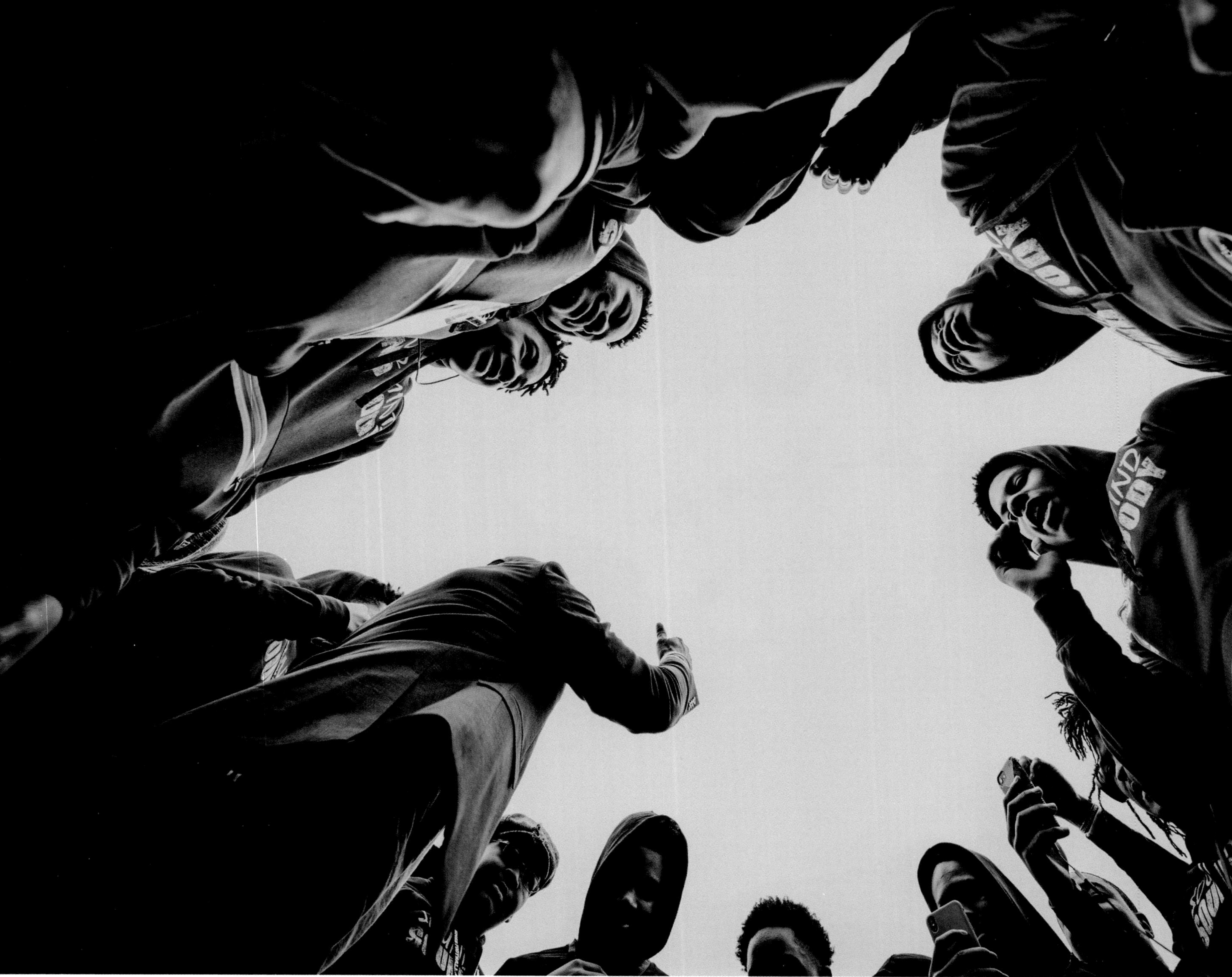

“All good leaders must learn to follow first.” Dr. William Dunn (*bottom left*) leads a call-and-response during a Sound Mind Sound Body college tour. Lincoln Memorial, Washington, DC, 2018.

IT'S YOUR TURN, DADDY

KHARY MASON

She's up on Sunday morning, just like every other morning. Except she gets to wake when she wants because it's not a school day. Able to grab breakfast on her own because it's not a school day.

She finishes and sits down to control the TV. Then I ask the usual question: "Did you brush your teeth yet?" She smiles and stomps away, mumbling beneath her breath.

Only to come back moments later and blow a minty breeze in my face to distract me while snatching the remote, saying, "We are watching something I want to watch today, Daddy." I smile and sit there gladly.

The sun pierces the blinds to kiss her curly crown as she sits immersed in the show of light, color, and sound that adorns the wall.

I smile again and tell her, "Mommy is going to braid your hair." She pauses for a moment. The words I've said begin to sink in, and her smile slowly begins to disappear. Her face falls into her hands.

Mommy grabs the spray bottle, the brush, the comb, and some rubber bands. That's when I tell her I've got a plan. I watch as Mommy's fingers dance between her curls like a spider weaving silk.

After several hours of face-twisting and wincing—bringing to light the pain of her coils being wound tight—and just when Mommy has a little more to go . . .

I tell her I'm going to set up the studio.

She responds in the most evil but beautiful voice a little one can muster: "I'm not taking any pictures today."

I grab the light stands. She hollers from the other room, "Daddy, I'm not taking any pictures today!" But I don't stop. I press on, grabbing the camera, the props, and the backdrop.

A little while later, my princess peeks around the corner, smiling, and I say, “Baby girl, your hair is beautiful. Please, please, step into my studio.” She tries to frown and walk away, but her smile refuses to leave. That’s when I say, “Please come and have a seat so that your loyal subjects can have a peek at what you look like today.”

She agrees after she learns that a fifteen-minute photo shoot will give her plenty of time to play.

This is how it always goes, and we pretend to powder her nose.

We get the light just right; that is when the magic begins. Still not sure if she wants her picture taken until the first click of the shutter. That’s when it happens. I know it’s coming, so my heart begins to flutter. Her false facade of apprehension vanishes in an instant. She leaps from the stool, smiling, saying, “Daddy, I wanna see my picture.”

This we do again and again. *Knit hood on, knit hood off, look at the light, look into the camera, glasses on, glasses off, Stetson on, hand on chin, legs crossed. Look at me.* “Smile,” I say. “Baby girl, I think that’s enough for today.”

She smiles and says, “Now, Daddy, you have a seat. It’s my turn to take your picture.” She then repeats back to me. *Look at the light, glasses on, glasses off, Stetson on, hand on chin, legs crossed. Look at me.*

And after another hour of me running over to the camera to see what she shot, she says, “I think we got it, Daddy. That’s a wrap.”

Every time we do this, the emotions run the same, but I don’t change or interrupt the process to explain. In a world filled with distractions, I often find myself competing for her time, but when the studio goes up, for a moment I am hers and she is mine.

“IN A WORLD FILLED WITH DISTRACTIONS, I OFTEN FIND MYSELF COMPETING FOR HER TIME, BUT WHEN THE STUDIO GOES UP, FOR A MOMENT I AM HERS AND SHE IS MINE.”

MAMA, I'M SORRY

KHARY MASON

"You are the man of the house now . . ."
He said to me . . .
I was eight or nine when he . . .
Placed that weight on my shoulders with little instruction as to what it meant.
I was twelve when he was taken from me, never to return.
Before he left, I'd see him on winter holidays, and more often in summertime.
He did the best that a grandfather could do as a surrogate father who lived across the bridge.
Even though he was less than an hour away,
His neighborhood seemed like it existed in a galaxy far, far away.
My father was a fighter, but he wasn't around,
The things I'd seen him do as the "man of the house"—
The unending combos of shouting his traumas, followed by a perceived permission to be violent,
Initiated in the name of ego and problem-solving
That were aimed at us,
The because I said so of it all
Cloaked beneath a guise of protection—
Those were the examples of what it meant to be a man that were activated by my grandfather's words to me that day.
My grandfather as a father—he was a fighter, too.
Now, as a father, I'm a fighter.
Although I've never hit my wife—that I learned not to do—
I know that I haven't always been the best son.
I miss the way we used to be.

I know I'm not the son I used to be . . .

Not the brother I used to be . . .

But truthfully . . .

I have been upset ever since we left Gilchrist for the first time . . .

Of all the things we left behind,

I'd be okay if it was a book or a chair we kept on moving, but my childhood . . .

was forced to stay right there.

I return to the block from time to time, hoping a chest filled with my innocence

I'll find.

I know that, for you, life hasn't been fair, and the reason I was mad at you and

not Grampa or him is simply because

You were there . . .

LISTEN TO THE LESSONS OF THE FALLING FEATHERS

KHARY MASON

In 1995, I turned eighteen, my wife graduated from Mumford High School, and Mobb Deep released their second album titled *The Infamous*. On the song "Survival of the Fittest," they say:

"There's a war going on outside no man is safe from."

In our culture, it is cool and common to be entertained by the pain of our brothers and sisters, but it's never okay to talk about that pain in an open and productive manner,

Not during the work or school day, not on Saturday, not in my house, not in god's house, not during the tailgate or even on the couch.

"Shhhhhhhhhh, bro, I don't have time to hear what you talkin' 'bout or what's going on. I'm trying to hear my favorite rapper's new noose song."

Man walked up to me the other day trying to figure out why the child in his arms wouldn't stop bleeding.

My chest got tight, it was hard for me to breathe, and then

The man began to dance in the street to a dope beat.

Before I could proceed, the boy started seizin',

Then the man ran off before I could tell him

The reason . . .

Hood anthems glorifying the mass murder of Black people by Black people are placed on tracks and pressed in wax long before they put the needle on the record.

We get infected by the DJ who commands us to bounce and sway

To a soundtrack played again and again,

Before the porch-jumper gives it another spin,

Amped to go on a search-and-destroy mission,

In search of a boy lookin' just like him so he can make him listen

To the hollow sounds that make Black boys go missin',
A boy who has accepted that, because of the things he has seen and the things he has done, he might not live much longer;
He just didn't think his last day would be today.
He is unaware that he is about to die on beat, at the hands of a brother he's never known, while they both shake and shimmy to the same damn song,
My attempts at addressing the matter head-on are met by . . .
The sobering sounds of teeth getting sucked, showing their disgust,
Turning to sighs from the side,
Followed by a side eye
Before disappointed words begin to fly,
"Read the room,"
They say,
"You're spoiling the mood,"
They say,
"This is not the place to have that conversation,"
They say,
Like a sports fan who has more in common with a protest about police brutality saying, "I just want to watch this game. Fuck reality."
I search for the meaning in what they mean, wondering if they seein' the shit I've seen,
I feel like these two conversations are the same,
Man, to keep it one hundred, fuck "yo" game . . .
We out here dying every day; you wouldn't think it was still this way, 'cause we keep dancing, performing, proudly prancing and drinking to the rhythms of our own extinction.

Instead of figuring out how to take the whip they beat us with, we out here partying with masa on the same slave ship,
Streaming selfies, sayin',
"Look, Ma,
We made it . . ."
Today ofay don't need to use his hands to kill you quicker; he just lay the weapons on the table and watch you kill yo'self,
Nigga . . .
And while he smiling and he clapping, I see you clappin', too,
I'm lookin' out at the crowd, wondering what y'all rockin' to, and you steady staring back, askin' who the fuck I'm talkin' to.
I plant my feet to come in peace before I say to you,
"Man . . .
This whole time y'all been dancing,
I just been trying to talk to you . . ."

TREVON BLONDET

Self-taught portrait photographer constantly in search of quiet moments that reveal his subjects as their truest selves

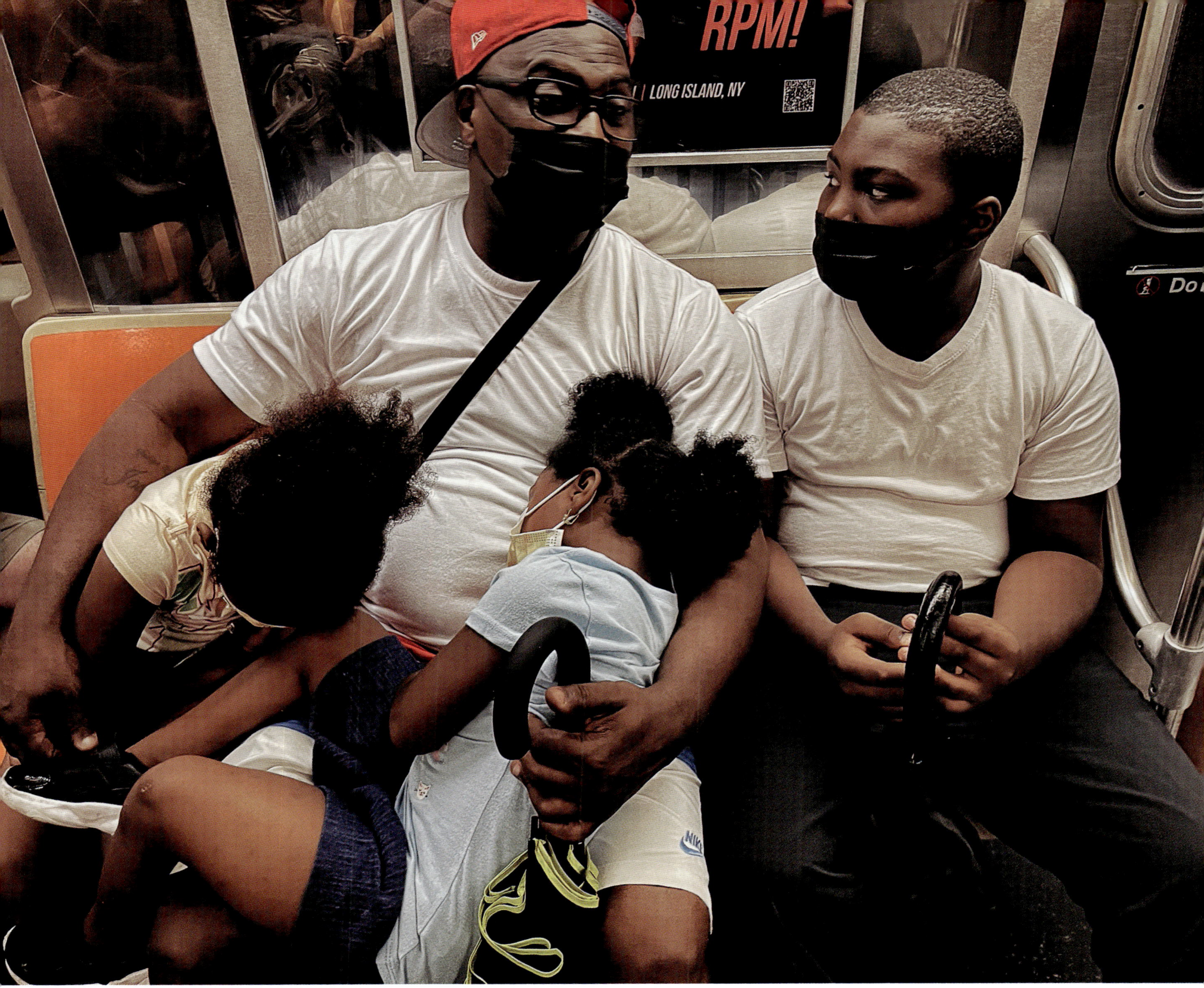

A father of three cradles his daughters on a crowded D Train to the Bronx.
He shares some wisdom with his son during the 2020 pandemic.

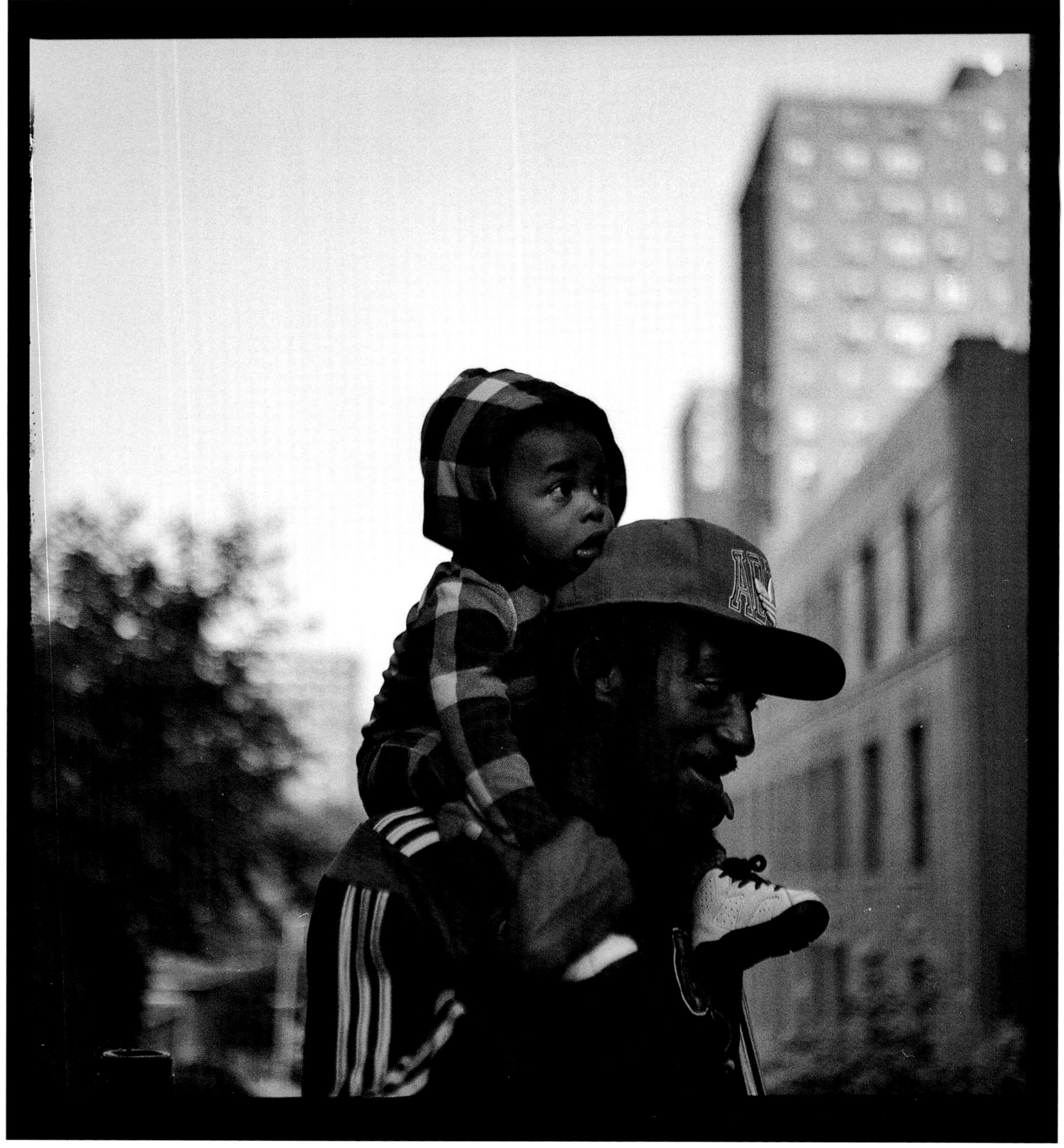

“Crossing paths on Webster Avenue in the Bronx, I met a brother whose pride radiated as he cared for his two little girls with his sun on his shoulder. His name escapes me, but his presence was unforgettable. Captured on a Hasselblad 500 with expired film, this moment tells a story of love and legacy.”

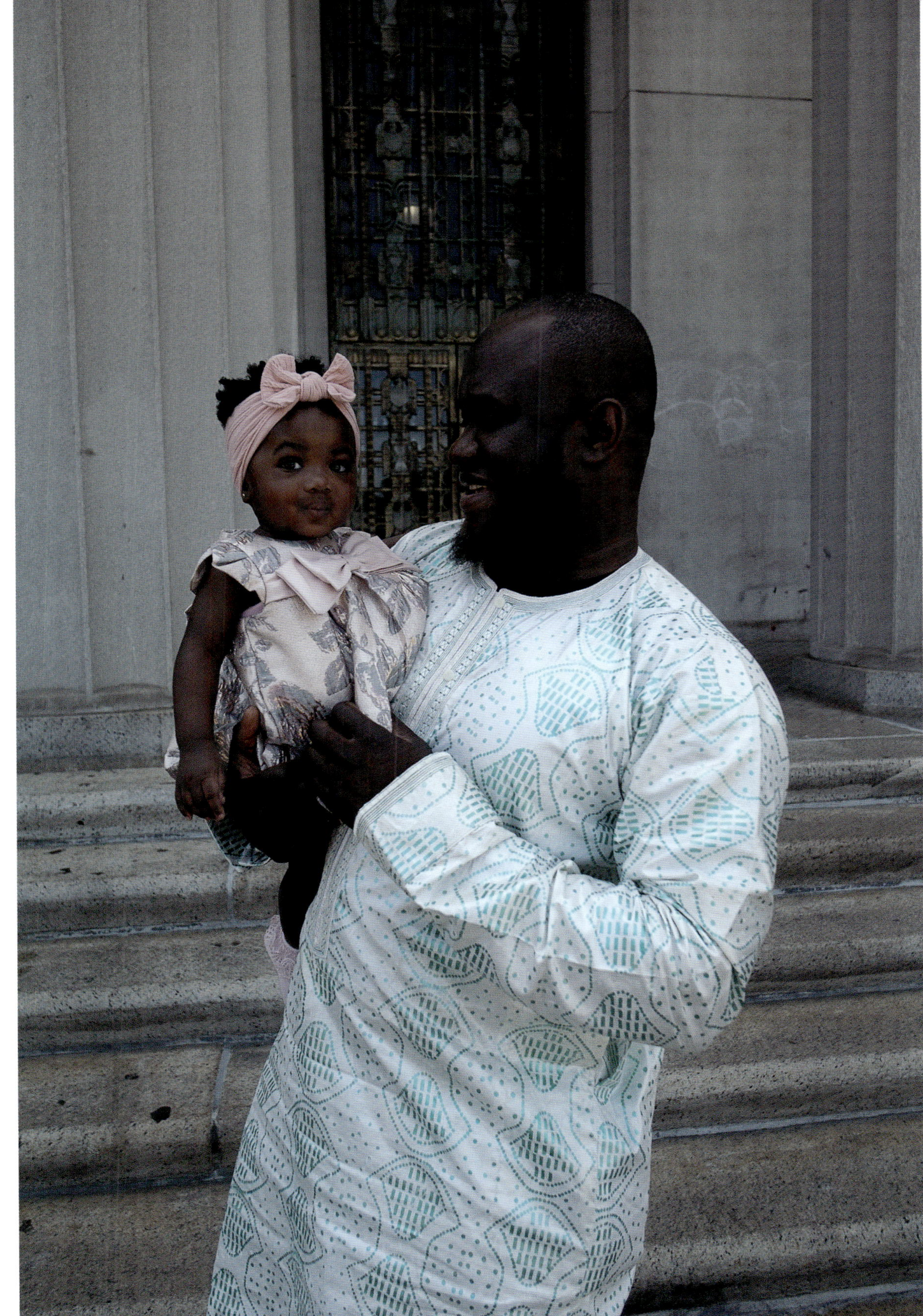

Rooted in tradition, nurtured by love— an African father and his daughter, a bond as strong as the boabab tree

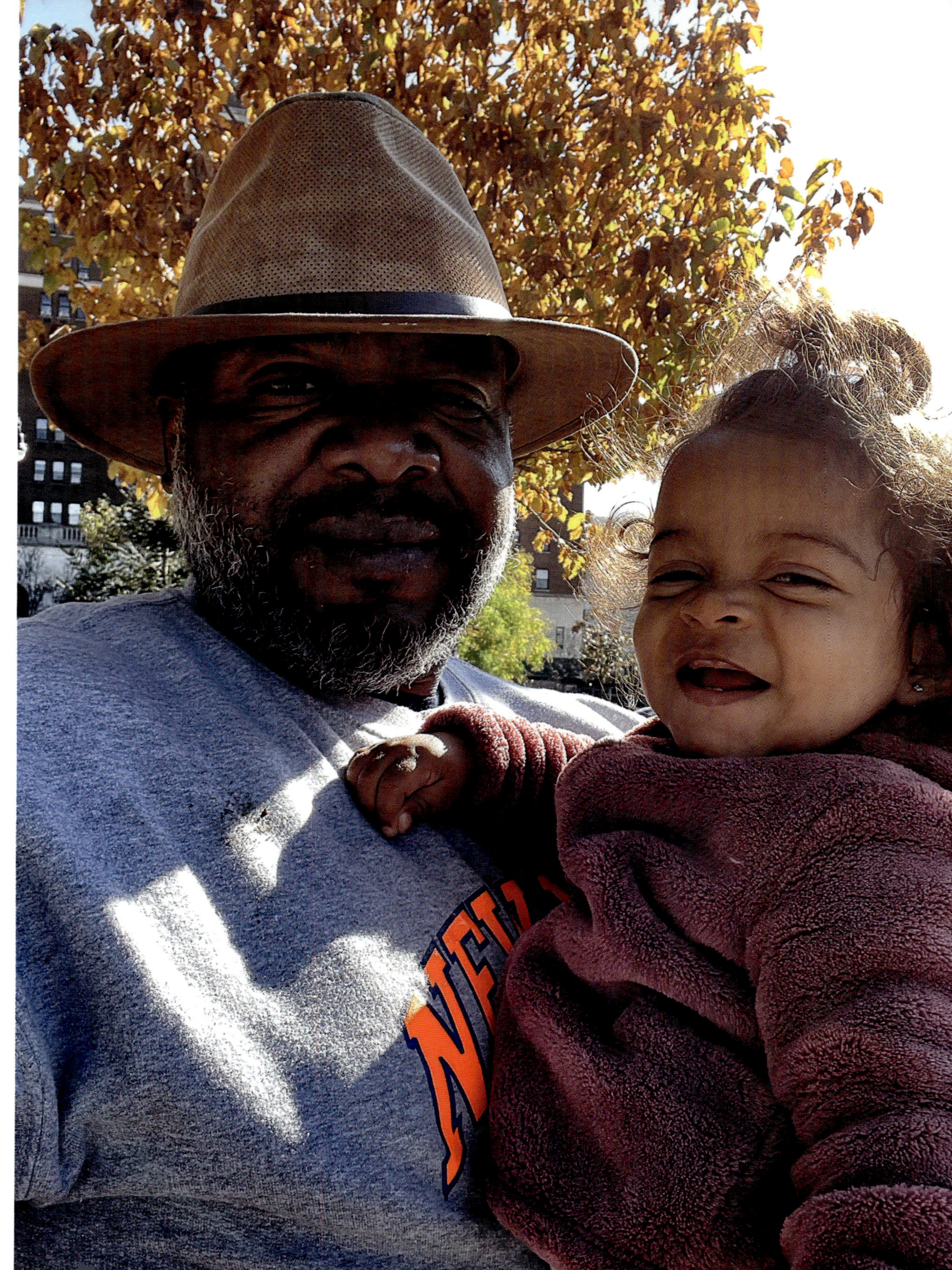

Guided by love, strengthened by laughter—dad and daughter creating memories on the Grand Concourse in the Bronx.

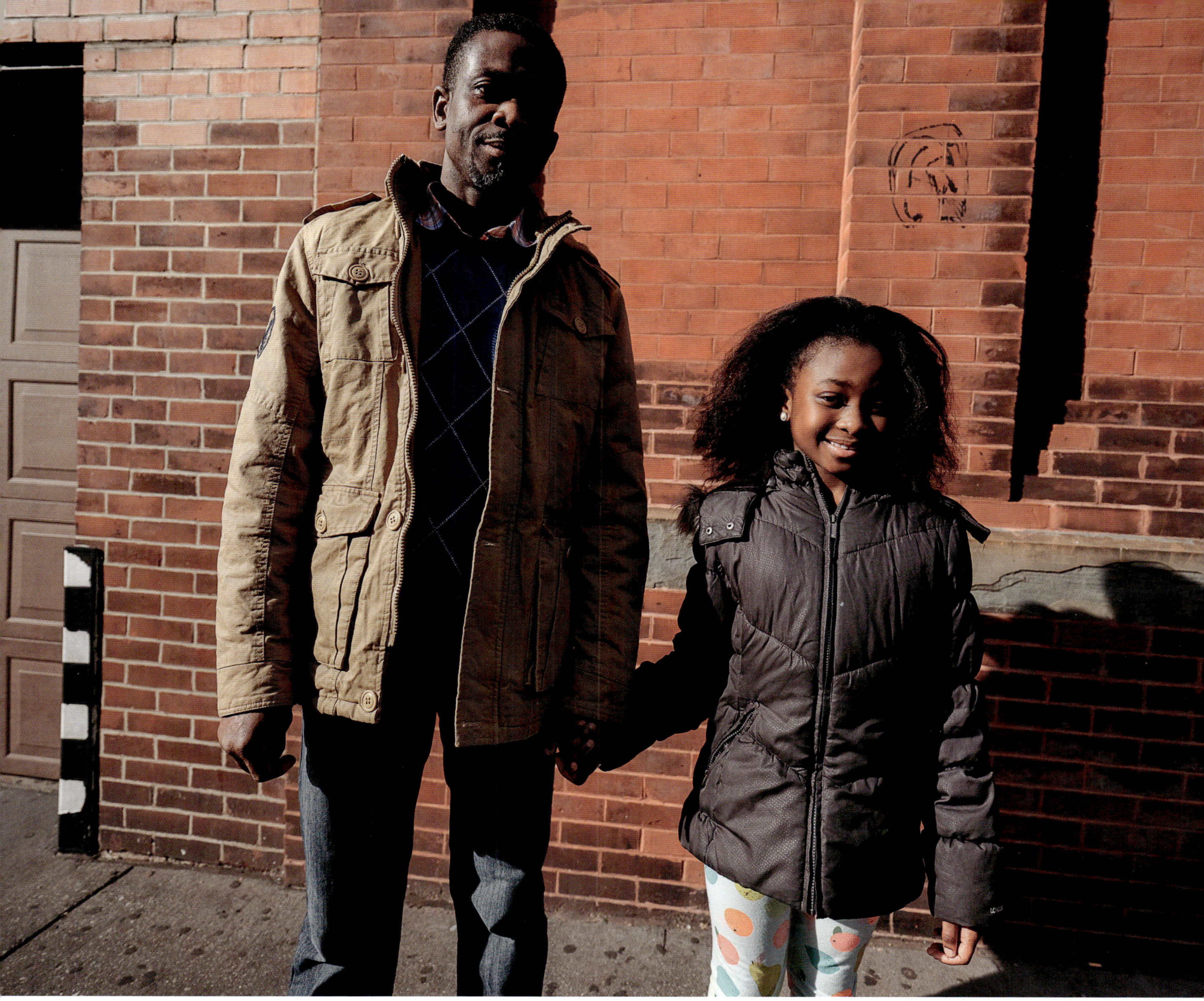

She's his greatest joy, and he's her unshakable hero. Together they share a bond that grows stronger with every laugh, every lesson, and every moment.

RAYMOND HOLMAN

Documentary photographer whose work places a focus on Black and brown communities, telling the stories of their struggles, their successes, and their joys

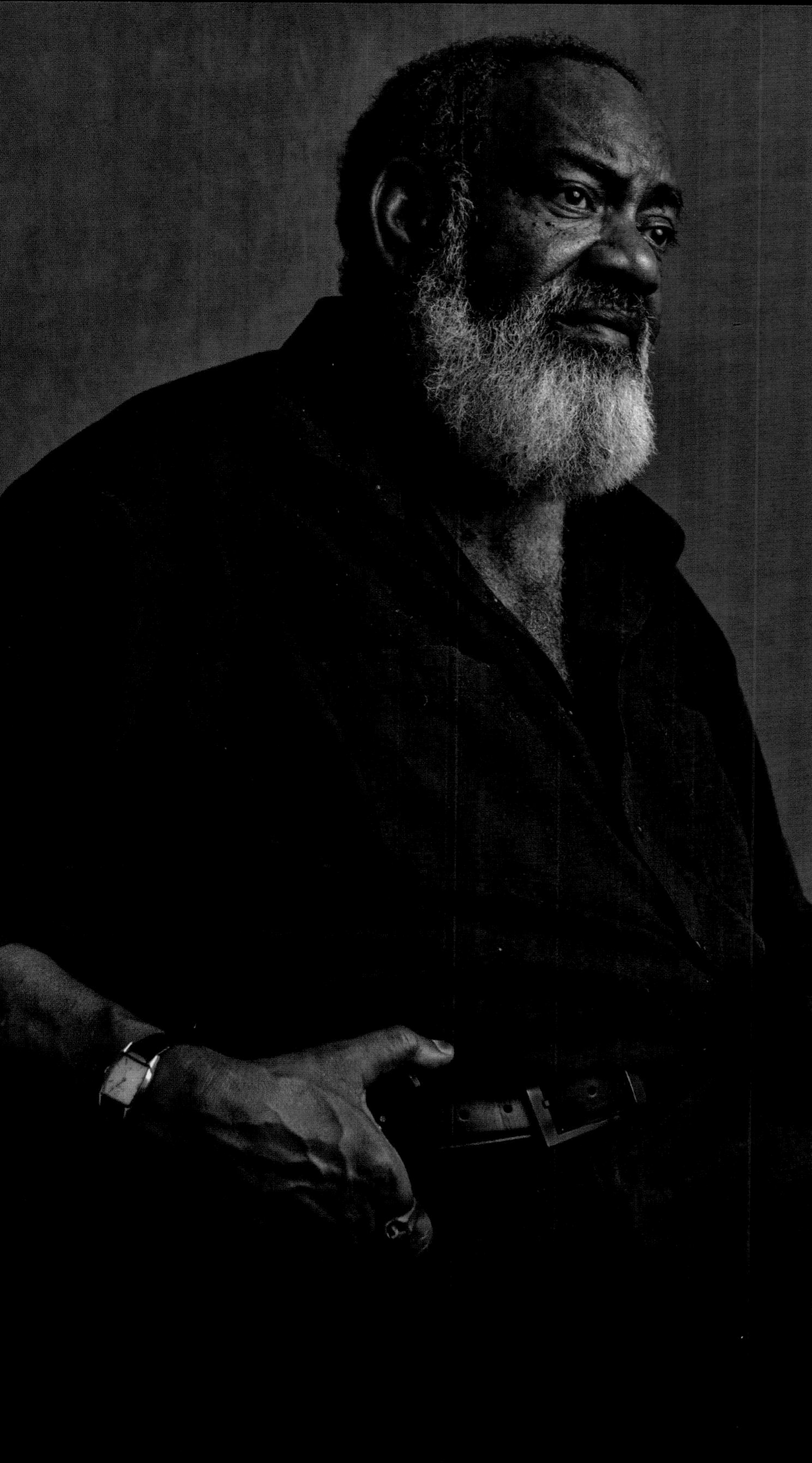

“Being a father is a gift that keeps on giving. I have a beautiful daughter and [an] amazing grandson. I love family time. We enjoy talking to each other every day. I take pride in being a family person. I enjoy driving my daughter and grandson around while listening to music, talking, and laughing. Though being a parent and grandparent, life is full of surprises—the good, bad, and ugly—I stand firm on always keeping God primary. I was raised that way and raised them just the same. I love them dearly, and our bond is unmatched. I thank God for blessing me with a daughter and [a] grandson that keep me on my A game.” —Lumpkin

RAYMOND HOLMAN

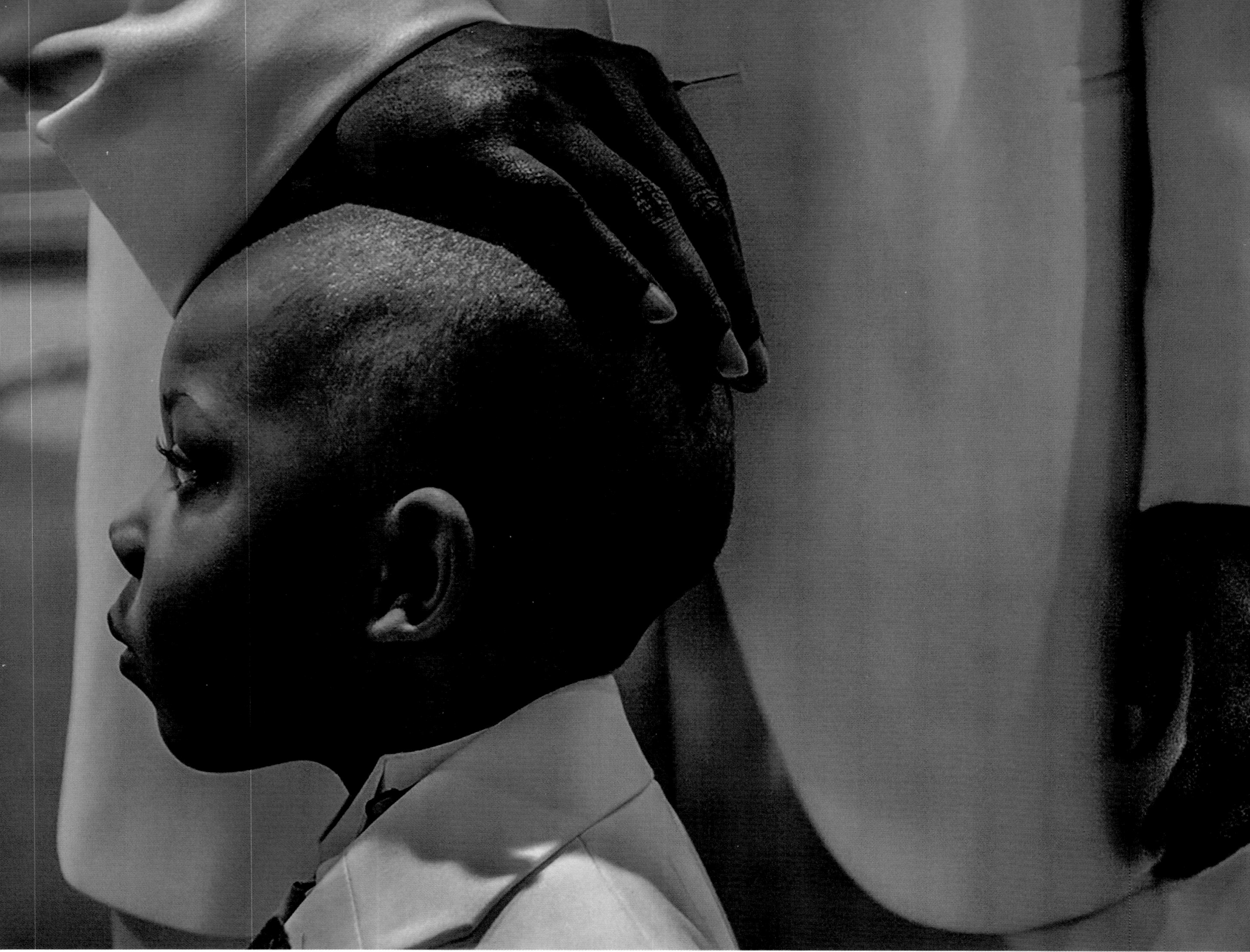

“Being a father has been the most important thing I have ever done in my life. There is no class or instructional manual that could prepare me for [the] experience, but I knew that love, dedication, and commitment were necessary in playing a significant role in my children’s lives. I was very immature entering fatherhood, but through them I was able to really become a ‘grown-up.’ For that I will be forever thankful to them. Raising a child from infant to adulthood has to be one of the most incredible experiences in life. Watching [them] grow and learn and develop a personality has given me a completely different outlook on life. I love my son and daughters more than anything, and nothing I’ve done compares to being their dad.” —Dante

RAYMOND HOLMAN

FATHERHOOD IS AN HONOR
MARTIN COPELAND

You know those little girls who dream of their weddings? They use their dolls to imagine their dream ceremonies, or, when they become teenagers, they discover their favorite designers and choose a dress. Or do you know those boys who have dreams of throwing that game-winning touchdown in the Super Bowl or of hitting a buzzer-beating three-pointer in game seven of the NBA finals? You know those boys. They can't put anything in the trash without yelling, "Kobe!"

Well, as a kid, I had different dreams. I know it sounds crazy—probably because it's rare—but I dreamed of being a dad. I actually liked playing house! I loved movies and TV shows with dads in them because I wanted to be those guys. I was probably the only ten-year-old who didn't want to "Be Like Mike." I wanted to be like Uncle Phil, Carl, and Pops from *The Wayans Bros.*, which explains *so* much about me. I loved how those guys loved their kids. I loved how safe they made their children feel and how their children respected and admired them. I loved the bonds they had and how they could make their kids laugh uncontrollably at times. I had that. My dad was and is one of "those guys." I was surrounded by amazing Black dads in real life and on TV. So that's what I wanted to be. I dreamed about it. So, for me, fatherhood is the fulfillment of a lifelong dream. Fatherhood is the blessing of an answered prayer. Fatherhood is the opportunity to stand with and on the shoulders of giants. Fatherhood, to me, is an honor.

REESE BLAND

Visual documentarian who views life as a composition of narratives, moments, and perspectives that he hopes to capture and share with the world

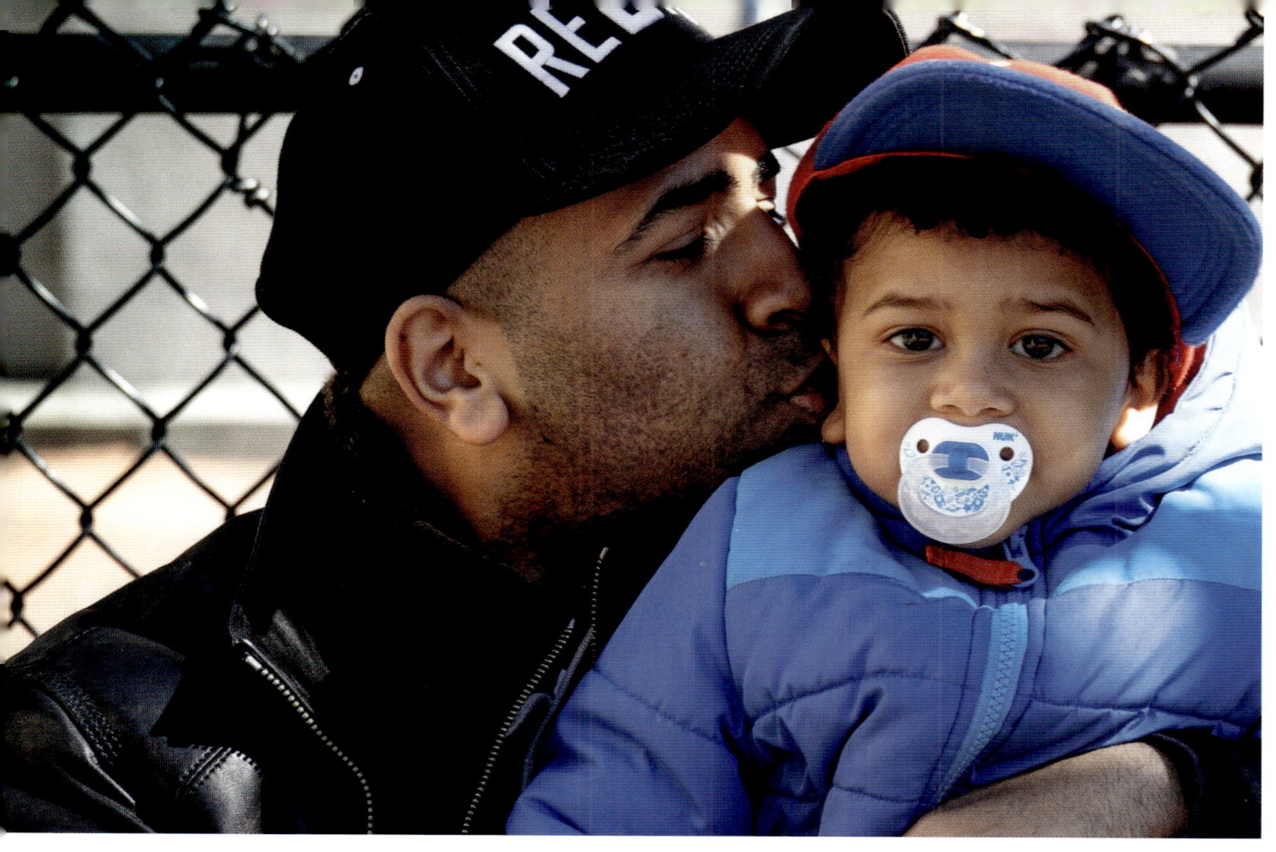

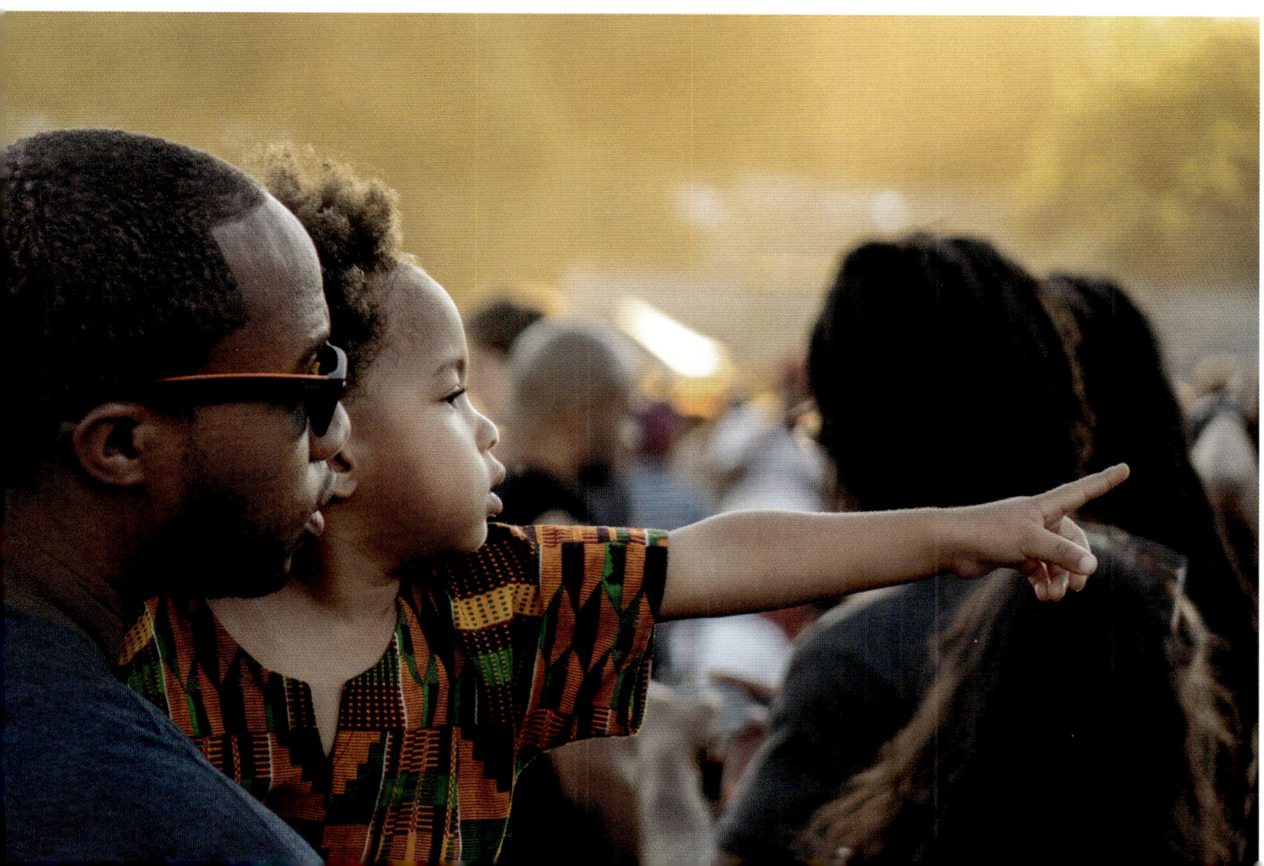

**Through your eyes,
we see the future.**

REESE BLAND

DARIUS LYLES

Photographic and cinematic artist with a passion for promoting Black excellence through art and contributions within the community

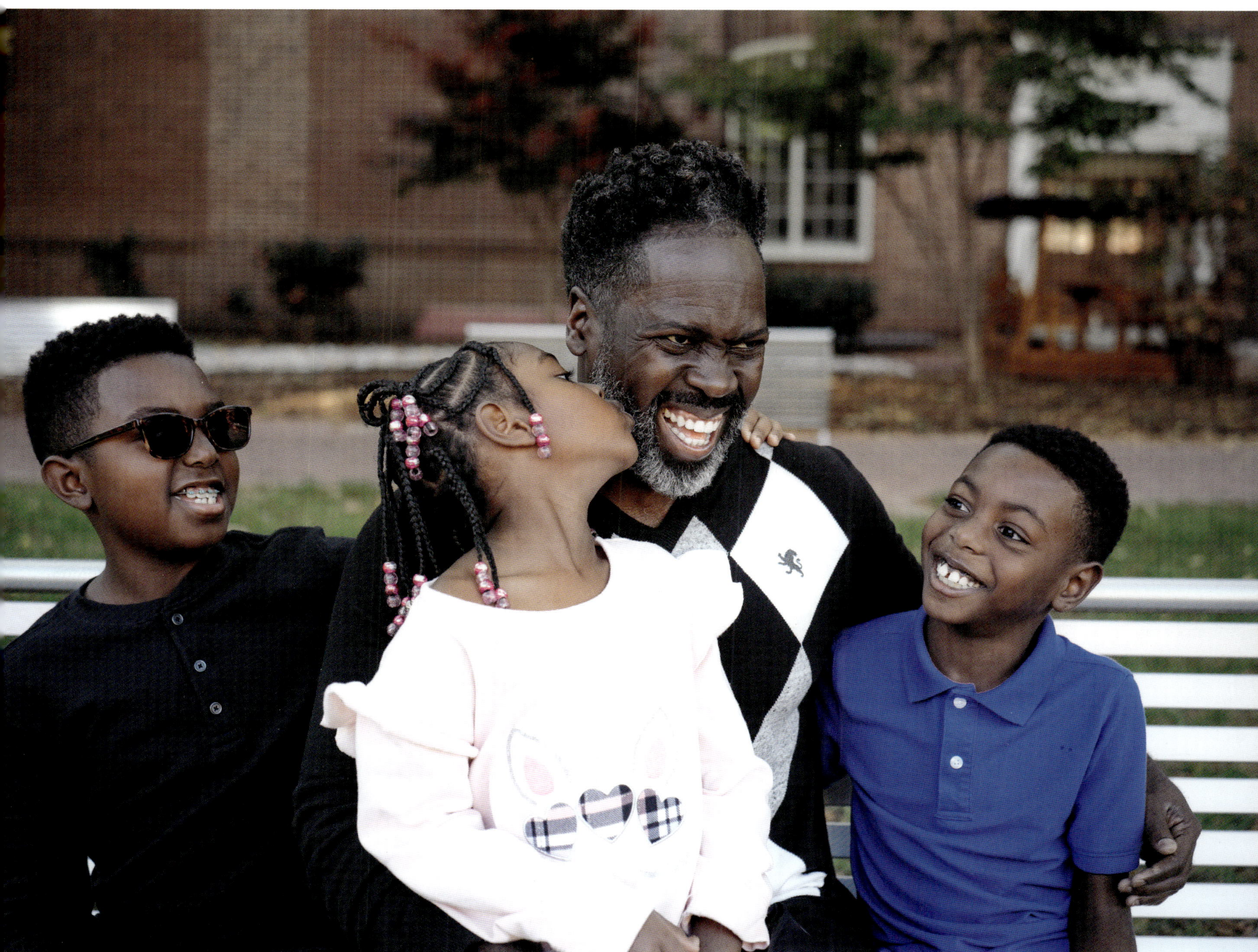

Afternoons with Dad

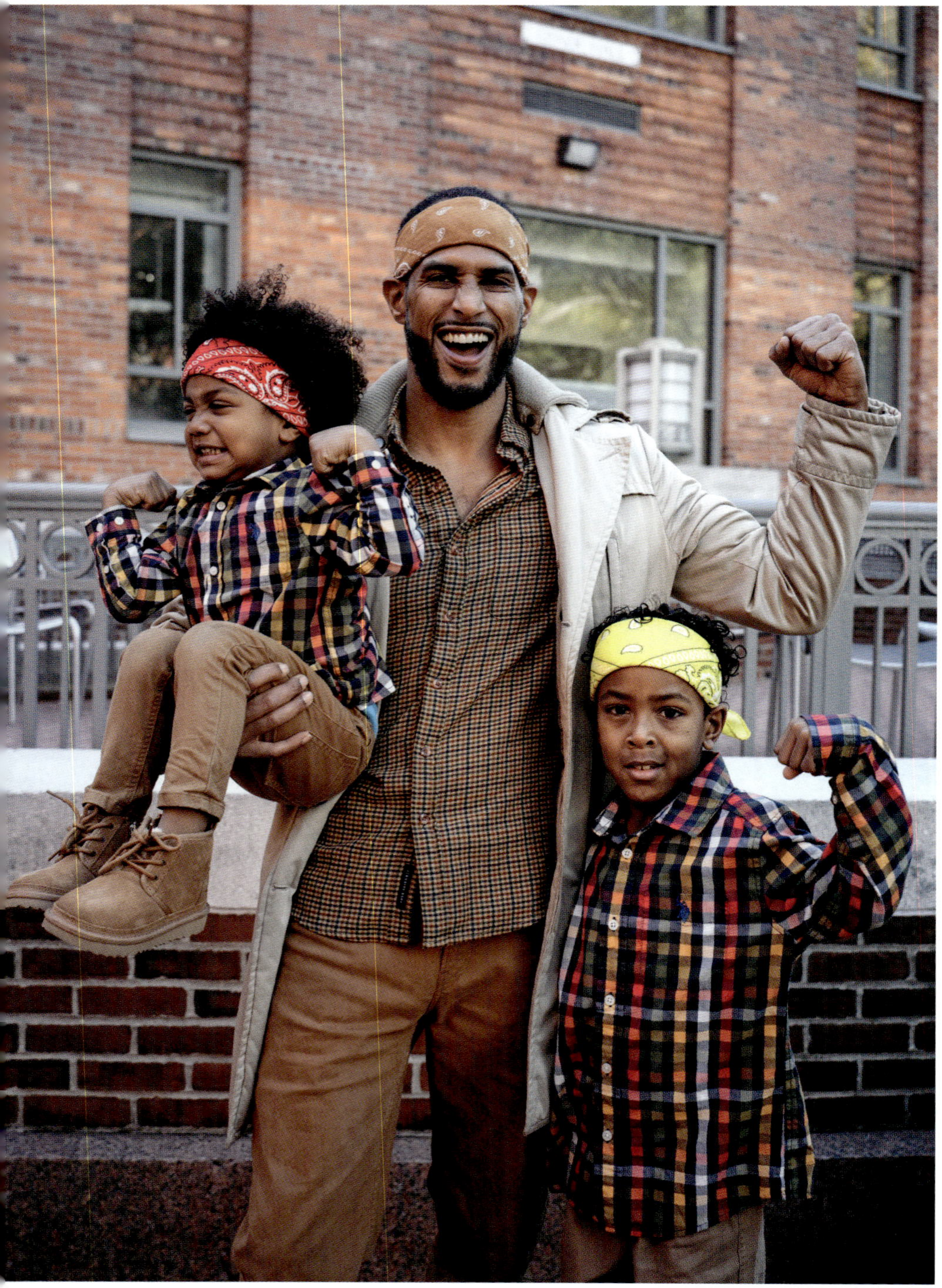

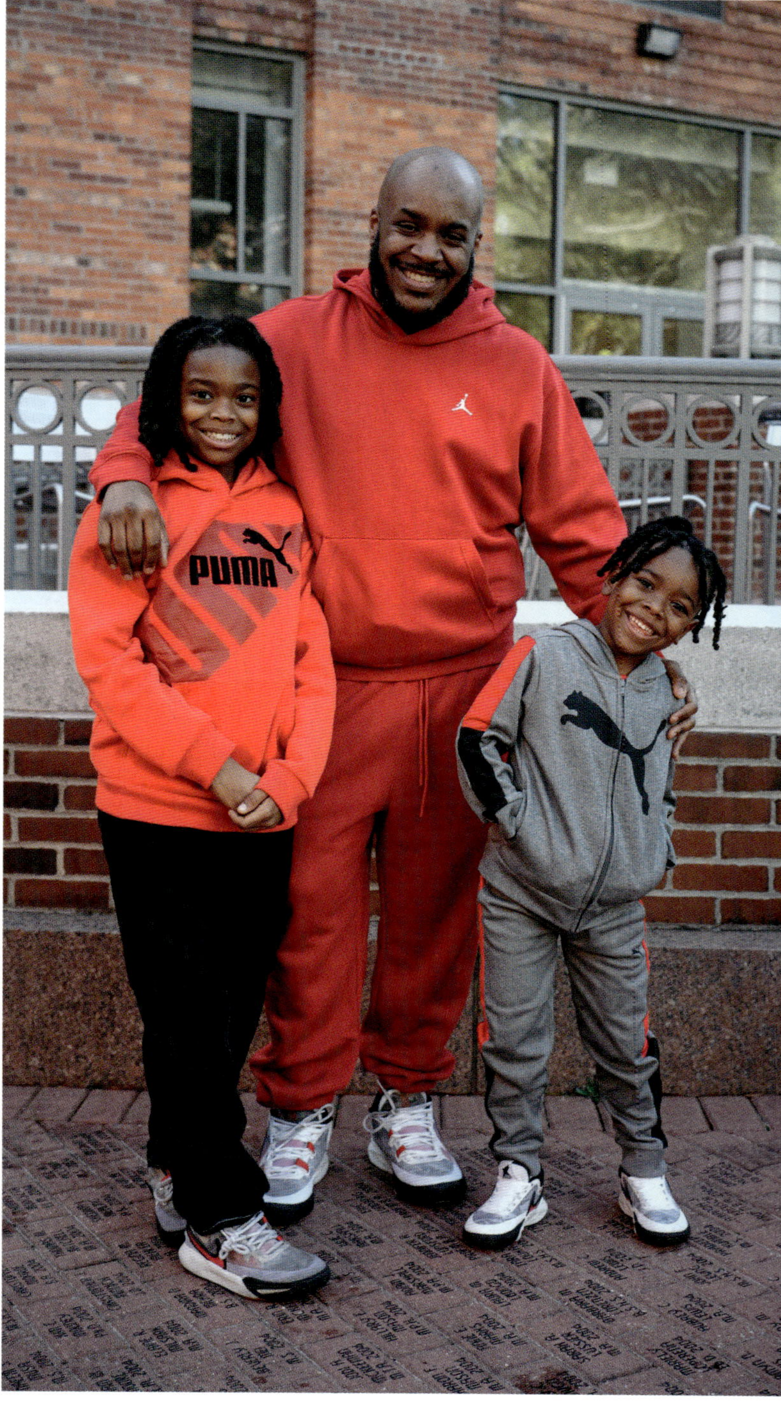

Family makes us strong.

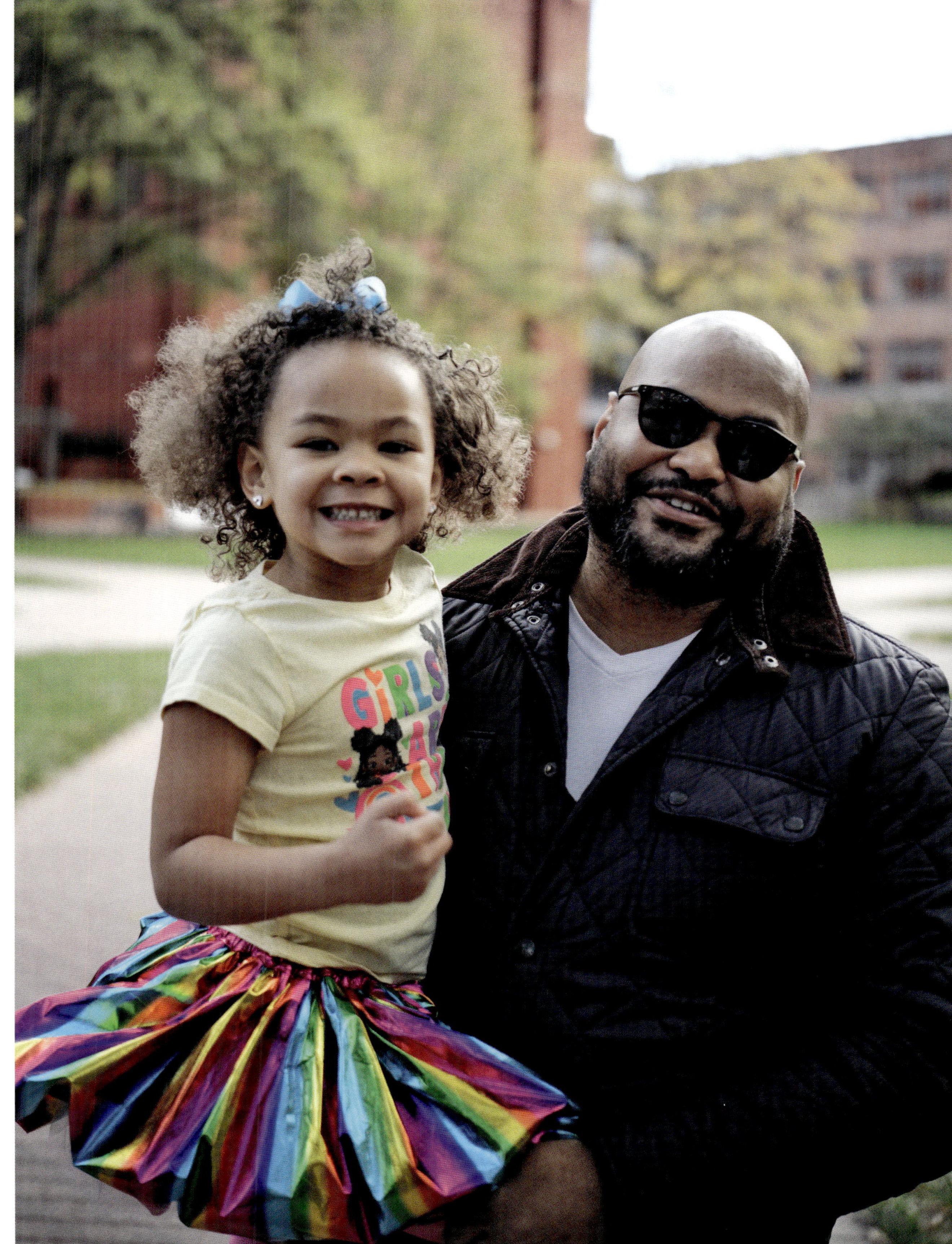

Girls just want to be celebrated.

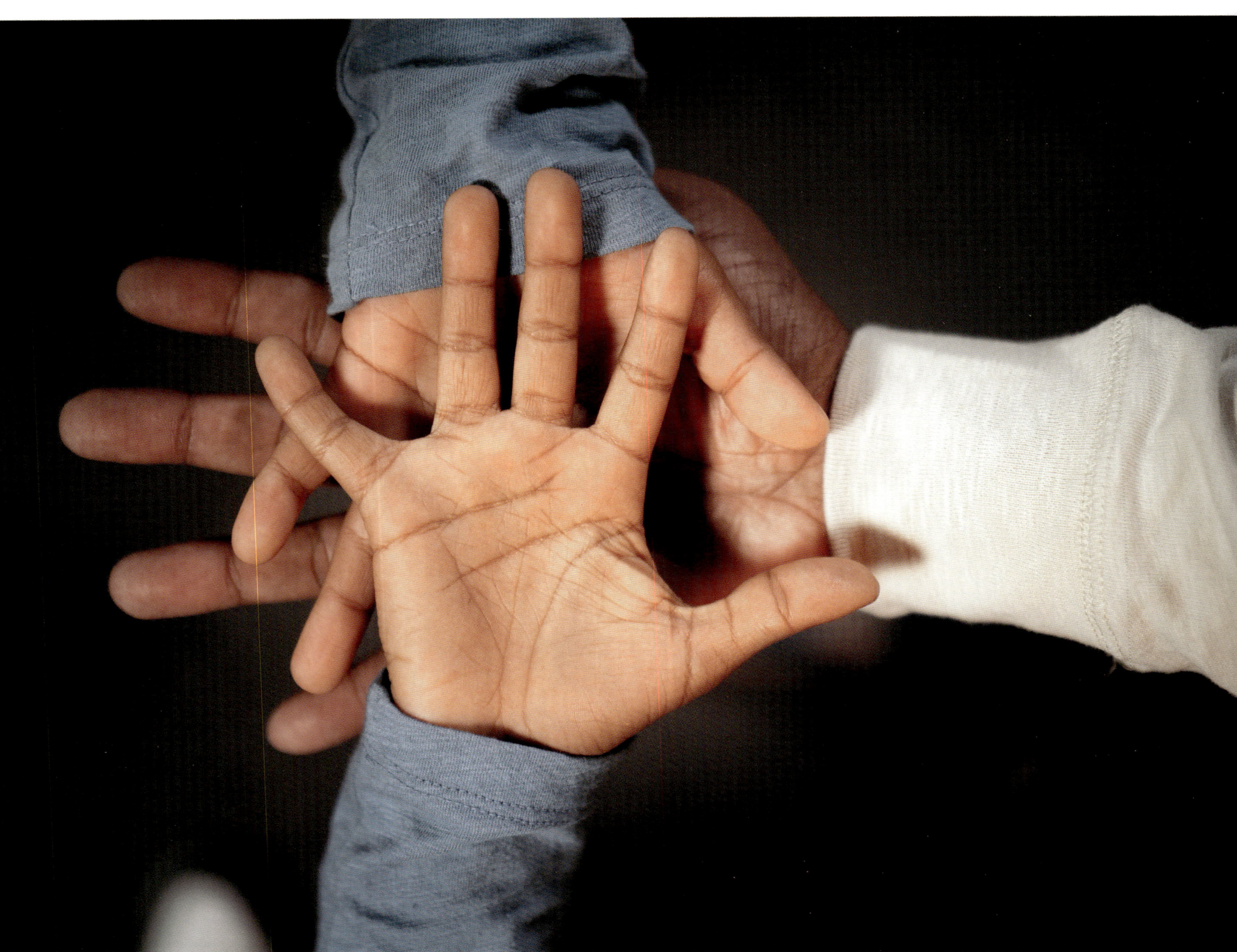

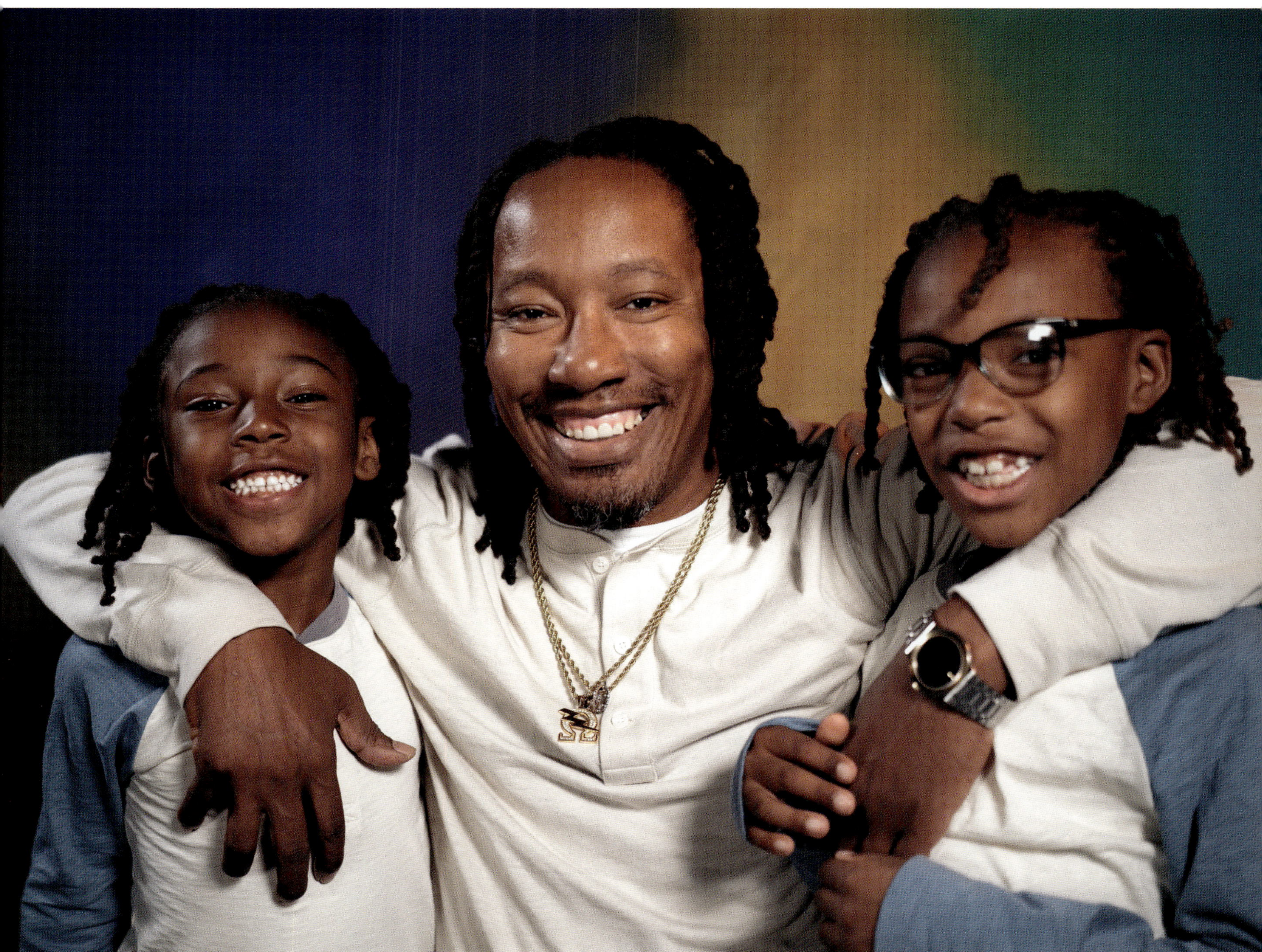

Forever protected by Dad's hands

KIRK SHARP

Museum director working to highlight the work of Black male photographer Gordon Parks at the Gordon Parks Museum in Kansas

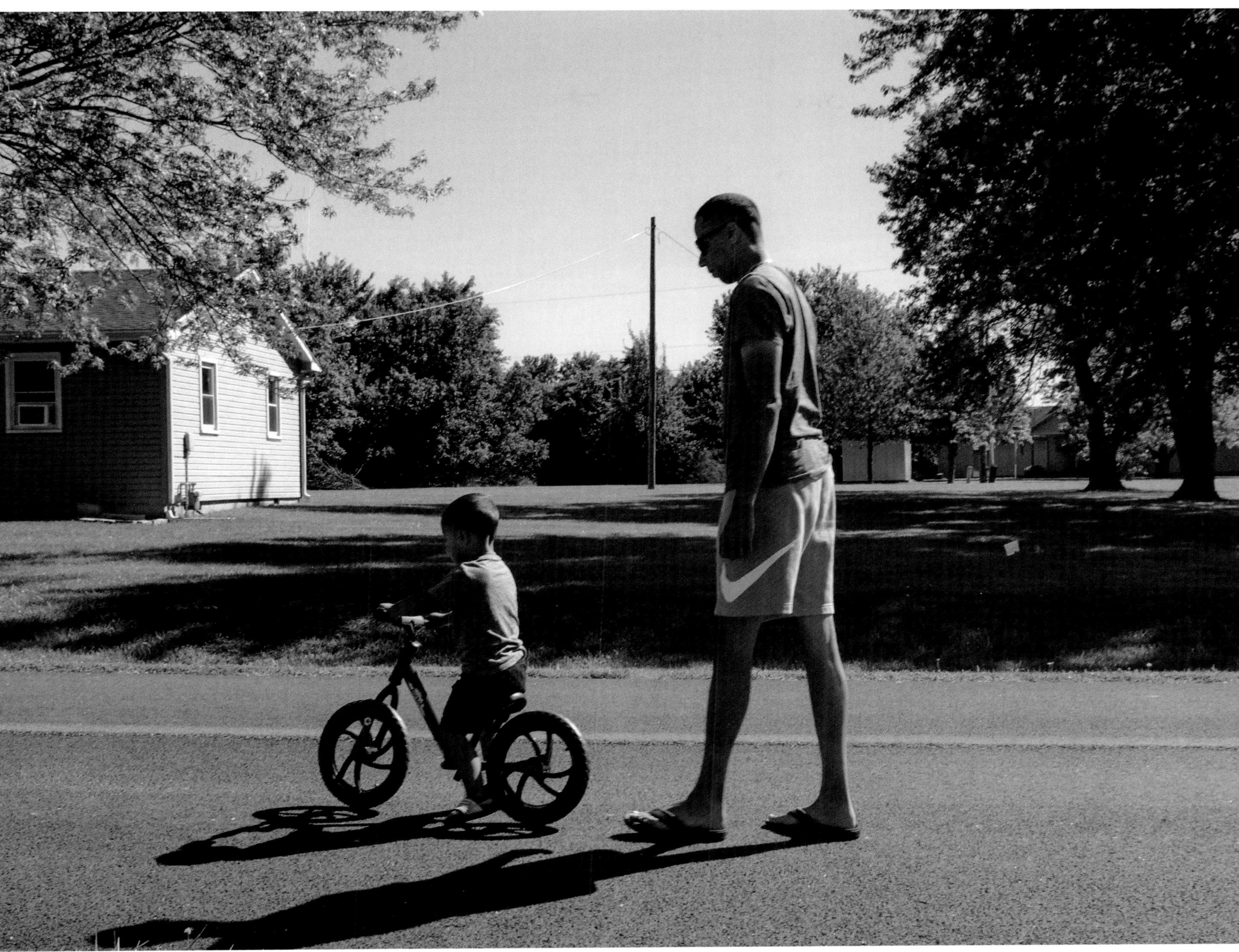

Trey Sharp follows his son, Lacari, with a loving, watchful eye, giving encouragement and support while he learns to ride a bike in Fort Scott, Kansas.

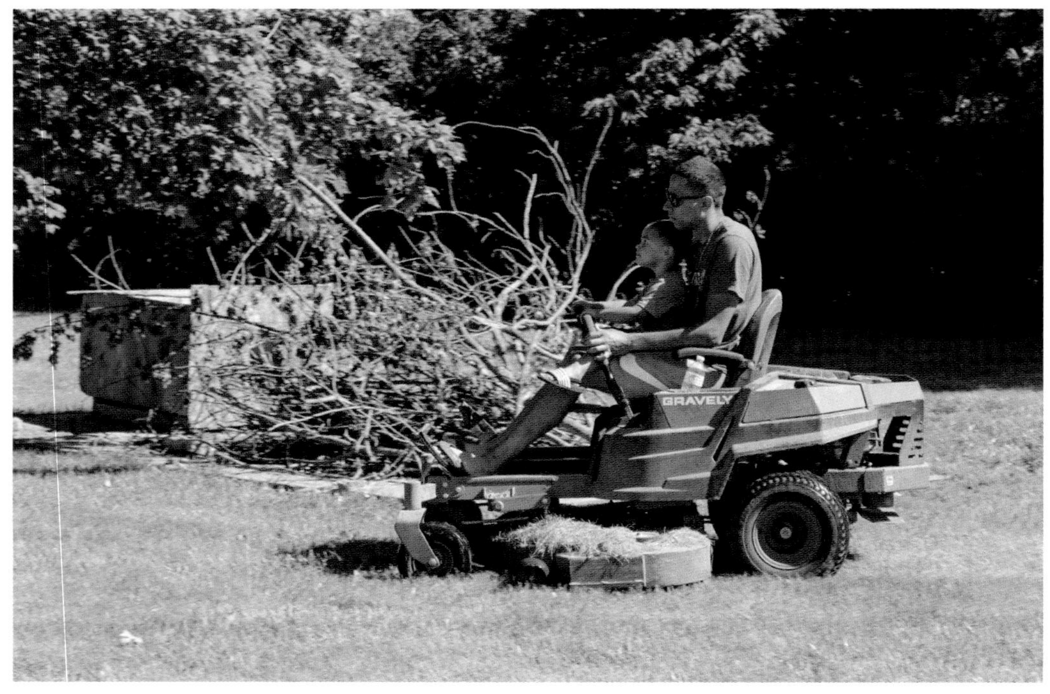

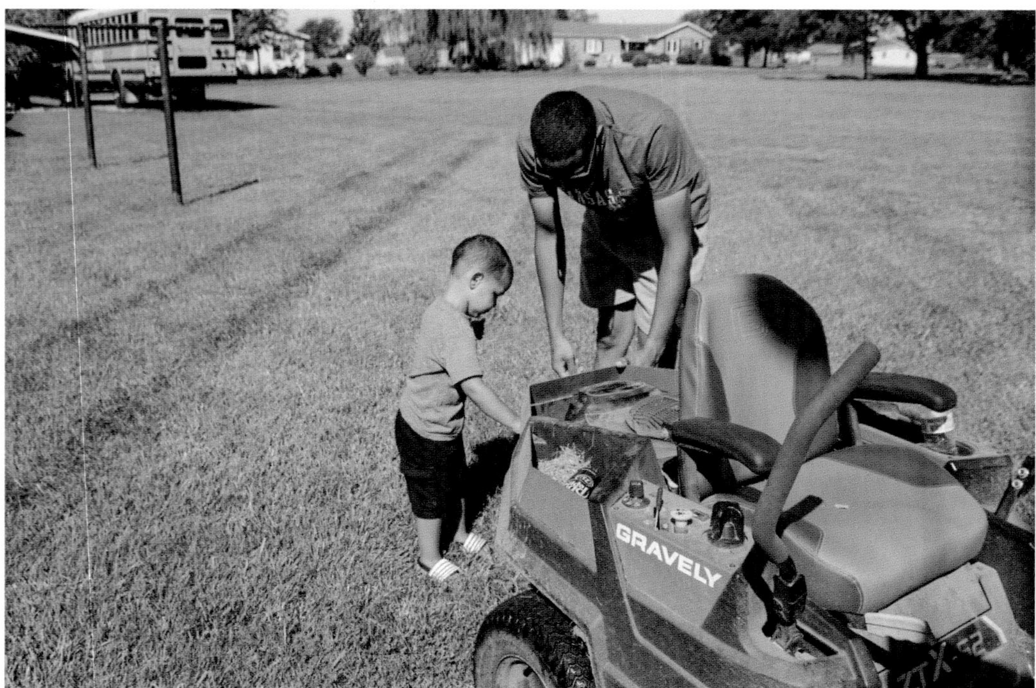

Trey teaches Lacari preparation and problem-solving through a hands-on learning experience.

BLACK FATHERHOOD: A JOURNEY OF PRESENCE AND PURPOSE

MARKUS TYREE

Fatherhood is a profound journey, especially for a Black man. It carries unique responsibilities, challenges, and rewards. For me, it means guiding, protecting, and providing strength to my children while constantly learning and evolving to be the best example I can be. In a world that presents extra obstacles for my children, particularly as they grow up as Black individuals, fatherhood becomes a calling to equip them with the values, confidence, and resilience they'll need to navigate life.

At its core, fatherhood is about presence. While financial support, discipline, and teaching life skills are important, nothing compares to being fully involved in every second. From the significant milestones to the quiet, everyday moments, the relationship I build with my children is shaped by my presence. Many Black men may not have had a consistent male role model due to systemic issues or personal circumstances. This only strengthens my resolve to be there for my children in every way. My presence is the foundation upon which they will build their understanding of love, family, and self-worth. By simply being there, I show them they are valued and loved.

Fatherhood also means protecting my children—not only physically but emotionally and psychologically. The world can be harsh, and as a Black father, I recognize that my children may face prejudices and injustices that can undermine their self-confidence. Part of my role is to shield them from negative influences and prepare them to face adversity with strength. I want them to feel secure in their identity, and I hope to help them build a sense of pride in who they are. By fostering this foundation, I hope they will grow into individuals who are self-aware, resilient, and unshaken by the pressures around them.

But protection doesn't mean hiding them from the realities of the world. There will come a time when I must have difficult conversations with them about race, identity, and how they may be perceived by others. These conversations are not easy, but they're crucial. They're about more than just preparing them for the world; they're also about helping them embrace their culture, history, and identity. I want my children to see their Blackness as a source of strength, beauty, and resilience. They should hold their heads high, knowing that their heritage is filled with creativity, excellence, and pride.

As a father, I'm also committed to being a role model. My children learn more from my actions than my words. It's my responsibility to model the values I want them to adopt: integrity, humility, respect for others, and a commitment to self-improvement. I want my sons to learn how to treat people with kindness and empathy, and I want my daughter to feel empowered and confident in her own worth. Modeling these values is one of the most effective ways to teach them, as children often emulate what they see more than what they're told.

Fatherhood has profoundly impacted my perspective, especially on time. Before becoming a father, I often viewed time as a resource to be spent efficiently on personal pursuits. But fatherhood taught me to prioritize moments of connection over productivity. I recall an evening when my youngest child struggled to fall asleep. Instead of rushing through the bedtime routine, I held them a bit longer, singing softly until their breathing steadied. That moment taught me that my presence and patience were the greatest gifts I could offer. I realized that these quiet moments are just as important as the big milestones.

Another defining moment came when my eldest child faced unfair treatment at school. The disappointment in their eyes and the confusion in their voice were heart-wrenching. In that moment, fatherhood compelled me to be both a protector and a teacher. I reassured them that while the world may not always be fair, their worth is never determined by others' opinions. Together we talked through how to handle the situation with confidence and respect. That experience reminded me that fatherhood is not just about shielding my

> **I WANT THEM TO LOOK BACK ON THEIR CHILDHOOD AND KNOW THEY WERE LOVED UNCONDITIONALLY.**

children from the world's challenges but about giving them the tools to face those challenges with pride and resilience.

Fatherhood also involves vulnerability and honesty. Black masculinity is often associated with strength and stoicism, but I believe there's power in showing my children that emotions are natural and that it's okay to express them. By being open about my feelings, I help them understand that vulnerability is not a weakness but an essential part of being human. I want to create a home where they feel safe to express themselves without fear of judgment. In doing so, I'm not only teaching them how to manage their emotions but also how to form healthy, loving relationships in the future.

Finally, fatherhood is about creating a lasting legacy. This isn't about wealth or status but about imparting values, memories, and life lessons that my children will carry forward. I want them to look back on their childhood and know they were loved unconditionally, that their father believed in their potential, and that they have the strength to accomplish anything they set their minds to. My hope is that the lessons I teach them will inspire them to be positive role models in their own families and communities.

Fatherhood as a Black man means embodying everything my children need from me while helping them discover the strength and confidence to become the best versions of themselves. This journey continually challenges me to grow—not only as a father but also as a person. Through love, guidance, and unwavering commitment, I strive to give my children the best foundation in life, empowering them to reach their full potential.

In essence, fatherhood is about more than just providing; it's about being present, nurturing resilience, and fostering pride in one's identity. The challenges and responsibilities that come with being a Black father are many, but they offer unique opportunities for growth and connection. Through my example, I aim to raise children who are not only prepared to face the world but are equipped to thrive in it. By embracing the role of a father, I'm not just shaping their futures—I'm shaping my own as well.

PRINCE JOHNSON

Self-taught Ghanaian photographer sharing the beauty of life on the West African coast

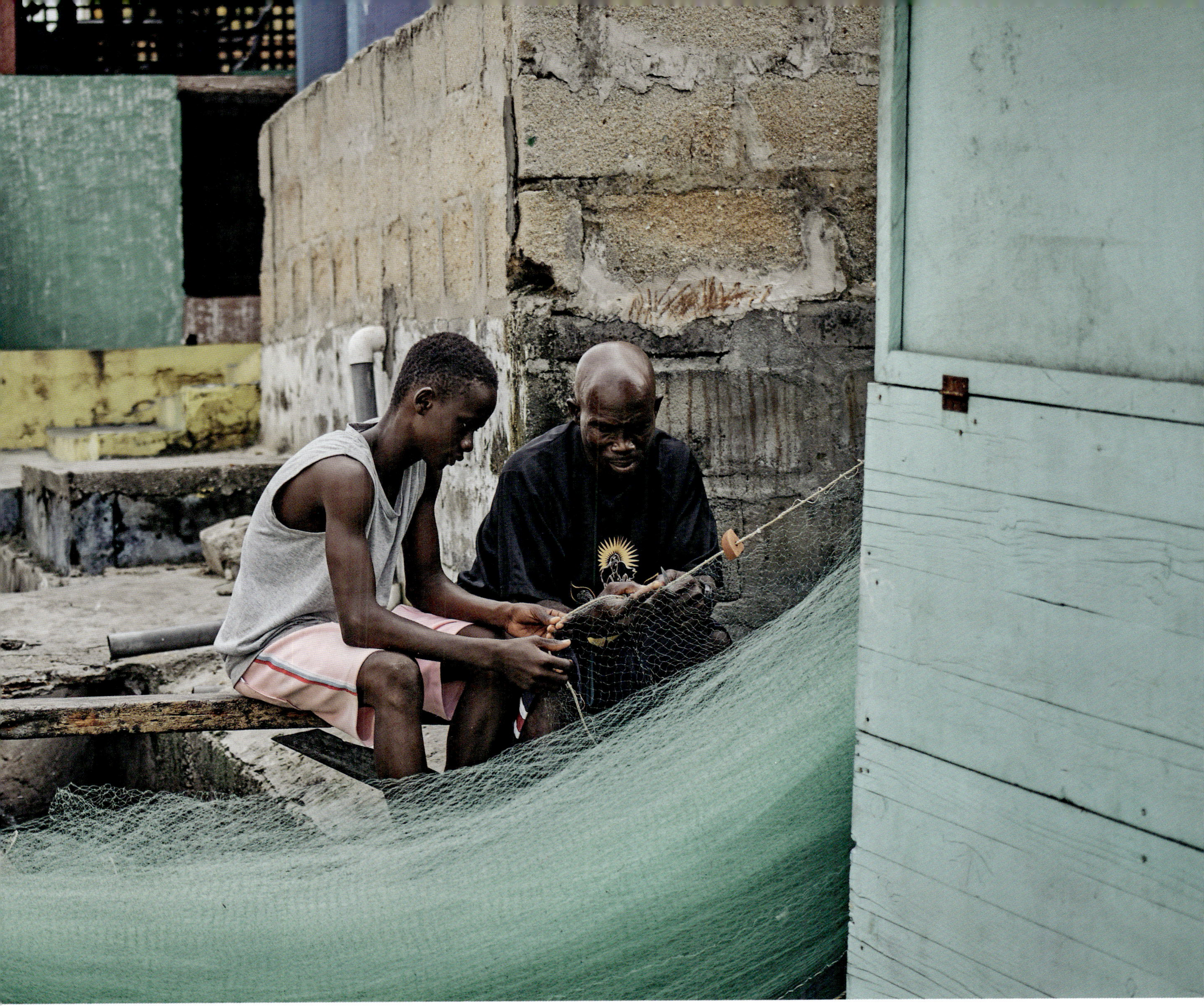

A father teaches his son how to patch a fishing net after returning from sea.

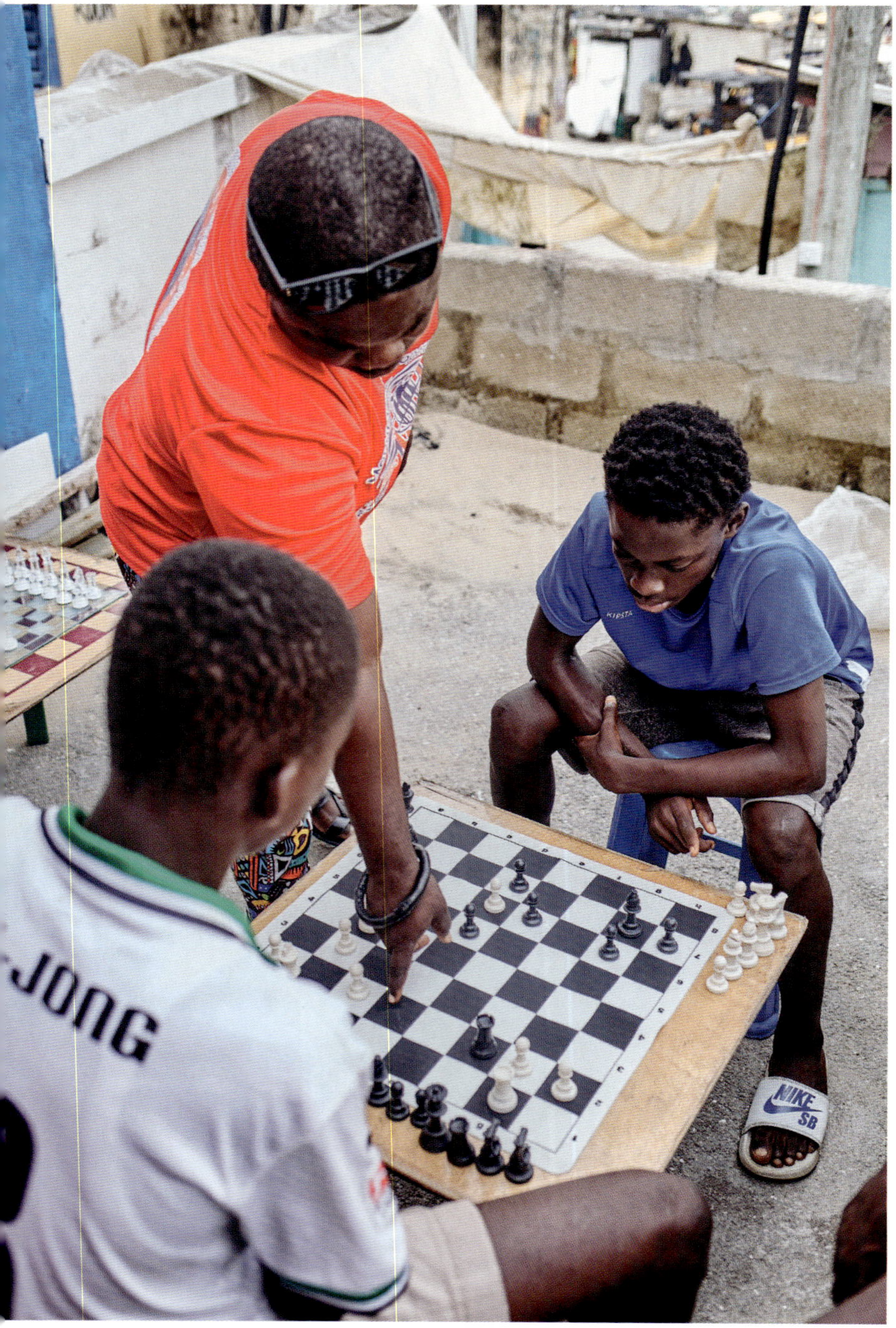

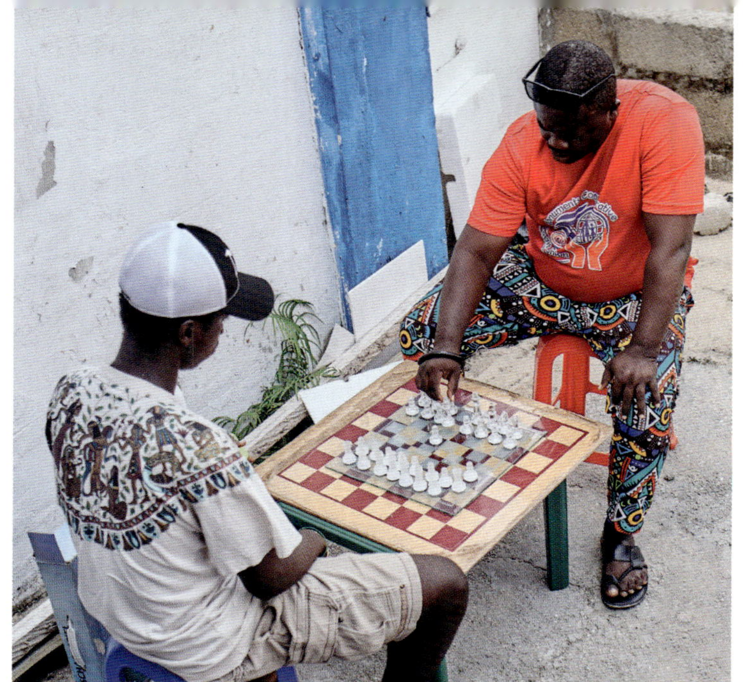

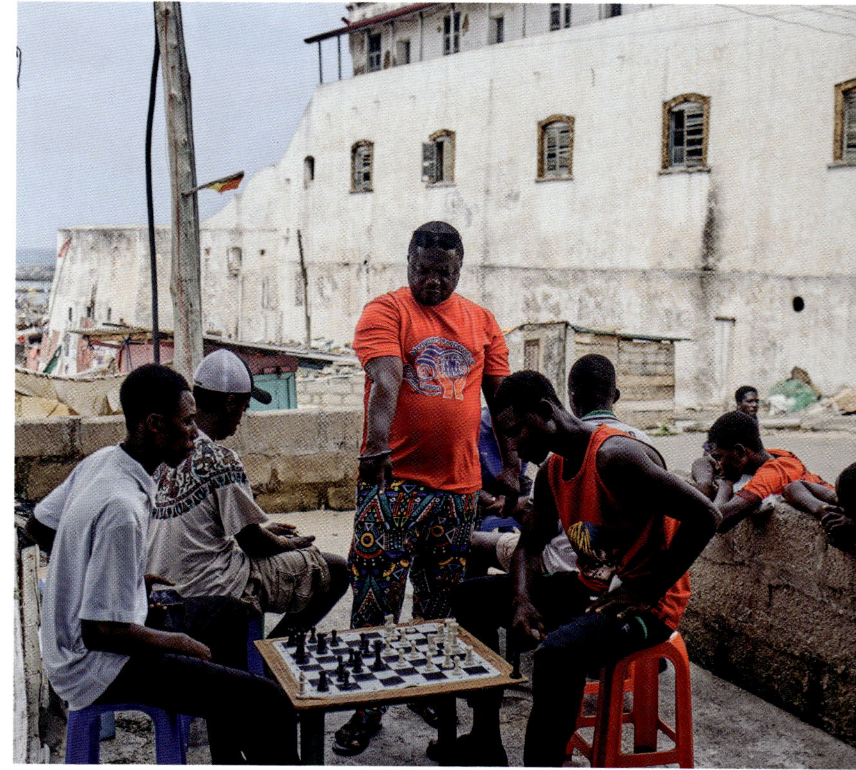

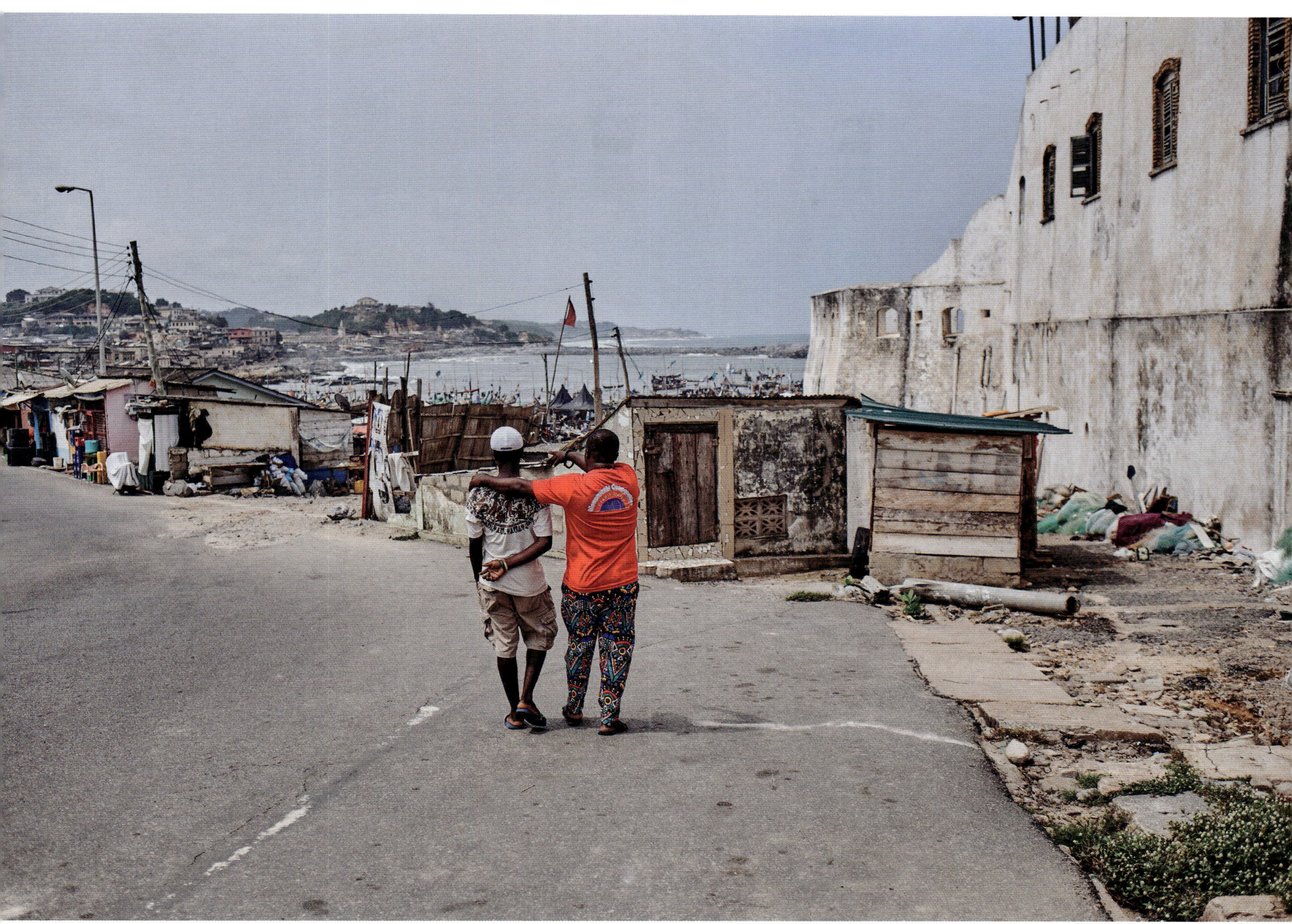

opposite: **A father shares his knowledge about chess with his son and some children who have shown interest in learning the game.**

above: **Coming of age. A father shows his son around town to equip him with the necessary knowledge to go about in the society.**

ADAM DANIELS

Washington, DC, producer and director dedicated to inspiring the Black community

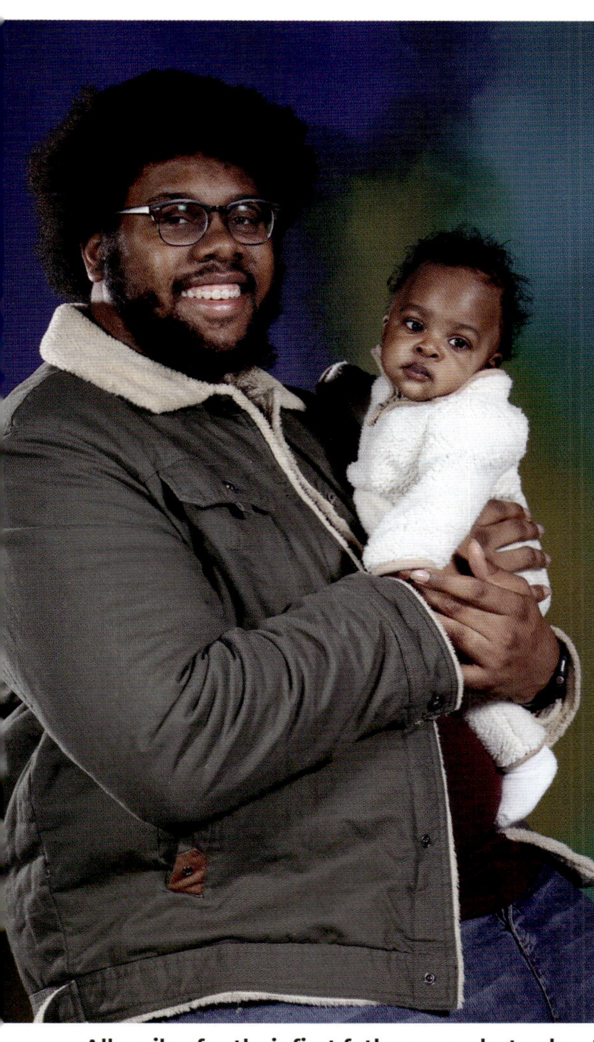

All smiles for their first father-son photo shoot

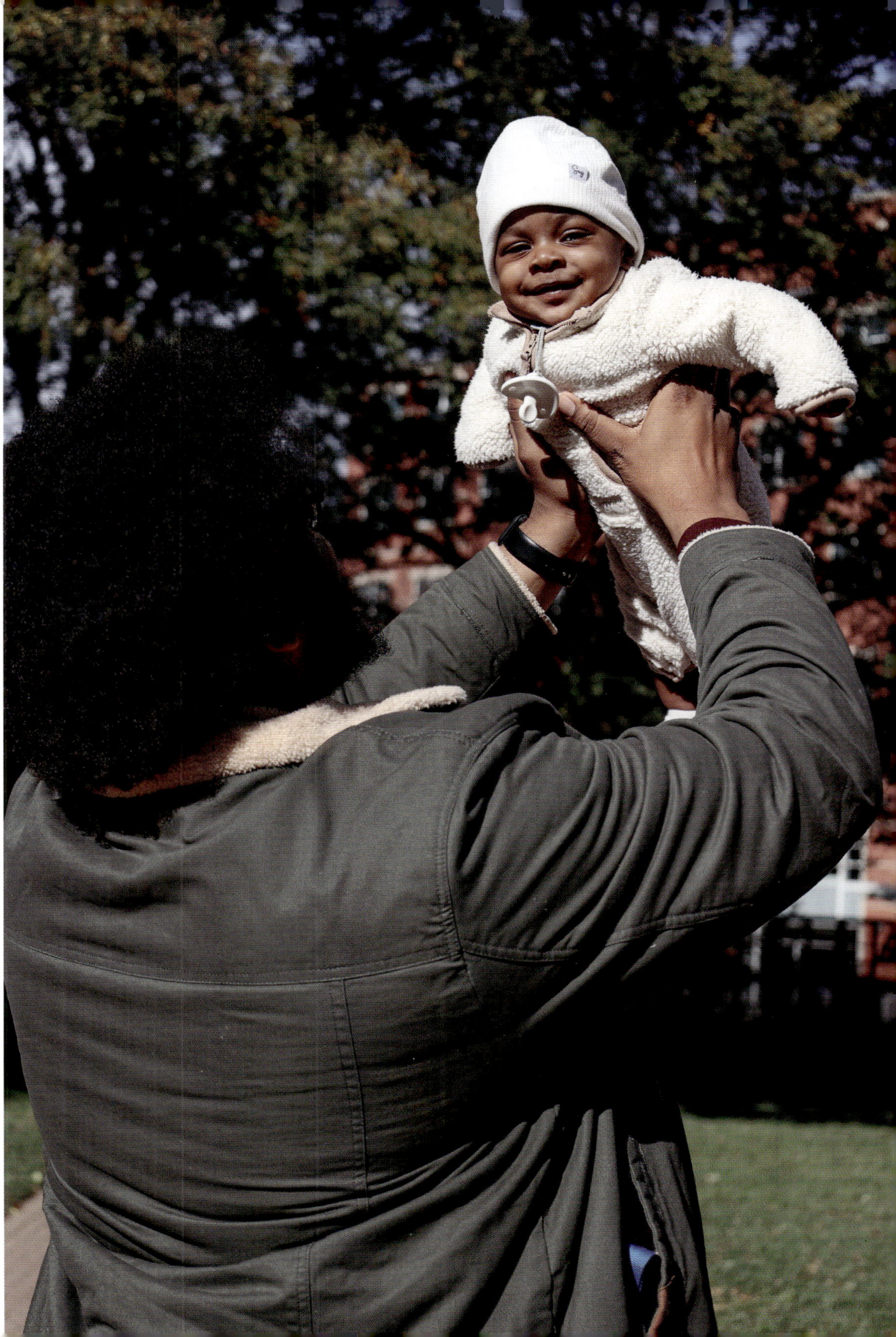

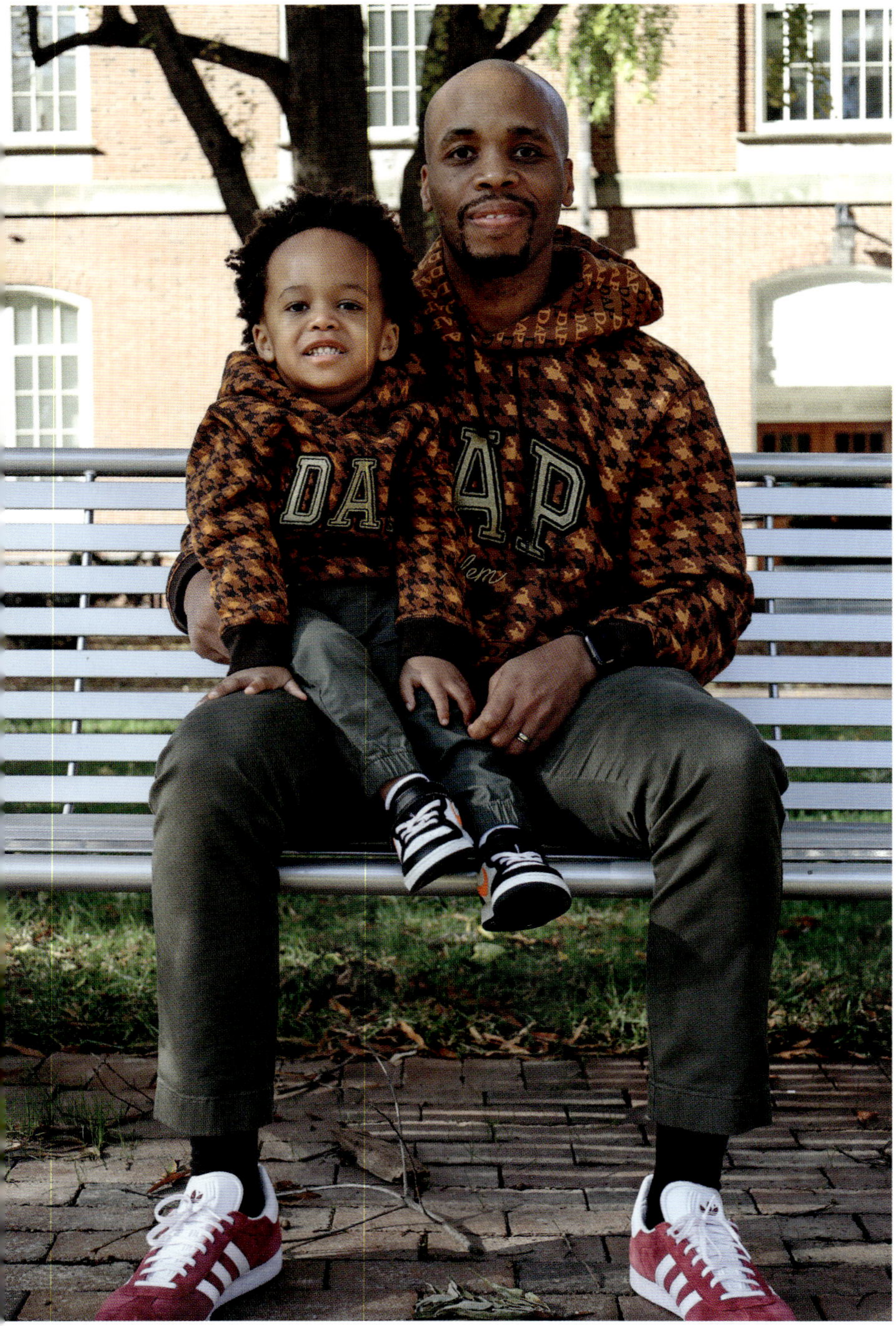

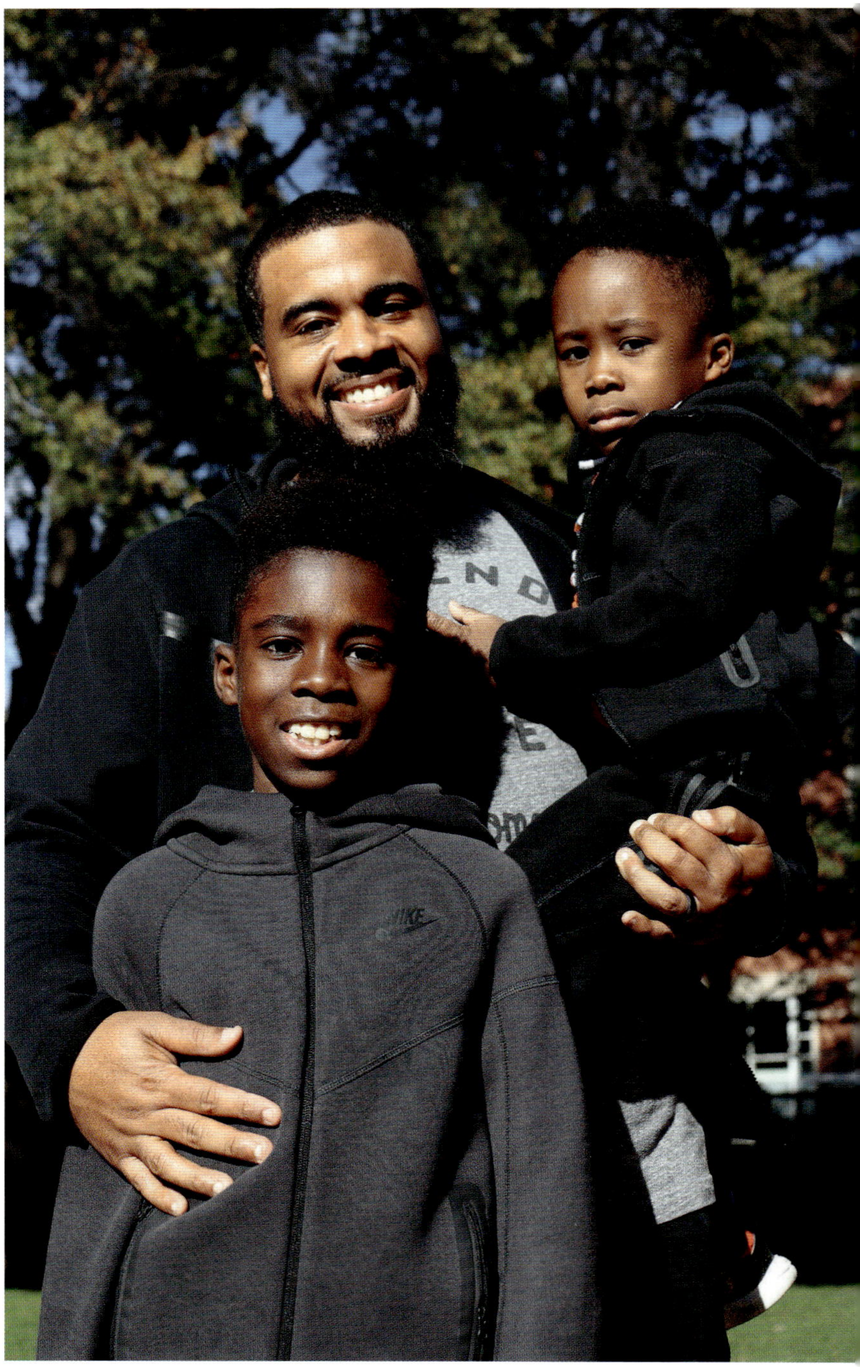

As fathers, sons are a mirror of who we want to be.

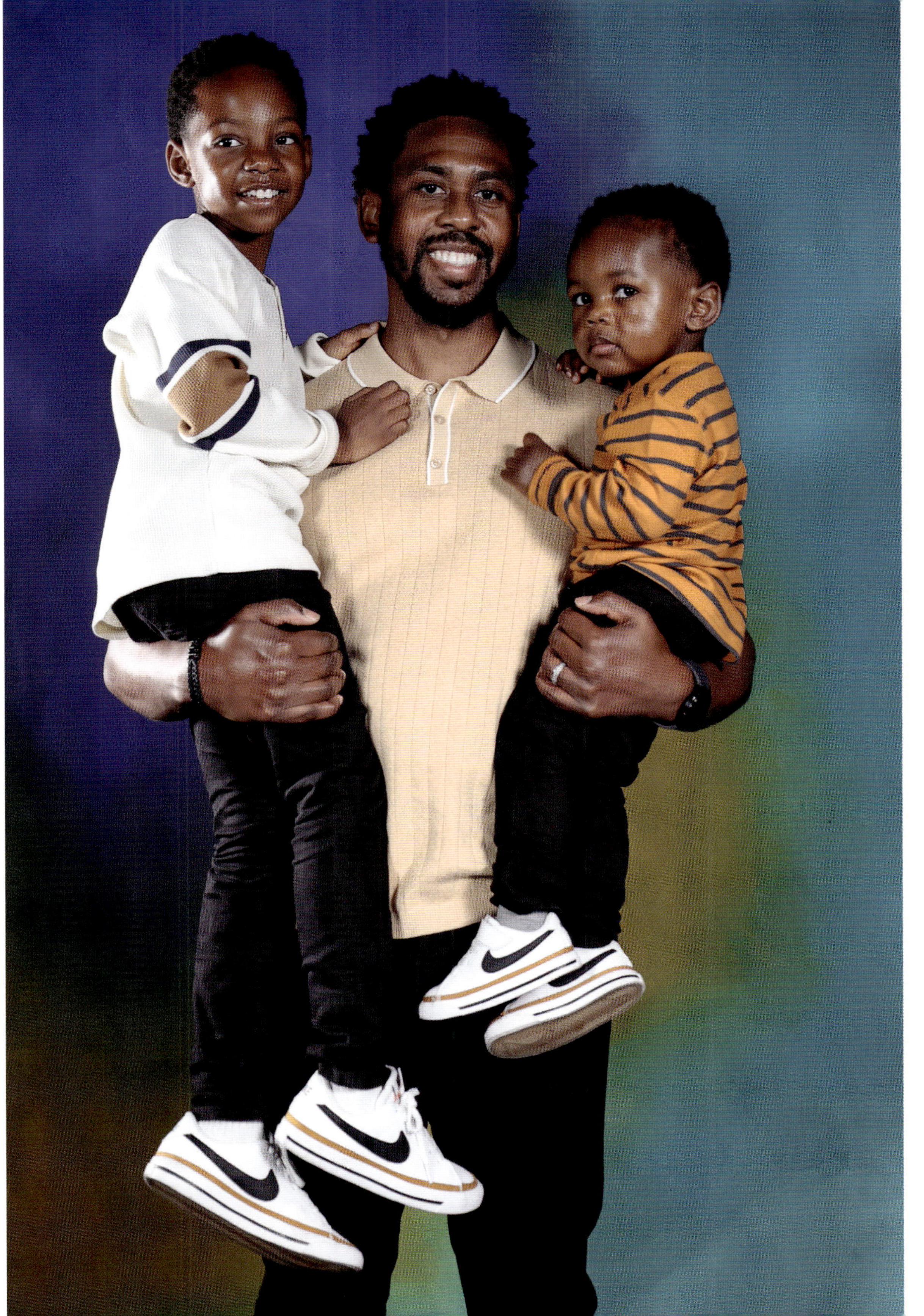

MICHAEL A. McCOY

Prominent photojournalist recognized for capturing historic moments in American politics and Black culture

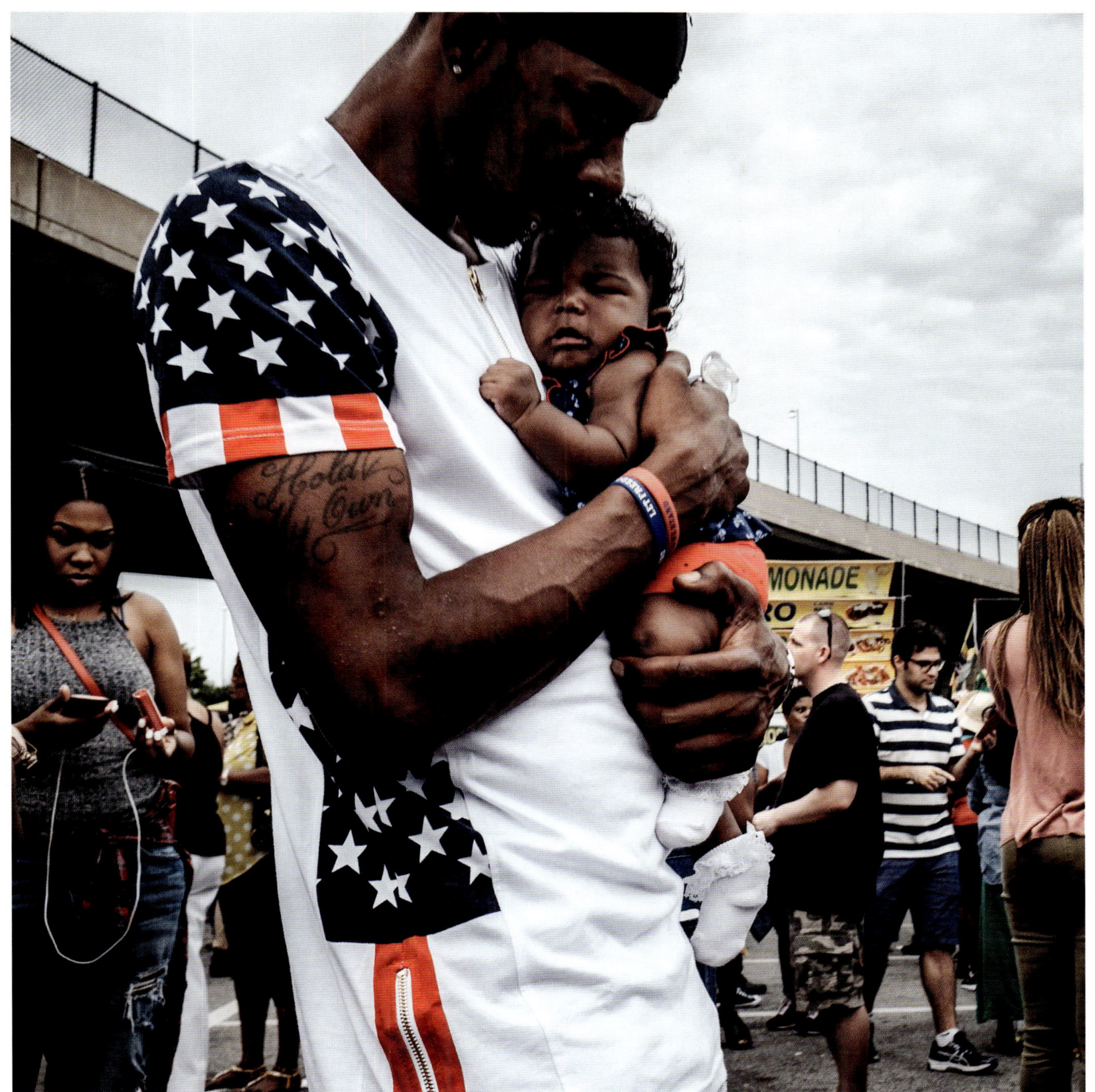

Holding my own

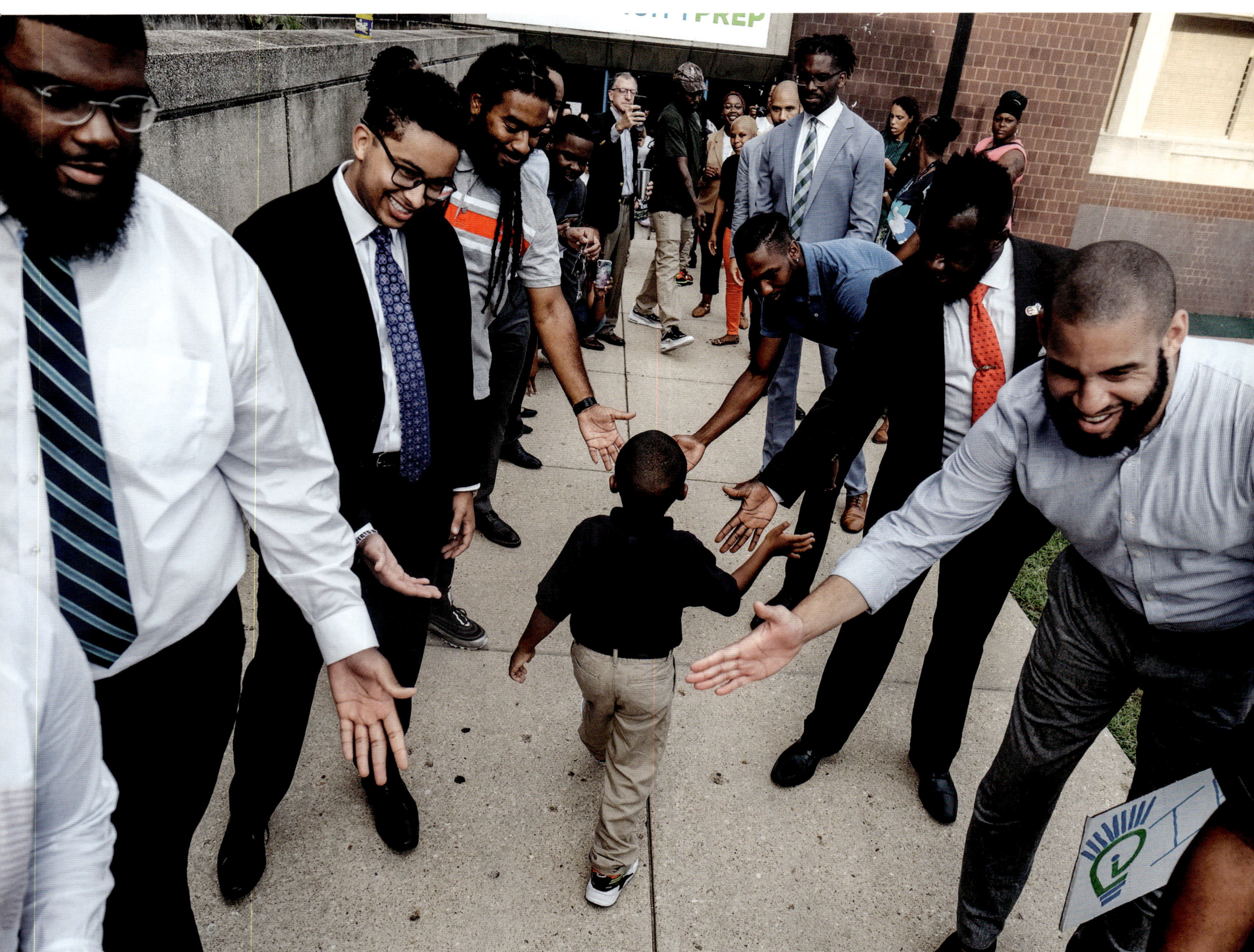

Uplifting the next generation of Black men

MY FATHER'S FACE

LAWRENCE WARE

For the past forty years, the day designated to celebrate the investment that fathers had in their children has not brought me a great deal of joy.

In 1988, just two weeks after Father's Day, my dad was convicted for stealing money from his place of employment. I was just seven years old and did not know what the word *embezzlement* meant. I just knew that he was going on vacation for a long while. For the next five years, Father's Days were spent at the Joseph Harp Correctional Center.

Every year my mother and I would leave the house at the break of dawn to make the hour-long drive from Oklahoma City to Lexington, Oklahoma, the site of the facility. Upon entering the center, men and women who smelled of cigarettes and old coffee rifled through our things, making sure we were not sneaking in drugs or contraband. I remember the sense of dread that washed over me when I learned that my Transformer toys were made of metal and, therefore, not allowed into the penitentiary. I tried to explain my need to show them to my dad, but after listening to my tearful plea, the officers explained that metal was not allowed and threw Optimus Prime and Megatron into a plastic bin. They promised my belongings would be by the entrance when I returned, but I did not pick up the toys when we left. I'd brought them to show my dad. I had no use for them anymore.

My father met us in the family room of the facility. Clothed in a gray prison uniform, he smiled widely when we saw us, shamelessly showing the perfectly aligned gaps between his middle teeth on the top and bottom rows. For some ungodly reason, he'd trained his hair to be brushed backward, but that aesthetic choice did not matter to me then. Spending time with him was like spending time with the divine, and the fact that I saw him infrequently only added to the mystique. I hung on his every word and cried every time I had to leave.

Unfortunately for him, I grew up, and my admiration did not last.

My father was paroled just before I entered the sixth grade, and we spent the summer before I attended Webster Middle School eating Big Macs and taking monthly trips to the comic book store. I was so overjoyed he was back home that I did not think too much about how he left home every night around eight p.m. to go to "work."

Most nights he did not come home, but when he did, I'd jump out of bed and run into his arms. Each time he'd kiss me on my forehead and call me his "bigheaded boy." I remember those nights fondly. They were the last times when I loved him with no reservations.

Life was simpler then.

Not long after I started middle school, he was sent back to prison. Parole violation, they said. I remained his son, but because of my anger and resentment, I lost my dad. He never returned.

He finished serving his time in prison when I was a sophomore in high school, but it was too late. He tried to treat me like he'd done before he'd gone back to prison, but things had changed.

I had changed.

I was not interested in a relationship with him. I did not want to spend time in his presence. "Dad" was a title he'd forfeited; it was "sir" from then on. Inclusion into the circle of family was something to be earned, not given. It was not dependent on blood but, instead, on commitment. That's what fatherhood meant to me, and when he failed in his commitment to be present in my life, he lost his right to call me "son." I was a boy without a father, and he was a man who'd fathered a child but lost his son.

“I WISH MY HEART WOULD LISTEN TO WHAT MY HEAD HAS TO SAY.”

That’s why I was caught off guard when I began to see him every time I looked in the mirror. I don’t have his brushed-back hair, and I don’t have a perfect symmetrical gap between my front teeth. But I cannot deny that I am my father’s son. I see him in my high cheekbones, my deep and intense eyes, my full lips. I am my father’s son, no matter how much I hate it.

I now have children—three boys—and when I see him in the mirror, I am terrified that I will repeat his mistakes, that I will give my sons a reason to hate me, that I will fail them as he failed me. These are the unacknowledged ramifications of institutional racism.

Amid talk of systemic racism and policies meant to be tough on crime, there is rarely an acknowledgment that children with incarcerated parents grow to be adults. I am a psychological prisoner of the war on crime, an unseen victim of what Michelle Alexander calls “the New Jim Crow.”

Intellectually, I know that my father stole money because of the pressure he felt to put food on the table. My head knows that if he’d had a better lawyer, he might have received a lesser sentence. As a scholar of race, I teach my students about the way Black men and women are imprisoned at disproportionate rates in America and how important it is that we see the humanity in those who have been incarcerated.

I wish my heart would listen to what my head has to say.

My story is not unique. It is representative of the reality faced by millions of other Black boys and girls. I’m just tired of seeing the man who failed me as a father every time I look in a mirror—and I wish that each time I saw him in my reflection, I was not reminded of how much I loved him.

He is my father, after all.

ACKNOWLEDGMENTS

To my mother, Darline M. H. Cheers: At the opening reception for the exhibition on June 18, 2022, you remarked, “This feels like a book!” Thank you for always supporting me and believing in my dreams. It’s bittersweet that you’re not here to hold this book in your hands, but I feel your love in every smile I see and your light shining down on me.

I am extremely grateful for the photographers who have trusted me and my vision since the inception of this project. Specifically Jamel Shabazz and D. Michael Cheers, who have been influential in the success of this endeavor. I would also like to thank the authors and poets who contributed their heartfelt reflections. Special thanks to my literary agent, Kathy Green; my editor, Danys Mares; and my publisher, Andrews McMeel Publishing, for supporting this book.

ABOUT THE CURATOR

Imani M. Cheers is an award-winning cultural curator, director, producer, and filmmaker, as well as an associate professor of digital storytelling in the School of Media and Public Affairs at the George Washington University. She is also the director of academic adventures for Planet Forward, an environmental storytelling initiative dedicated to solving the world's most complex and complicated climate change challenges.

Dr. Cheers is an award-winning cultural curator, director, producer, and filmmaker. She received her BFA in photography from Washington University in St. Louis and an MA in African studies and a PhD in mass communication and media studies from Howard University. As a professor of practice, she uses a variety of mediums including video, photography, television, and film to document and discuss issues impacting and involving people of the African Diaspora.

In 2021, she created "It Takes A Village: Basics of Boyhood and Messages for Manhood," an interdisciplinary research initiative that explores Black masculinity in mainstream multimedia. Dr. Cheers curated the photography exhibition *Framing Fatherhood* in 2022 and launched the podcast *The Basics of Boyhood* in 2024. This work has been profiled by CBS, NBC, and *The Washington Post*, reaching an estimated fifty thousand households.

Dr. Cheers is also an expert on diversity in Hollywood, specifically the representation of Black women in television and film. She is the author of *The Evolution of Black Women in Television: Mammies, Matriarchs, and Mistresses* and the forthcoming *Sacred Sisterhoods: A Celebration of Black Women's Friendships on Television and in Film.*

Dr. Cheers is also a regular contributor for international outlets including the BBC, CGTN America, and CTN Canada as well as national networks NBC, ABC, and CBS, offering insight into American race relations, popular culture, and African politics. She lives in the Washington, DC, area with her son, Isaiah.

ABOUT THE CONTRIBUTORS

Adam Daniels is a producer and director based in the Washington, DC, area.

Amir Nasser is a self-taught software developer currently contributing code to startup app GreatNight. Amir also enjoys spending time with his amazing wife, Fabienne Antoine-Nasser, and their energetic children, Eva and Khari Nasser.

Anthony Geathers is a documentary and portrait photographer from Bedford-Stuyvesant, Brooklyn, New York. He is also a Marine Corps veteran.

Brandon Ruffin is an Oakland-based, multidisciplinary artist best known for his visual storytelling in the mediums of photography and film under the moniker Ruff Draft. Brandon attributes his style of storytelling to the exploration of identity as well as how identity influences the movements and cultures of people within society.

D. Michael Cheers is a teacher of visual journalism at the School of Journalism and Mass Communications at San Jose State University. A documentary filmmaker, Cheers was coeditor and contributing photographer to the best-selling books *Songs of My People: African Americans, A Self-Portrait* and *Still Grazing: The Musical Journey of Hugh Masekela*. Cheers most recently produced and directed the documentary *I Needed Paris, Inspired by Gordon Parks*.

Darius Lyles is a Washington, DC–based filmmaker and photographer who has been working in production for eighteen years. He is an award-winning cinematographer who has worked on network TV shows and films for HBO, Showtime, NBC/Peacock, Amazon Prime, PBS, The History Channel, and BET. He is the epitome of a camera nerd who loves to talk codecs and image quality.

Delan Stone is a marketing manager and loves music. Originally from Portland, Oregon, he now lives in Bowie, Maryland, with his family.

Derek Morgan is a husband, father, and writer.

Derrel R. Todd is a photographer, cinematographer, and lighting instructor based in Washington, DC.

Jamel Shabazz is a documentary, street, and fashion photographer from Brooklyn, New York. He has authored twelve books.

Jason Miccolo Johnson is a Savannah, Georgia–based author and award-winning photojournalist. He captures the essence of his subjects through their "eyes and hands" while conveying layers of subtle information.

Khary Uché Mason is a retired Detroit Police homicide detective. His visual and written works focus on underrepresented narratives that exist within the Black community.

Kirk Sharp is a veteran, a Pittsburg State University graduate, and the executive director of the Gordon Parks Museum in his native town of Fort Scott, Kansas.

Lawrence Ware is the associate director of the Center for Africana Studies at Oklahoma State University. He is also a professor of philosophy at the school.

Leo Aristilde is a husband, father, and writer.

Markus Tyree is a Maryland-based artist and entrepreneur and a proud father of three. He is a driven and visionary artist who is passionate about creative expression and building meaningful community connections.

Martin Copeland is a community organizer and mental health advocate from Prince George's County, Maryland. He lives in the Washington, DC, area with his two sons.

Michael A. McCoy is a Washington, DC–based photojournalist known for his compelling visual storytelling. An avid golfer, he brings focus and precision to every frame.

Michael Young is a Bronx-based street and documentary photographer. His passion for light and shadow informs his imagery, which has been featured in *The New York Times* and exhibited at the former Corcoran Gallery of Art at George Washington University, the Wilmer Jennings Gallery at Kenkeleba, and Medgar Evers College.

Prince Johnson is a self-taught event and portrait photographer who lives in Accra, Ghana.

Quinton Pete is a passion-driven San Jose, California–based photographer who documents emotion through portraits and street photography, honoring his late father who first ignited his passion for the artform.

Raymond Holman is a documentary photographer based in Philadelphia with more than twenty years of experience. His most recent project is *Covid-19 in Black America.*

Reese Bland is a documentary photographer from Pittsburgh, Pennsylvania, currently working in Washington, DC.

Reginald Cunningham is a concert and event photographer originally from St. Louis, Missouri. He currently resides in the Washington, DC, area with his wife and two sons.

Russell Frederick is a self-taught Afro-Latino photographer, educator, and filmmaker from Brooklyn, New York, with more than twenty-five years of experience. Over the past two and half decades, Russell's work has been published and exhibited extensively in some notable establishments such as *The Washington Post*; *The New York Times*; NBC News; NPR; BK Reader; ESPN; Numéro; the former Corcoran Gallery in Washington, DC; the Visa Pour L'image Foto Festival in Paris, France; Addis Foto Fest in Addis Ababa, Ethiopia; and the Museum of Contemporary African Diaspora Arts in Brooklyn, New York.

Tau Battice is a New York City–based photographer from St. Kitts and Nevis.

Tony Mobley is a Washington, DC, native and Navy veteran. He has dedicated himself to capturing the raw emotion, resistance, and power of people demanding change. Through his lens, he has been blessed to document and create moments that define movements and amplify unheard voices.

Trevon Blondet is a self-taught portrait photographer from the Bronx whose creative journey began with capturing the energy of concerts, basketball, and football. Over time, he found his true passion in medium-format film portraits—drawn to the quiet moments where trust builds and subjects begin to reveal their truest selves.